Carolin Overhoff Ferreira

Identity and Difference

Postcoloniality and Transnationality
in Lusophone Films

LIT

Coverpicture: *Hans Staden* (Courtesy Jorge Neves Produções)

Gedruckt auf alterungsbeständigem Werkdruckpapier entsprechend
ANSI Z3948   DIN ISO 9706

Bibliographic information published by the Deutsche Nationalbibliothek
The Deutsche Nationalbibliothek lists this publication in the Deutsche
Nationalbibliografie; detailed bibliographic data are available in the Internet at
http://dnb.d-nb.de.

ISBN 978-3-643-90217-7

A catalogue record for this book is available from the British Library

©LIT VERLAG GmbH & Co. KG Wien,
Zweigniederlassung Zürich 2012
Klosbachstr. 107
CH-8032 Zürich
Tel. +41 (0) 44-251 75 05
Fax +41 (0) 44-251 75 06
e-Mail: zuerich@lit-verlag.ch
http://www.lit-verlag.ch

LIT VERLAG Dr. W. Hopf
Berlin 2012
Fresnostr. 2
D-48159 Münster
Tel. +49 (0) 2 51-620 320
Fax +49 (0) 2 51-23 19 72
e-Mail: lit@lit-verlag.de
http://www.lit-verlag.de

Distribution:
In Germany: LIT Verlag Fresnostr. 2, D-48159 Münster
Tel. +49 (0) 2 51-620 32 22, Fax +49 (0) 2 51-922 60 99, e-mail: vertrieb@lit-verlag.de

In Austria: Medienlogistik Pichler-ÖBZ, e-mail: mlo@medien-logistik.at

In Switzerland: B + M Buch- und Medienvertrieb, e-mail: order@buch-medien.ch

In the UK: Global Book Marketing, e-mail: mo@centralbooks.com

To my husband Luiz for accompanying me on this journey
and to my son Cauã for having joined us with his light

Contents

List of figures

List of tables

Preface and acknowledgments

This book is the result of a decade of research and teaching on lusophone films. It all began when I moved to Portugal in 1999 and started working as Assistant Professor at the *Escola das Artes* of the *Universidade Católica Portuguesa* in Oporto. In the department of *Som e Imagem* I taught dramaturgy and scriptwriting, as well as film history, film and script analysis. I am grateful for having had the chance to discuss many films of this study with my students. Several of them were challenging for a generation not accustomed to discuss their parents' vivid memories of the Salazar dictatorship. The participation as soldiers in the colonial war was still a tabu, while talking about the active participation in the anti-colonialist struggle for independence in Africa seemed easier. The debates on authoritarianism, colonialism and post-coloniality in Portuguese and Luso-African films were, nonetheless, always rewarding.

In 2006 I was invited to teach a course on contemporary Brazilian cinema at the *Universidade de Coimbra* in the context of its newly established *Curso de Estudos Artísiticos*. This gave me the opportunity to study films of which many were co-produced with Portugal. The concept of transnationality was gaining importance and my classes became the starting point for a research project on Luso-Brazilian and Luso-Afro-Brazilian films.

The project was accepted in 2008 by the *Departamento de Cinema, Rádio e Televisão* of the *Escola de Comunicações e Artes* (CTR/ECA) at the *Universidade de São Paulo* and I received a two-year grant as Senior Post-Doctoral Fellow from the *Conselho Nacional de Desenvolvimento Científico e Tecnológico* (CNPq). I am much obliged to both the CTR and the CNPq, since the Fellowship made it possible to finalize this book project and to discuss parts of it in a post-doctoral seminar organized by the CTR.

Much of my research took place at the library of the *Cinemateca Portuguesa* in Lisbon and its *Arquivo Nacional de Imagem em Movimento* (ANIM), as well as at the *Instituto de Cinema e Audiovisual* (at the time ICAM, now ICA), and I am indebted to the helpful assistance of their staffs. The *Cinemateca Brasileira* in São Paulo was equally supportive when I did research on Luso-Brazilian films.

The *Instituto Camões* in Brasília sponsored an exhibition of films by Manoel

14

de Oliveira that I organized at the *Cinemateca Brasileira* for his centenary in 2008 (with additional funding by the *Universidade Federal de São Paulo*), and a course on post-coloniality in Portuguese-speaking cinemas at the *Instituto de Educação Superior de Brasília* (IESB) in 2009. Both events were important opportunities to present parts of my research to different audiences.

All of the chapters that are united in this book have been published in shorter or different versions in peer-reviewed journals or as book chapters. I am grateful to the reviewers and editors of *Adaptations*, *Camera Obscura*, *Journal of African Cinemas*, *Studies in European Cinema* and *Third Text* for their important suggestions and critical input. I also would like to acknowledge the valuable contribution of Yoram Allon and the staff at Wallflower Press who invited me to edit *Dekalog2: On Manoel de Oliveira*, as well as of Renata Junqueira, editor of *Manoel de Oliveira: Uma Presença*, and Verena Berger and Miya Komori, editors of *Polyglot Cinema*. In fact, I cannot stress enough how vital their thoughtful comments have been to my writing.

Introduction

The Portuguese Carnation Revolution on 24 April 1974 had two emblematic historical results: it ended the longest lasting European dictatorship and the oldest empire of the modern age. Portugal had been under dictatorial rule ever since the 'May Revolution' in 1926. The 'New State' regime, masterminded by António Oliveira de Salazar, endured from 1933 until the peaceful uprising of the Portuguese military, which occurred after thirteen years of colonial war/wars of independence in Africa (1961–1974). As a result, the country's remaining ultramarine territories in Africa and Asia were finally decolonized in 1975 and Portugal returned to its original boundaries from 1415, when expansionism initiated with the conquest of Ceuta.

Film production was deeply affected by this change of political paradigm. On the one hand, democracy and freedom of expression offered a chance to assess the past and to inquire the socio-political transformation process. Throughout the 1970s and in the early 1980s documentaries scrutinized the Salazar dictatorship or sketched out the construction of a more just society. Fiction film production took somewhat longer to gain impact. But in the middle of the 1980s contemporary film productions were already being celebrated internationally as the *escola portuguesa* (Portuguese school). The 'school' consisted of a loose set of filmmakers from all generations, who received much attention for their authorial style and particularly visual outlook on national idiosyncrasies. While the 1990s saw a diversification in terms of styles and themes, and a crystallization of commercial cinema, a new generation of *auteurs* kept the idea of a particular Portuguese art house cinema alive.

In terms of production processes, the post-revolutionary governments took measures to improve film funding. Film partnerships, especially agreements on co-productions with the ancient colonies, were set up. Brazil, independent since 1822, signed as early as 1981, followed a decade later by the *Países Africanos de Língua Offical Portuguesa*/African Countries with Portuguese as Official Language (PALOP): Angola signed in 1992, Cape Verde in 1989, Mozambique in 1990 and São Tomé and Principe in 1994.

In 2001, due to the creation of the *Comunidade de Países de Língua Portu-*

guesa/Community of Countries with Portuguese Language (CPLP),[1] a multi-lateral agreement on co-productions followed that aims to foster audio-visual productions between all lusophone partners. While these political steps are part of a generalized reaction to the globalized film market, they are, above all, a product of Portugal's desire and need to bond with the former colonies after introducing restrictive immigration measures such as the Schengen Treaty in 1993. The creation of the CPLP in 1996, which generated a symbolic supranational space modelled after the EU, was designed to deal with this moral debt and must be understood as part of Portugal's process of redefining and redeeming its identity after the end of its empire.

This book aims to discuss the impact of the Portuguese Carnation Revolution on fiction feature production[2] by looking at films that discuss the legacy of Portuguese colonialism in the context of the current globalization process, that is, the post-colonial *and* trans-national condition of Portugal and its ex-colonies. It includes studies of national productions from Portugal, but also of films that have been co-produced with Angola, Brazil, Cape Verde, Guinea Bissau and Mozambique and are considered national productions by both financial partners.

Over the last three decades Portuguese production companies have engaged on a large scale with these important issues and the reformulation of national identity has been addressed in a vast number of film narratives – as much in national as in co-productions. While the colonial history is still a rare topic in the national films, especially when it comes to the colonial war/wars of independence in Africa, post-coloniality is either the key subject or present

---

[1] The CPLP presents as its main objectives a political-diplomatic awareness, co-operations in diverse fields (education, health, science and technology, defence, agriculture, public administration, communications, justice, public security, culture, sports and social communication) and the organisation of projects to promote and propagate the Portuguese language.
[2] It is worth noting that there has been a proliferation of trans-national short-film and documentary productions for cinema and television that deserve attention, but have not been part of my research so far.

through secondary characters. It takes centre stage in films on African immigrants – both first and second generation – but even more so in productions that engage with the difficult adaptation process of the homecoming soldiers or the *retornados* – the Portuguese colonizers that returned from Africa after decolonization – as well as in the portrayal of adolescent characters whose difficulties in constructing their subjectivity serves as an allegory for the country's reorientation process. In fact, the search for a new identity that deals with the tensions between colonial past and European future is the subtext in the majority of Portuguese fiction films since the 1980s.

Since the number of co-productions with the former colonies – Brazil and the PALOP – is growing, they offer a parallel and perhaps even more significant arena for these issues. The provision of funding depends, according to the regulations of the agreements on co-productions, on the relevance of the project in terms of cultural relationships. In the case of the twenty Luso-African features produced between 1988 and 2010, this rule has been followed consistently. The Luso-Brazilian productions, on the other hand, demonstrate that economic interests can overrule in productions with minor sponsoring, namely, where only 20 per cent of the money comes from the co-producing country. Ten out of the twenty-six films released between 1995 and 2008 do not present any, or only irrelevant references to either colonialism or post-coloniality.

Nonetheless, a large number of the lusophone co-productions choose the colonial past in Brazil or Africa as their topic. When the subject matter is not historical, the co-productions engage with situations marked by post-coloniality and globalization, especially with migration. The PALOP co-productions frequently depict the conflicts that arise from the encounter between traditional African values and Western ideas, or they deal with the delicate subject of civil wars (in Angola and Mozambique), while Brazilian co-productions tend to engage mainly with the legacy of authoritarianism. By and large, due to the history of colonial relationships, the forty-six or so lusophone co-productions, especially those on the colonial past, offer as much ideological traps as opportunities to develop what I would like to call a transnational dialogue and will define in a moment.

Portugal's self-image, which is based on its past as a seafaring nation, has always stressed the country's difference from other European countries.

Fernando Pessoa's poem *Mensagem/Message* from 1934 is telling about the singular position that Portugal attributed to itself for centuries, in addition to its mission to lead the old and tired Europe to a new existence:

> A Europa jaz, posta nos cotovelos: / De Oriente a Ocidente jaz, fitando,/
> E toldam-se romanticos cabelos / Olhos gregos, lembrando.
> O cotovelo esquerdo é recuado; / O direito é em angulo disposto./
> Aquele diz Italia onde é pousado; / Este diz Inglaterra onde, afastado,/
> A mão sustenta, em que se apoia o rosto. /
> Fita, com olhar sphyngico e fatal, / O Ocidente, futuro do passado.
> O rosto com que fita é Portugal.[3]

Pessoa fundaments the idea of Portugal's exceptionality by associating its front-line geographical position with a vanguard disposition of projecting an unknown and outstanding identity into the future, which is thought to reveal itself in the New World, namely Brazil. This idea of being the chosen nation and future leader of the world due to the country's influence on other nations has been formulated throughout Portugal's cultural history and solidified first and foremost in its canonical literature, being Fernando Pessoa, Luís de Camões and António Vieira the country's most powerful visionaries (see Lourenço 1999a). Their literary works – that belong theoretically to the patrimony of all countries with Portuguese as official language – as well as political and academic discourses from the beginning of the twentieth century have participated in developing two potent and persisting concepts that celebrate hybridization and 'inter-identities' (Sousa Santos 2001) in order to distinguish Portuguese colonialism from its European counterparts: luso-tropicalism and lusophony.

---

[3] ('Europe is lying propped upon her elbows: / From East to West she lies, staring / Out, reminiscent, – Greek eyes from the shelter / Of romantic hair. / Behind her back the left elbow is cast; / The right has the angle place. / That one says Italy in its repose; / This one says England where, gathered apart, / It holds the hand up to support the face. / She stares, her gaze doom-heavy, sphingical, / Out at the West, the future of the past. / The face with which she stares is Portugal.')

Luso-tropicalism propagates Portugal's outstanding accomplishments – the discoveries of sea routes, islands and 'continents' – as a consequence of the country's desire to convert the world to Christianity in a peaceful manner. In contrast to the Spanish conquerors, Portugal's colonialization process is interpreted as having been guided by religious instead of material interests and understood to have been conducted in a non-violent way, by engaging, living and mixing with the most diverse cultures and ethnicities from the southern hemisphere. The concept is based on the idea that the Portuguese people, due to their own cultural miscegenation that suffered influences from Europe and Africa, are transnational in their essence. It is not surprising that luso-tropicalism regained importance in the 1950s when the empire was coming under threat since the decolonization processes in the anglophone and francophone colonies began to abolish colonial rule around the globe.

Lusophony was first developed in the late 1950s but entered the lusophone stage for good after Portugal finally let go of its 'ultramarine provinces' in the early 1970s, which brought a feeling of loss to the core. Its defenders believe that the utopia of constructing a harmonious transnational community in the colonies is a reality that survived the end of the empire. It is identified mainly by the common language, which is used as a metaphor for culture. By ignoring regional and national linguistic, cultural and historical differences, the Portuguese language is identified as the unifying principle and corner stone of a cultural identity, which – due to its transnational dimension – is considered superior to any national identity. Both concepts are powerful tools to convert the colonial history into a shared cultural history.

Only in the last decade or so have Portuguese literary criticism and social sciences started to translate the insights from post-colonialism and the awareness of a post-colonial national identity crisis into the critical assessment of concepts and ideas associated with the country's supposed singularity and humanistic colonialism. Scholars have questioned the national predisposition for transnationality and the celebration of its post-colonial cultural legacy, laying bare luso-tropicalism's and lusophony's intent to camouflage difference by acknowledging that they were designed to maintain the imaginary of Portugal as a great nation. In my film analyses I will rely heavily on the key authors of this undertaking, namely Eduardo Lourenço, Boaventura Sousa Santos, Margarida Calafate Ribeiro and José Gil.

International film studies began somewhat earlier to spotlight questions related to post-coloniality and national identity and has produced a vast bibliography on national and regional cinemas, as well as on anglophone and francophone films. Many insights from these studies have been of great significance for this book and will be addressed in the different chapters.

The recent efforts to turn transnationality into a critical concept for film analysis have inspired much of my study of the lusophone co-productions. Will Higbee and Song Hwee Lim (2010: 8) explain why the concept has been welcomed by a variety of fields within academia:

> One immediate response is to view this shift towards the transnational as encouraged by a wider dissatisfaction expressed by scholars working across the humanities (in particular sociology, postcolonial theory and cultural studies) with the paradigm of the national as a means of understanding production, consumption and representation of cultural identity (both individual and collective) in an increasingly interconnected, multicultural and polycentric world.

The concept is employed in film studies so as to question the idea of national cinema, to inquire its presence in film history, or in its post-colonial or diasporic dimension. It is not free of controversy, since it is being used in an almost inflationary way and sometimes uncritically, demonstrating that border crossing is often rather wishful thinking than an actual fact.

Transnationality's affirmative employment within European or North American academic circles reveals similarities with the celebratory tone related to the concepts of lusophony and luso-tropicalism that equally depict the encounter between cultures, even though exclusively those colonized by Portugal. The critical work that has been accomplished to challenge the propagation of Portugal's harmonious co-existence with its colonized can, in fact, help to shed more light on transnationality's ambivalence. I hope that my definition of transnationality and its study in the lusophone co-productions will participate in further clarifying the dangers and potentialities of the concept in film studies, as well as in other areas.

My analysis of the trans-national films and their comparison with the national productions indeed demonstrates that transnationality is ineffective when based on the idea of identity within a world of difference – namely in those films where the discourses on lusophony and luso-tropicalism are unfiltered – but turns into a powerful tool when their ambivalence – the complicated net of identity and difference that results from the multi-faceted encounters during colonialism and post-coloniality – is paid attention to. Accordingly, I will only consider those films transnational that offer a critical perspective or dialogue on the relationship between identity and difference in the lusophone world. Following the distinction common in post-colonial studies, I will use a hyphen to differentiate the trans-national condition from transnational as a critical potential that emerges when two parties engage on a non-governmental basis in order to discuss their complex relationship.

In accordance with the different modes of production of the lusophone films under analysis – the national and the trans-national – this book is divided into two parts. The first is devoted to Portugal's national films and the second to its co-productions with the former colonies. While the first part consists of comparative studies that feature in-depth analyses of either two or three films, the second part uses a different methodology. Since it introduces new fields of study that still need to be mapped out – the trans-national productions between Portugal and the PALOP, the Luso-Brazilian literary adaptations and the comparison of national and trans-national lusophone films – it offers panoramic views and only one in-depth analysis of a particularly remarkable Luso-Brazilian production. By pointing out productions that are more successful in their transnational dialogue, I hope to encourage others to conduct further in-depth analyses and comparisons.

In the first part of the book dedicated to Portugal's national film production, 'Facing authoritarianism and the end of the empire: in search for an alternative identity', four important issues will be discussed in exemplary Portuguese films, according to the order of their historical appearance: 1) the foregrounding of authoritarian structures, 2) the representation of the colonial war, 3) the assessment of the European expansions and 4) the use of the adolescent as post-colonial allegory.

The first chapter, 'Non-canonical adaptations: Non-inscription and dictatorship in *A Bee in the Rain* (1968–71) and *The Dauphin* (2001) by Fernando Lopes' compares the filmmaker's adaptation of two books that challenged the hegemonic identity of Salazar's regime and became canonical novels after the Carnation Revolution. While both films use diverse adaptation strategies, they remain true to the same methodology. The diverging aesthetics express, nonetheless, rather contrasting points of view – before and after the end of the dictatorship – on the possibility of taking action through the arts. In fact, I get to the conclusion that after the experience of thirty years of democracy, Lopes presents a less innovative film but a more mature standpoint on the persisting need of political action.

The following chapter, 'Attempts to decolonize the mind: The representation of the African colonial war in Portuguese cinema', is again a comparative study, but of two films made by different filmmakers. I show that both João Botelho in *Um Adeus Português/A Portuguese Farewell* (1990) and Manoel de Oliveira in *NON, ou a Vã Glória de Mandar/No or the Vain Glory of Command* (1995) wish to interrogate hegemonic memories and assumptions about the war but get to the conclusion that they do not free themselves completely from colonialist/imperialist discourses. As a matter of fact, they present a double consciousness in which the African other is of no importance and serves mainly to come to terms with what is perceived to be an exclusively national issue.

In the third chapter, 'The discovery of paradox: The European expansion in six films by Manoel de Oliveira', I argue that the filmmakers ambiguous perspective on the subject does not change substantially in other films (*O Sapato de Satin/The Satin Slipper*, 1985; *Palavra e Utopia/Word and Utopia*, 2000; *Um Filme Falado/A Talking Picture*, 2003; *O Quinto Império – Ontem como Hoje/The Fifth Empire – Yesterday and Today*, 2004 and *Cristovão Colombo – o Enigma/Christopher Columbus – The Enigma*, 2007). Although Oliveira exposes the inconsistencies in Portugal's, Europe's and the United States of America's imperialist and religious expansionist politics over the last centuries, he confirms, in the tradition of Luís de Camões and António Vieira, Portugal's singularity and special mission.

In the last chapter of the first part, 'The adolescent as post-colonial allegory: Strategies of inter-subjectivity in Portuguese films of the 90s', I analyse three outstanding films that challenge this perspective: *Ossos/Bones* (1997) by Pedro Costa, *Corte de Cabelo/Hair Cut* (1995) by Joaquim Sapinho and *Os Mutantes/The Mutants* (1998) by Teresa Villaverde. The film's adolescent characters are used to demonstrate how the post-colonial situation makes the search for inter-subjectivity obligatory, since it engages with the

Other in a compassionate and respectful way. I argue that the allegory of the adolescent is designed to offer the spectator the possibility to come to terms with the current identity crisis that is portrayed as a result of the uneasy transition between colonial legacy and uncertain European future.

The second part, entitled 'Facing past and present from a trans-national perspective: between identity and difference', is dedicated to the co-productions based on agreements between Portugal and its former colonies. It presents a survey of all Luso-African productions released so far, concentrates on one particularly accomplished Luso-Brazilian film, analyses all literary adaptations produced with Portuguese and Brazilian subsidies and concludes with a comparison of the national and trans-national films that focus on migrating characters.

The first chapter, 'Ambivalent transnationality: Luso-African co-productions after independence (1988–2009)', presents an analysis of sixteen out of twenty trans-national productions. It seeks to assess whether the evident dependence on financial, material and human resources has an effect on the identity discourses in the films. My findings indicate that most Luso-African feature productions directed by Africans or by filmmakers with a trans-national biography actually present compelling multilateral perspectives, whereas unilateral identity discourses are almost the rule among European directors. Only a small number of films, namely *Na Cidade Vazia/Hollow City* (Maria João Ganga 2004), *Comboio da Canhoca/Canhoca Train* (Orlando Fortunato de Oliveira 2004), *Os Olhos Azuis de Yonta/The Blue Eyes of Yonta* (Flora Gomes 1992) and, with some restraints *Moia ou O Recado das Ilhas/Message From The Islands* (Ruy Duarte de Carvalho 1989)*, O Herói/The Hero* (Zezé Gamboa 2004) and *Comédia Infantil/Nelio's Story* (Solveig Nordlund 1998) offer transnational dialogues.

The second chapter, 'The limits of Luso-Brazilian brotherhood: Fortress Europe in *Foreign Land* (1995) by Walter Salles and Daniela Thomas', presents one of the most persuasive co-productions between Portugal and Brazil. I suggest that this example demonstrates that co-productions have the potential to deal with the contradictory legacy of colonialism, since this particular film opens up a space to discuss and examine the historic and cultural ties by rejecting out-dated discourses on inter-identity.

In the following chapter, 'Lusophone monologues or transnational dialogues: Luso-Brazilian literary adaptations (1995–2008)', my results are less affirmative. Among the eleven films under analysis less than half do factually engage with unbiased perspectives (*Bocage – O Triunfo do Amor/Bocage – The Triumph of Love*, Djalma Limogni Batista, 1995; *Hans Staden*, 1999; *Desmundo*, Alain Fresnot, 2002; *Estorvo/Turbulence*, Ruy Guerra, 2000 and *O Judeu/The Jew*, Jom Tob Azulay, 1995) that bypass lusophony and luso-tropicalism. Myths and mythmaking are actually perpetuated in *Word and Utopia* (2000), *Diário de um Novo Mundo/New World Diary* (Paulo Nascimento, 2006), *Amor e Cia./Love and Co.* (Helvécio Ratton, 1999) and *A Selva/The Forest* (Leonel Vieira, 2002).

In the final chapter, 'Identities adrift: lusophony and migration in national and trans-national films', I conclude that co-productions are no guarantee for multilateral views on the complex bonds and historical relationships between Portugal and its ex-colonies in films that feature immigrant characters from Africa and Brazil. The perspectives vary greatly and often reveal a critical stance, but many films are still based on the belief in cultural identity. Within the group of films discussed (six national and five co-productions), there is only one co-production, *Foreign Land*, and two national productions, *The Mutants* and *Juventude em Marcha/Colossal Youth* (Pedro Costa, 2006), that can be considered examples of a transnational cinema coming to terms with the burden of lusophony.

The end of Portugal's dictatorship and empire opened up a new chapter in film history, not only in terms of the profound changes that occurred in Portuguese national film production, but, more significantly, in offering for the first time a chapter on lusophone co-productions. This book is a first attempt to study both production modes and offers a lance at their relationship. It needs to be stressed that many films are still waiting to be studied in detail and that a number of questions are in the open concerning the relation of commercial and authorial films, the comparison of national and co-productions, the categorization of the co-productions and so forth. I genuinely hope that this book will stimulate further the ongoing research in this fascinating field of study.

Part I: Facing authoritarianism and the end of the empire: in search for an alternative identity

Non-canonical adaptations: Non-inscription and dictatorship in *A Bee in the Rain* (1968–71) and *The Dauphin* (2001) by Fernando Lopes[4]

Introduction

Fernando Lopes (b. 1935) is one of Portugal's most esteemed film and television directors and producers. He was a key filmmaker of the country's *novo cinema*[5] (new cinema) and one of the founders of the *Centro Português de Cinema* (Portuguese Centre for Cinema), established in 1968, an association of filmmakers responsible for the proliferation of this new cinema's second wave in the last years of the dictatorship. As a founding member and director of the journal *Cinéfilo* he participated in the development of serious film criticism, and as a lecturer at Lisbon's film school, *Escola Superior de Cinema*, inaugurated in 1973, had an impact on following generations. Moreover, Lopes set off the cooperation between public television and cinema as program director of the country's public channel, RTP (*Radiotelevisão Portuguesa*), between 1978 and 1980.

Lopes' filmography includes a vast number of documentary, fiction and essay films[6], both for the small and the big screen[7]. Two of his features are literary adaptations of canonical twentieth century Portuguese novels that engage in unprecedented ways with Portugal's dictatorial *Estado Novo* re-

---

[4] This chapter was previously published with the same title in a slightly different version in *Adaptation*. 3.2 (2010): 112–131. There is a shorter Portuguese version, published as 'Pouco canónicas – As adaptações de Fernando Lopes *Uma Abelha na Chuva* (1972) e *O Delfim* (2001)'. *Narrativas em Metamorfose: Abordagens Interdisciplinares*. Ed. Irene Blayer and Francisco Cota Fagundes. Cuiabá: Cathedral Publicações, 2009, pp. 319–338. Reprinted by permission of Oxford University Press.

[5] In order to distinguish the movement more clearly from the Brazilian *cinema novo*, it has been referred to as *novo cinema* in recent years.

[6] His most famous documentary and essay films are: *As Pedras e o Tempo - Évora* (1961), *Belarmino* (1964), *Nacionalidade: Português* (1972), *Nós Por Cá Todos Bem* (1975), *Altitude 114* (1984), *Se Deus Quiser* (1996) e *Cinema* (2001).

[7] His eight feature fiction films are *Uma Abelha na Chuva* (1971), *Crónica dos bons malandros* (1984), *Matar Saudades* (1987), *O Fio do Horizonte/On the Edge of the Horizon* (1993), *O Delfim* (2001) and *Lá Fora* (Out there, 2003), *98 Octanas* (98 octanes, 2006), *Os Sorrisos do Destino* (2009).

gime, which lasted from 1933 until 1974 and was predominantly shaped by the dictator António de Oliveira Salazar[8]. Lopes adapted *Uma Abelha na Chuva/A Bee in the Rain*, written by Carlos de Oliveira in 1953, under authoritarian rule between 1968 and 1971 and *O Delfim/The Dauphin*, written by José Cardoso Pires in 1969, more than two decades after the reinstauration of democracy in 2001.

Like many other national cinemas, Portugal's film history has been shaped to a large extent by literary adaptations[9], and literature has been vital in offering stories and reputation to the medium[10]. Literary texts by renowned writers such as Abel Botelho, Alexandre Herculano, Bernardo Santareno, Carlos de Oliveira, Fernando Namora, Ferreira de Castro, Guerra Junqueiro, Jorge de Sena, José Rodrigues Miguéis, José Cardoso Pires, José Régio, Júlio Dantas, Júlio Diniz, Mário de Sá Carneiro, Prista Monteiro and Virgílio Ferreira, or by national monuments such as Camilo Castelo Branco, Almeida Garrett, Eça de Queirós and Fernando Pessoa inspired numerous film narratives[11]. Contemporary authors of national and international reputation, such

---

[8] Ever since the 'May Revolution' in 1926 Portugal had been under dictatorial rule. The 'New State' initiated a new period with a proper ideology, focused on the nation, the family and the church. It was conservative, authoritarian, nationalistic and corporativistic.

[9] The first example is a production from 1912, *Carlota Ângela*, which is based on a novel by nineteenth century writer Camilo Castelo Branco. Silent cinema drew heavily on national authors: seven of the twenty five silent feature films were based on canonical books, next to popular melodramas, comedies, theatre plays and feuilleton stories. Portugal's first sound film, *A Severa* (1931), by Leitão de Barros drew on the highly popular book with the same title by Júlio Dantas, considered the most important writer at the time.

[10] The national treasures *Amor de Perdição/Doomed Love* by Camilo Castelo Branco and *As Pupilas do Senhor Reitor/The Pupils of the Dean* by Júlio Diniz have been adapted several times. The former is one of the country's most respected books and the latter one of its most popular.

[11] José Régio, Júlio Diniz and Eça de Queirós have been adapted five times to the big screen, Camilo Castelo Branco four times, and Fernando Pessoa, Ferreira de Castro, José Cardoso Pires and Júlio Dantas three times. The other authors have been adapted only once (see José de Matos-Cruz 1999).

as Agustina Bessa-Luís[12], Lídia Jorge and Mário de Carvalho have also seen their works adapted with frequency.

When publications on literary adaptations started to proliferate in recent years, James Naremore (2000: 11–12) indicated the analysis of films based on canonical texts as a relevant issue:

> (...) we need to ask why certain canonical books have been of interest to Hollywood in specific periods, and we need more elaborate investigations into the historical relation between movies and book publishing. (...) we need writings that address the uses of canonical literature by specific filmmakers. Some directors have been intent on faithfully illustrating their sources, whereas others have been motivated by a desire to interrogate or 'read' the prior text. Along similar lines, many directors have used canonical literature for politically or culturally resistant purposes, sometimes filming it more or less faithfully and sometimes radically changing it.

Fernando Lopes' adaptations demonstrate how complex the negotiations with the canonical status of an original text can get. The fact that the novels only became part of the canon after the Carnation Revolution of 25 April 1974 turns the filmmaker's engagement with their identitarian projects into elucidative examples of how aesthetic approaches can shift when the hegemonic identity changes. Before the Revolution, the cultural establishment ignored the novels since they opposed the archaic values of the dictatorship and its agrarian and industrial bourgeoisie[13]. By questioning the dominant discourses and power relations of the dictatorship, both Carlos de Oliveira[14]

---

[12] Agustina Bessa Luís is with six adaptations the most notorious author in terms of literary adaptation (including novels, short stories and original ideas).

[13] Boaventura Sousa Santos (1998: 18–19) argues that the agrarian bourgeoisie lost its economic hegemony in the beginning of the 1960s, but managed to remain its ideological hegemony until the end of the decade. The industrial bourgeoisie, started to control the small and medium industries and some parts of the agrarian bourgeoisie with credits in the 1960s.

[14] Lourenço (1999b: 289) considers Carlos de Oliveira to be a representative of the dictatorship's anti-culture and gives an early example of his criticism: his *Canções Heróicas/Heroic Songs* (lyrics together with José Gomes Ferreira and João José Cochofel, music by Fernando Lopes-Graça). The songs were performed on the streets of Lisbon in 1946 (and again in 1960) and then forbidden.

and José Cardoso Pires[15] faced repression because of their resistance identity[16]. The change of political paradigm turned both into hegemonic authors and their texts into canonical books, which came to represent the values and ideas of the young democracy and its intellectual elite.

Three decades separate the two adaptations and they bear the marks of opposite political regimes. The film *A Bee in the Rain* was based on a dissident text and both book and film saw their status changed after 1974. The film *The Dauphin*, conversely, was already based on what had become a classic text with a dissident past in a moment when Portugal was settling in as a modern member of the European Union.[17] The comparison of the two adaptations therefore offers a case study for how the status of a book might interfere in the adaptation process of a filmmaker.

To grasp the importance of Lopes' choices, one can draw on the definition of canonical books by the American literary critic Harold Bloom, the most influential and polemical defender of the relevance and existence of a Western canon. When isolating the qualities that make books indispensable within a certain culture, the author states: 'The answer, more often than not, has turned out to be strangeness, a mode of originality that either cannot be assimilated, or that so assimilates us that we cease to see it as strange' (Bloom 1994: 2). It is the aesthetic value of a literary work that leads to the immor-

---

[15] Even though Liberto Cruz (1972: 31) pointed out the importance of *The Dauphin* quite early, saying that the novel was 'obra maior da literatura portuguesa do nosso século' ('a major Portuguese literary work of this century'), Pires suffered direct and indirect censorship and had to live in exile in Paris and Brazil between 1959 and 1961. He chose voluntary exile between 1969 and 1971, following a call to teach Portuguese and Brazilian literature at London University's King's College. His first book *Os Caminheiros e Outros Contos* (1949) and his second collection of short stories, *Histórias de Amor* (1952) were confiscated by the secret police PIDE (*Policia Internacional e de Defesa do Estado*) and forbidden. Based on this experience, Cardoso Pires wrote and spoke extensively on censorship during the dictatorship (see Cândido de Azevedo 1999: 99–112).

[16] Manuel Castells (1997) refers three modern categories of identity: resistance identity, legitimising identity and project identity.

[17] It must be noted that when Cardoso Pires' text was first published, the dictatorial regime was already facing a deep crisis, due to the social contradictions created by the colonial war (1961–74) and inner pressure for democracy (see Santos 1998).

tality of its writer: 'One breaks into the canon only by aesthetic strength, which is constituted primarily of an amalgam: mastery of figurative language, originality, cognitive power, knowledge, exuberance of diction' (Bloom 1994: 29).

While Bloom has been criticized for his perspective on canonical books – especially for his belief that aesthetics are rather an individual than a social concern –, film studies have been interested in a larger picture and focused increasingly on the relationship between cinema and national or cultural identities over the last two decades.[18] As already indicated by Naremore, due to literatures' and films' unquestionable impact on the imaginary of a nation, which has come to the foreground in the wake of Benedict Anderson's (1983) insight that nations are imagined communities, the study of films based on canonical texts is an important site for the understanding of the construction and renegotiation of identity.

Even Bloom hints at this fact when he remembers that literature is driven by a longing for figuration and cites Friedrich Nietzsche's definition of metaphor as the desire to become someone different or to be in a different space. From this results another characteristic considered essential for canonical texts: their anxiety of influence. This anxiety reflects arts' intertextuality, given that outstanding artists always search for a dialogue with earlier key texts in order to exceed them:

> This partly means to be different from oneself, but primarily, I think, to be different from the metaphors and images of the contingent works that are one's heritage: the desire to write greatly is the desire to be elsewhere, in a time and place of one's own, in an originality that must compound with inheritance, with the anxiety of influence. (Bloom 1994: 12)

In Fernando Lopes' case, the adaptation strategies are strongly related to their political context. Keeping this in consideration, two hypotheses for the comprehension of his films can be developed from Bloom's rather apolitical affirmation, which has also been criticized for being oedipal.[19] First, if a

---

[18] See, for example, Mette Hjoert and Scott MacKenzie (2000).

[19] See Robert Stam (1994: 211): 'This view has been rightly critiqued by feminists as masculinist (exclusively concerned with oedipal struggles between men), leaving no place for the quilt-like intertextuality of women's dialogue with their literary

canonical novel wants to be in another place, that is, project an unfamiliar imaginary, it is likely that the filmmaker will try to offer a self-image that differs from the hegemonic identity of its time. Second, the longing for figuration will remain a crucial reference point for the adaptation process, even when the dictatorship's dominant identity ceases to exist and, especially, when a young democracy has difficulties of affirming itself. This is to say that Lopes' reading of a famous text will, most likely, question a novel's aesthetic and its construction of identity, indifferent to, or rather because, of its canonical status.

In view of that, the following questions will guide me in my endeavour to comprehend Lopes' adaptation processes: What is the significance of the resistance against the hegemonic identity for the adaptation strategies and aesthetic decisions in *A Bee in the Rain*, produced during the dictatorship? What does the now hegemonic identity of the novel represent for the adaptation of *The Dauphin* during democracy? What are the differences and similarities in terms of aesthetic choices? How do the films deal with the cultural importance of the originally dissident texts? Does it make sense to speak of an anxiety of influence?

In order to describe their identity politics, I will first contextualize the novels on which the films are based and introduce the concept 'non-inscription', coined by Portuguese philosopher José Gil. Subsequently, the analyses of each adaptation and its aesthetic strategies will lead to a concluding comparison. My main interest here is to understand how Lopes deals with the change of political paradigm and its effects on the status and the identity politics of the books he adapted.

Original texts on non-inscription

The novels adapted by Lopes, *A Bee in the Rain* by Carlos de Oliveira (1921–1981) and *The Dauphin* by José Cardoso Pires (1925–1998), are both considered innovative successors of neo-realism, the mythical Portuguese literary movement from the 1940s that set out to reflect on and transform its society. A return to reality by means of an authentic portrayal of repression

---

mothers. It can also be see as Darwininan (literary survival of the fittest) and Eurocentric, and certainly lacks the amiable generosity of Bakhtinian dialogism. Nonetheless, Bloom's approach does at least bring desire, and even passion, into the question of intertextuality'.

and the disfavoured has been described as its major trait, first in literature and then in cinema. But according to Eduardo Lourenço, the Portuguese neo-realist style is often wrongly defined in ideological terms, without taking into consideration the complex relationships between Marxist ideology and the fictional works. Neo-realism was, in fact, a counter-culture movement, which assigned a new role to the writers by turning literature into a means of resistance against the dictatorial regime. This occurred in a moment when the Salazar dictatorship started to enhance repressive mechanisms and to loose its strong popular approval in Portugal and abroad:

> Nesse momento adquiria tal regime, sem vontade nem possibilidade de emenda, aquele carácter organicamente repressivo e institucionalmente anquilosado que até então mascarara com mais talento e sucesso. Apesar disso, até aos fins dos anos 44, o Regime gozou de um virtual consenso público, conferido pela nota modernista dos anos 30, a sua própria novidade, o dinamismo de certos quadros e a maturidade do seu chefe super-carismático. Sem esquecer que a pulsão do Ocidente ainda não contrariava, de frente, o esquema que era o seu. (Lourenço 1993: 289)[1]

Carlos de Oliveira's writings pick up on the suffocating atmosphere of these years. The portrayal of Portugal's ambiguous and repressed society and a glimpse of hope are referred as outstanding qualities of his texts (Magalhães 2002: 1039). *A Bee in the Rain* is the author's most celebrated text, since it marked an extension of neo-realist concerns and aesthetics. Magalhães (2002: 1031) emphasizes that the book has a density rarely associated with neo-realism: 'se revela inaugural é na recusa absoluta da imposição de uma perspectiva simplificadora, o que implica uma construção rigorosa capaz de jogar com todos os meios susceptíveis de contribuir para a apresentação de

---

[20] ('At that moment the regime acquired, unwillingly and incapable of changing it, the organically repressive and institutionally paralyzed character which it had been able to mask earlier with more talent and success. Moreover, until the end of 1944 the regime had enjoyed almost complete public approval, earned by its modernist stance in the 1930s, by its very novelty, by its dynamic in certain cadres and by the maturity of its super-charismatic leader. It should also not be forgotten that the Western world did not yet question directly this kind of scheme.')

uma realidade complexa, construída de múltiplas forças contraditórias'[21]. It was canonized a masterwork once the dictatorship had been abolished.

José Cardoso Pires' *The Dauphin* is also considered a masterpiece and responsible for much of the author's reputation. Dietrich Briesemeister (1997: 377) praises the way in which the novel unmasks the myths of a society based on power, violence and the arrogance of class difference. The topic of Portugal's underdevelopment is, according to Eunice Cabral (1999: 8), one of the semantic and discursive axes of the book: 'a impossibilidade de realização das potencialidades de uma formação social, a portuguesa, por falta de recursos ou por uma utilização incorreta destes'[22]. In Carlos Reis' (2000: 657) understanding, this and other issues are explored through a much-acclaimed multi-vocal narrative, which dares to question neo-realism's constraint rhetoric.

This is to say that Fernando Lopes chose for his literary adaptations two aesthetically innovative texts associated with neo-realism that defy the ruling class during the dictatorship by accusing her of being responsible for misery and social stagnation. This critique is put forward with great originality. Instead of focusing on the common neo-realist protagonists from the lower classes, the books use allegorical couples from the upper class, whose vicious and (self-) destructive relationships turn the oppressive mechanisms under dictatorship visible.

The dilemma faced by these couples can be described with Portuguese philosopher José Gil's (2004) term 'não-inscrição' (non-inscription). The author argues that non-inscription occurs when individuals are deprived of any kind of action, affirmation or decision with which they would usually achieve their autonomy and sense of existence. Although his definition centres initially on the deficiency of subjectivity in adult individuals, his aim is to explain Portuguese national identity.

My following chapters, especially the one on films that use adolescent char-

---

[21] ('it proves to be novel in its complete refusal to impose a simplifying perspective, which implies a rigorous construction capable of bringing into play all susceptible means that contribute to the representation of a complex reality, constructed by multiple contradictory forces')
[22] ('the impossibility to fulfil the potential of a specific social formation, the Portuguese, due to the lack of resources or because they are wrongly applied.)

acters as an allegory for post-coloniality, will show that I question authors or filmmakers who consider identities as essential or fixed. I do not think that this is Gil's case. Rather, he tries to alert that Portugal's long history of authoritarianism has made self-affirmation – which is the basis of a healthy identity project – almost impossible. The disease that he diagnoses for his country consists in the difficulty to construct an individual identity, since it was more often than not sacrificed for a higher ideal: the national identity. In relation to the theoretical framework from my forth chapter, one could say that Gil points out that the skills for inter-subjectivity – to accept the constant tension between self-affirmation and the recognition of the Other – is compromised and that identification, that is, inscription, is problematic – not only in relation to oneself (desire) but also in relation to the Other (real).

Gil stresses that Portugal's non-inscription differs from that of other countries because it works with peculiar mechanisms. In any case, it is the opposite of inscription:

A inscrição abre os corpos. Se a potência de vida aumenta, a inscrição incorpora-se no desejo de tal maneira que a sua 'marca' ou 'selo' desaparece. Se se mutila ou esmaga o desejo, fica apenas um corpo-objecto marcado a ferros – corpo aprisionado. Quando o corpo se fecha, há não-inscrição. A inscrição é pois a condição da produção do desejo e do real (ou da sua destruição). A não-inscrição suspende o desejo, e vai provocar, mais cedo ou mais tarde, violência física. Equivale a uma 'má inscrição'. (...) Portugal forjou uma bem específica, para o seu uso próprio. (Gil 2004: 49)[23]

Non-inscription occurs in places where desire(s) – or self-affirmation – have been shattered because consciousness – namely language, images, feelings and sensations – live in a kind of fog. Gil (2004: 19) relates it to an original

---

[23] ('Inscription opens the body. When the potential of living increases, inscription is incorporated into desire in a way that its "mark" or "sign" disappears. When desire is mutilated or smashed, the only leftover is an iron-branded body-object – an imprisoned body. When the body shuts down, non-inscription occurs. Thus, inscription is the condition in which desire and reality are produced (or destroyed). Non-inscription suspends desire and provokes, sooner or later, physical violence. It is the equivalent of a "bad inscription" (...). Portugal forged a very specific type, for its particular use.')

trauma, but also to historical, social and individual events, that escaped inscription: 'Qualquer coisa como um Alcácer-Quibir (...) Um "branco
psíquico", ou melhor, uma multiplicidade de brancos psíquicos atravessam a
consciência clara, de tal maneira que, sem que ela se aperceba, formam-se as
maiores obscuridades e confusões'.[24]

Even though Gil does not establish a specific moment in which Portugal's
dilemma of non-inscription began, the reference to the battle of Alcácer-
Quibir in Morocco, in 1578, is telling. I will mention this battle quite often
in the following chapters, since it was the most decisive event in modern
Portuguese history after which the country lost its independence to Spain,
and thus, factually, the capacity to act on the political stage. Non-inscription
is, therefore, 'um velho hábito'[25] (Gil 2004: 17), a deeply rooted problem
within Portuguese society. The absurd idealization of national identity not
only favoured authoritarianism but worsened during the almost fifty years of
dictatorship. And the phenomenon survived the Carnation Revolution because the transition process towards democracy did not escape its influence.
Gil (2004: 16) insists that non-inscription remains a problem, since nobody
wanted to identify with the past:

O 25 de Abril recusou-se, de um modo completamente diferente, a inscrever no
real os 48 anos de autoritarismo salazarista. Não houve julgamentos de Pides
nem de responsáveis do antigo regime. Pelo contrário, um imenso perdão reco-
briu com um véu a realidade repressiva, castradora, humilhante de onde provín-
hamos. Como se a exaltação afirmativa da 'Revolução' pudesse varrer, de uma
penada, esse passado negro.[26]

---

[24] ('Something like an Alcácer Quibir (...) A psychic "blank", or rather, a
multiplicity of psychic blanks cross the lucid consciousness in a way that, without it
noticing, major obscurities and confusions are formed.')
[25] ('an old habit')
[26] ('The 25 April refused, in a completely different way, to inscribe 48 years of
Salazarist authoritarianism into the real. There was no judgement of either PIDE
agents or people involved in the former regime. On the contrary, a massive pardon
covered like a veil the repressive, castrating, humiliating reality from where we
came. As though the affirmative exaltation of 'Revolution' could wipe out the
sinister past in one strike.')

Eduardo Lourenço (1999a: 18) would probably agree with this analysis of political amnesia, but he establishes, less metaphorically, a direct relationship between Portugal's most profound trauma, the battle of Alcácer-Quibir, and the beginning of its political passivity: 'Quase sem transição, Portugal deixa de se viver como actor e sujeito da sua própria história, entra no tempo do seu apagamento politico próprio'.[27] The author's analysis is prior to the concept of non-inscription, but his explanation is similar. It is of particular importance, since Lourenço gives an idea of how Portuguese culture was used as a powerful surrogate to idealize the country's identity.

The phenomenon of *Sebastianismo* (Sebastianism) demonstrates how Portugal learned to project its desires after Alcácer Quibir into a flashy utopia. The myth suggests that the young King *dom* Sebastião, who disappeared during the battle in Morocco, would resurrect and guide Portugal to a glorious future as spiritual and political leader of the world: 'Tudo se passou como se Portugal tivesse ficado com um presente virtual, um passado morto, embora glorioso, e um future onírico'[28] (Lourenço 1999a: 19). Given the incapacity to act, action was postponed to the future.

Canonical literature was a key tool in this undertaking and became the preferred place for the inscription of historical and social processes. Bloom's definition of immortal texts as places that express the desire to become someone different or to be in a different space, proves to have a point – a very political one indeed – when one considers how literature offered the Portuguese nation a stage for its imaginary self-affirmation. This becomes particularly clear in Lourenço's observation that *Sebastianism* had a powerful predecessor in the most important Portuguese book of all times: *The Lusiads*. Luís de Camões sings the glories of Portugal's discoveries and describes the recognition of the exploring navigators by the gods: 'o verdadeiro Sebastião é o *texto* dos *Lusíadas* que desde então (...) se converteu na referência icónica da cultura portuguesa'[29] (Lourenço 1999a: 19). Many

---

[27] ('Almost without transition, Portugal ceases to be actor and subject of its own history and enters a period of political annihilation.')
[28] ('It seemed as though Portugal was living a virtual present, a dead past, even though glorious, and an oniric future.')
[29] ('The text of the *Lusiads* is the true Sebastian and it (...) became the iconic reference of Portuguese culture.')

other Portuguese writers would follow in Camões' footsteps, being Fernando Pessoa the internationally most celebrated. He is acclaimed for his mastery in retreating from reality and in entering a state – his famous heteronyms – in which he was at the same time absent from himself and omnipresent, as Lourenço (1999a: 89) claims.

Portuguese neo-realism and *novo cinema* were, on the contrary, movements eager to inscribe reality into culture by proposing an alternative to the canonical project associated with Camões or Pessoa. They engaged with the real conditions of Portugal's contemporary society, particularly with its social injustice and exploitation. Instead of concealing non-inscription or postponing inscription, they set out either to reveal the impossibility of acting politically or to demand it. Using Bloom's observation that immortal literature needs to present an alternative identity, the explanation to why neo-realism still faces strong reservations by literary critics becomes understandable.

New cinema, even though in demand of a profound assessment, has suffered a similar fate. Before I start with my analyses of Lopes' literary adaptations, I will briefly look at the relationship between the two movements. They have both been accused of being little successful in their inscription of reality, but what seems to be at stake is perhaps not the question of reality, but rather the lack of an original identity project. *A Bee in the Rain,* professedly a film of Portugal's *novo cinema*, is an exception since it proposes art as an arena for political action. *The Dauphin*, on the other hand, returns, even though in a different shape, to the necessity of unveiling non-inscription, because of the lost chances of inscription after the end of the dictatorship, without offering a palpable alternative.

Neo-realism and *novo cinema*

Novo cinema was set in motion with a film inspired by Italian neo-realism, *Dom Roberto* by José Ernesto de Sousa, produced by a cooperative in 1962. While it shares neo-realism's moral stance on the impoverished conditions of the lower classes, it is aesthetically still indebted to the Portuguese studio films, especially to its comedies from the 1930s and 1940s. The movement finally affirmed itself in 1963 with *Os Verdes Anos/The Green Years* by Paulo Rocha, inspired by the French *nouvelle vague* in its authorial style and elaborate *mise-en-scène* to narrate the clash between its character's rural and Lisbon's modern urban identity.

Like their French colleagues or those from other new cinemas around the world, the Portuguese filmmakers were looking for an aesthetic renewal and independent ways of production. Luís de Pina (1986: 139–40) sums up the characteristics of the movement: 'pretende-se, de um modo geral, obter mais liberdade para a criação, fugir dos temas e estéticas gastos do antigo cinema português (...), retomar, de certo modo, o entusiasmo e o "passo europeu" (...) da geração de 30'[30].

Except that *novo cinema* got wrapped up in artistic and political ambivalences. Many aspiring filmmakers accepted support from the dictatorial regime, which offered scholarships and loans. Trained at film schools in Italy, England and France and aspiring to create a Portuguese art house cinema, their innovative narratives found less approval than expected, or triggered off ideological disputes within the film circles. Based on critiques and essays from the period, Fausto Cruchinho (2001) describes in detail the complex debates and polemics, mainly related to the legacy of neo-realist literature. He argues that the majority of film critics who disliked novo cinema's films had a biased view, since they were either related to literary neo-realism or to the film club movement. Those related to neo-realism expected from the new cinema an alliance with and an improvement of the literary movement's aesthetic and ideological project, and rejected the filmmakers' search for modes of representation in the historic avant-gardes or the contemporary film movements.[31]

The paradoxical situation of *novo cinema* becomes even more apparent with

---

[30] ('They were trying to obtain more creative freedom, to break away from issues and aesthetics that had been exhausted by the previous Portuguese cinema (...), returning, in a certain way, to the enthusiasm and the "European way" of the generation from the 1930s.') The generation from the 1930s includes, for example, the filmmakers José Leitão de Barros and Manoel de Oliveira.

[31] Fernando Lopes (qtd. in Marques 1996: 8) attests, however, a more complex and ambiguous relationship between the filmmakers and neo-realist literature. Lopes' comparison of *A Bee in the Rain*, based on a novel considered neo-realist, with a film closer to neo-realist principles makes this clear: 'o filme *O Recado* de José Fonseca e Costa [1971], embora pouca gente tenha dado por isso, é uma obra com um grande peso da tradição moral do neo-realismo. Em *Uma Abelha na Chuva*, por outras razões, isso já se sente menos.' ('The film *O Recado* by José Fonseca e Costa [1971], even though nobody noted this, is indebted to neo-realism's moral tradition. For other reasons this is less perceptible in *A Bee in the Rain*.')

the help of the concept of non-inscription. Independently of its aesthetic strategies and its attempts to recover Portugal's hidden reality, the movement found it difficult to free itself from an imaginary impregnated with frustrations and lack of hope. The famous remark by Alberto Vaz da Silva (qdt. in da Costa 1991: 120) on *novo cinema*'s first fiction feature, *The Green Years*, is quite revealing of this double bind: 'um filme além do mais português, facto que se assinala porque muito raras vezes uma obra de arte deixou, entre nós, assim transparecer também além do mais todo o fatalismo, o tempo absorto e o peso surdo, pesado e prolixo que há tanto se enraizaram na terra e a vão definindo, no seu devir'[32]. *Novo cinema* can, in fact, be described as a cinema that tried to unveil and critique the non-inscription typical for Portuguese society, but rarely offered the outlook of inscription, that is, the possibility to overcome the repressive political and social situation.

The adaptation of *A Bee in the Rain* by Carlos de Oliveira

Lopes' literary adaptation *A Bee in the Rain*, based on a neo-realist novel, can, in fact, be regarded as one of the very few films that set out to bring the two paradoxes – the ambiguous relationship between film and politically inspired literature, and the lack of inscription – to a halt. Its mode of production[33] and the originality of the film's language that derives from its avant-garde style were crucial in this undertaking. Discontinuities of sound and image are used as equivalences for the novel's technique, but also for the development of a proper film style. The style is composed of lengthy shots showing fragments of the aristocratic couple's deserted mansion and of lingering travellings along the empty property. It makes use of repetitive montage, which, combined with freeze frames or inserts of stills, constantly in-

---

[32] ('The fact that it is a profoundly Portuguese film has to be singled out because there are few works of art that have turned perceptible the complete fatalism, the dead time and the deafening weight, heavy and diffuse, which is rooted in our earth and defines its development.')

[33] The film was produced without any state subsidies. Fernando Lopes told Vítor Tavares the epopee of its production. Further information on the production process can be found in Duarte. In earlier years, Lopes had received a scholarship from the National Film Fund (*Fundo de Cinema Nacional*) with which he studied at the *London School of Film Technique*.

terrupts the narrative flow. The vertical montage of sound and image also challenges conventional reception by discarding the reproduction of diegetic sound and speech usually employed with the intention of creating a reality effect. It desynchronizes sound and image by editing extra-diegetic sounds,[34] and the long interior monologues from the novel are reduced to fragments, either spoken in voice-over or translated into subjective shots from the point of view of the two main characters[35], Álvaro (João Guedes) and Maria dos Prazeres (Laura Soveral).

Figure 1: João Guedes and Laura Soveral in *A Bee in the* Rain (Courtesy Madragoa Filmes).

---

[34] One of the most famous scenes is the coach scene. Luís Miguel Pereira (1991) offers an excellent reading of the film's complex use of sound and the sound track by Alexandre Gonçalves.
[35] One example would be the memories of Álvaro's childhood that are substituted by shots in which he observes insistently photographs of himself as a child.

In the novel *A Bee in the Rain* the thoughts, memories and desires of the noblewoman Maria dos Prazeres Pessoa da Alva Sancho Silvestra and the anxieties and recollections of her husband Álvaro Silvestre, a rich farmer whom Maria dos Prazeres (Mary of Pleasure) was forced to marry when her family got bankrupt, construct a complex and contradictory reality. This reality does not follow the rules of realism, but 'dimana da subjetividade das personagens e de uma linguagem criativa simbólica, mais transfigurada do que mimética'[36] (Alves 2005: 13).

Prazeres and Álvaro are members of the small elite of the shire of Corgos and as much victims as agents of non-inscription. Prazeres is an embittered woman whose desire to marry out of love was frustrated, as are her romantic aspirations towards the coachman Jacinto or Álvaro's audacious brother. Imprisoned in her girlish dreams of romantic love, which she nurtures by reading romance novels, she perpetuates non-inscription by castrating others and abusing her position as powerful landlady in the region. Álvaro is her main victim, but although he tries to drown his wife's contempt in alcohol, his attempts to gain some sort of meaning for his existence are exercised without any scruples. There are two efforts of inscribing his desire – to be recognized by his wife: first, through a frustrated self-accusation of the couple's illegal undertakings at the local paper; and subsequently through a conspiracy against the coachman Jacinto.

His conspiracy initiates when he overhears a conversation between Jacinto and his girlfriend Clara. It reveals that Prazeres is in love with their employee. Álvaro's vengeance is to inform Clara's father, Master António, about the secret love affair between them. Since Master António desires a rich marriage for his daughter, he kills Jacinto with the help of a naïf peasant, Marcelo, who he seduces with the false prospect of getting Clara's hand in exchange.

But none of Álvaro's plans to inscribe his desire for Prazeres and to transfer his crisis to the dead Jacinto are successful. At the end of the novel nothing has changed for him; only the lower-class gets to feel the effects of his vicious plot: a maid is held responsible for the conspiracy against the dead

---

[36] ('stem from the subjectivity of the characters and from a creative symbolic language that is more transfigured than mimetic')

Jacinto and gets fired, Clara kills herself and her father has to go to prison. The little revolt, which results from these events and manifests itself in a few stones throws against the mansion, is promptly suffocated by another maid as 'coisas de garotos'[37] (Oliveira 2001: 160). The social order seems to have remained intact after Jacinto's and Clara's death when Prazeres, Álvaro, Dr. Neves, Dona Violante, Dona Cláudia and Father Abel gather around the fireplace. But the author carefully reveals the monstrosity of the small elite and its terrible deeds when he describes the characters as 'desfigurados, verdadeiros, sob o reflexo das chamas'[38] (Oliveira 179). The novel thus points towards the identity crisis of the agrarian elite and turns visible the vicious circle of non-inscription, perpetrated as much by the agrarian bour-geoisie and their power plays, as by the lower-class that is incapable of re-volt when it becomes the victim of jealousy or its own desire for class as-cendance.

Considered by many one of Portugal's best films ever (da Costa 1991: 138), Fernando Lopes' adaptation does not modify the novel's story in its major lines, but changes the way in which it is told. The film's plot condenses the novel's action by eliminating events and characters that serve to portray the shire's society in the novel. Consequently, the conflict between the couple is stressed and focuses more strongly on Prazeres' desire for the coachman and Álvaro's resulting resentment. There is also a shift of emphasis towards the character of Prazeres, resulting in the almost complete removal of her hus-band's feelings, desires and memories, especially those of his childhood.

The critical and creative reading of the novel is most perceptible in an added sequence in which a group of amateur actors performs a theatrical adaptation of Camilo Castelo Branco's famous romantic novel *Doomed Love*[39]. This

---

[37] ('childish pranks')

[38] ('disfigured, genuine, in the light of the flames')

[39] This sequence is not only an inter-textual reference to Camilo Castelo Branco's novel, but also, to a certain extent, to its cinematographic adaptations. José Manuel Costa stresses that the additional sequence results from an emphasis of elements encountered in Oliveira's novel that had been observed by Saraiva and Lopes: 'no filme, a exaltação da teia de sentimentos, a elevação deles e das pessoas no contexto do quadro histórico – de "classes" – em que também estão radicados, e, por essa via, a acentuação do lado camiliano do romance.' ('In the film, the exaltation of the net of feelings, their elevation and that of the characters in the historical context – of the

sequence works with the baroque metaphor of the world as stage and establishes a parallel between the on-stage performance and past, present and future of the narrative's characters. It begins with a long shot of the theatre booth in which the representatives of the agrarian bourgeoisie, Prazeres and Álvaro, are seated. This establishing shot emphasizes their central position in the rural society and is the starting point for the circular structure of non-inscription that becomes apparent at the end of the entire sequence. The beginning of the spectacle is stressed with shots of the diming lights and the rising of the curtain. The coachman Jacinto (Adriano Reys) enters the stage in the role of the tragic hero Simão who will kill his rival Baltazar, Teresa's cousin, who reveals their love affair to his uncle. When he speaks the lines 'Oh Teresa, Teresa, assim nos vão separar para sempre'[40], the vertical montage works against the realism established in the earlier shots: Jacinto's lines are echoed, repeated with variations and underscored with the pathos of the overture of Verdi's *The Force of Destiny*.[41] This has an ambivalent effect: it

---

"classes" – in which they find themselves, is, therefore, an accentuation of the Camilian side of the novel.' Fernando Duarte (1972: 2), on the other hand, points out the filmic inter-textual references, such as Fritz Murnau's *Nosferatu* in the coach scene, as well as films by Straub and Huillet. It is worth noting that Lopes' adaptation does not only use the novel *A Bee in the Rain* as reference but also much of Carlos de Oliveira's poetry (see Tavares 1968: 13–4).

[40] ('Oh Teresa, Teresa, this is how they will separate us forever.')

[41] Fernando Lopes (in Marques 1996: 40) described in detail the relation between sound and image in the film: 'pode dizer-se que a banda sonora adquire uma vida própria que sem se sobrepor à expressão visual, complementariza-a, acabando por aperfeiçoar a sua unidade. De facto, a memória que umas cenas ou situações conservam em relação a outras (…) acabam por estabelecer, ao longo do filme, um *eco* permanente e crescente. O exemplo mais flagrante é seguramente a tomada das palavras *Oh, Teresa, Teresa*, da representação teatral. Obviamente, o eco não pode ser entendido apenas ao nível de conotações de ordem musical ou sonora, em geral. Afinal, a leitura da riqueza expressiva de cada cena só é possível descobrindo-lhe as que com ela estão relacionadas, explicando-a ou completando-a. Não será essa única via de acesso ao conhecimento do naipe de significados que um filme, *construído e montado em mosaico*, contém?' ('You could say that the sound track has a proper life, which, instead of subordinating the visual, complements it and enhances its unity. In fact, the memory that some scenes or situations conserve in regard to others (...) establish, throughout the film, a permanent and growing echo. The most evident example is the use of the words *Oh, Teresa, Teresa* during the theatrical

highlights the character's feelings, while, at the same time, distances the spectator from them by making a perception of the scene's theatricality possible.

The same occurs on the visual level. The juxtaposition of the long shots of the stage and the long-lasting close ups of Prazeres and Álvaro, in which their gazes reveal her desire for Jacinto and his jealousy, and the medium shots of the spectators, especially of Clara (Zita Duarte) who observes with preoccupation these gazes, turn visible that Prazeres and Álvaro are not only spectators but also actors in the drama that repeats the plot of *Doomed Love*, and, to a certain extent, the story of Prazeres' forced marriage. The montage of the shots, together with the vertical montage of the sound foreground that we are watching the perpetuation of the hegemonic identity and the beginning of yet another drama of non-inscription as a result of the oppression of desire.

The *teatrum mundi* metaphor is again employed at the end of the film. After killing Jacinto with the help of Marcelo (Carlos Ferreiro), Master António (Ruy Furtado) goes to jail. Just like in the novel, this causes the insignificant upheaval mentioned before. In the film it is expressed in an abstract and hermetic fashion. A shot of the detonation of rocks is juxtaposed with the close up shots of their solidity. Ever since there is no real threat of a revolt, the detonation is only an extra-diegetic echo during these close ups. This lack of resistance emerges also in the following sequence that shows images of old peasants juxtaposed with the sound of people in oration. These people clearly do not represent any acute hazard for the agrarian bourgeoisie because they share their conservative and traditional values.

This sequence leads to the first of two closures. The first closure repeats the shots from the beginning of the film in inverted order. It emphasizes visually non-inscription's circular movement, described in the original text and further explored in the additional theatre sequence. After showing the improbability of a revolt on behalf of the peasants, the filmmaker now looks for rev-

---

performance. The echo obviously cannot be understood only on the level of musical or sound connotation. After all, the reading of the richness of each scene is only possible when you encounter those that are related to them and that explain or add something to them. Would not this be the only way of getting to understand this variety of meanings that a film, constructed and edited as a mosaic, contains?')

olutionary potential elsewhere. The circle of non-inscription closes only for a brief moment and opens up a new beginning that demonstrates that the self-referential film and its avant-garde strategies are themselves capable of changing the *status quo*.

The second circle reinitiates once more with the shots of the deserted landscape, which just closed the first circle. Then we see Prazeres in her living room where she resumes for her girlfriends the plot of a romantic novel that contains once again the well-known story of frustrated love. This shot is juxtaposed with the shots from the theatre sequence, in order to establish an analogy between the violent fate suffered by Jacinto and Clara, the characters in the just cited novel and the heroes from Castelo Branco's canonical book. But after having set up this relation, Fernando Lopes now freezes the shot when Álvaro enters the room. This image is followed by a freeze frame of Prazeres. Freezing the images of the perpetrators of non-inscription is an act of inscription by the filmmaker, suggesting that there is a possibility for revolt, which consists in singling out and thus stopping those responsible. Instead of a possible upheaval performed by the peasants of the shire insinuated in the book, it is the filmmaker who takes action, aesthetically and politically, by bringing the vicious circle and its actors to a standstill.

The closure of the film thus reveals the reason for the anti-illusionist style of the film that expands the symbolism of the original novel. Through its aesthetic and because of the second ending that follows the circular closure of Oliveira's text, the literary adaptation goes beyond the demonstration of non-inscription. In fact, the film *A Bee in the Rain* affirms the existence of a resistance identity and considers it possible to act with cinematographic means against repression. That is to say that the filmmaker inscribes his desire as an artist by declaring the autonomy of sound and image during the dictatorship. In vanguard tradition, this autonomy not only makes the actors and the mechanisms of non-inscription perceptible but presents the possibility of political action. It is not by chance that *A Bee in the Rain* is considered a canonical film.

The adaptation of *The Dauphin* by José Cardoso Pires

The Dauphin was written in 1968, in the same year in which the dictator Salazar left power after his grotesque fall from a chair. An auto-diegetic narrator from Lisbon examines the expectation that the dictatorial regime could come to an end, symbolized in this fall, in the famous novel. He is a writer by profession and thus Pires' *alter ego* who returns after a year of absence to Gafeira, a rural region with a mythical lagoon that belongs to the local aristocrat, the *fidalgo* Tomás de Palma Bravo. The invented place is an allegory of Portugal and, as Eduardo Prado Coelho (2002: 10) remarks, still representative for its contemporary society: 'todos nós, de José Cardoso Pires, escritor, até aos narradores em que o escritor se representa, dos tipógrafos aos capistas, dos editores aos livreiros, dos críticos aos leitores, dos professores aos estudantes, todos continuamos a ser, de certo modo, súbditos dessa lagoa'.[42] Like José Gil, the late literary critic advocates that at the beginning of the new millennium and almost three decades after the end of the dictatorship, Portugal remains under non-inscription because the power mechanisms of the dictatorship, represented by the novel's aristocracy, survived.

Lopes' adaptation from 2001 was applauded by the press and well received by the public.[43] Just like in *The Bee in the Rain*, the filmmaker does not change the general story, but changes the way in which it is told. In terms of plot, the story concentrates again on the conflict between the couple, except that it maintains all the secondary characters. The complexity of the book that results from the reflections and memories of the narrator is, on the other hand, simplified as far as possible. Indeed, the temporal and spatial come and go, which characterizes the novel's style, disappears almost completely.

In the book, the narrator/writer is confronted with the news of a crime when he returns to Gafeira for the hunting season: Maria das Mercês (Mary of Grace), the wife of the *fidalgo*, and his African servant, Domingos, were found dead. The people from the village accuse the aristocrat of being the murderer. This hypothetical crime gives the narrative, whose main interest consists in lifting the fog around the accusations, the touch of a detective

---

[42] ('All of us, from José Cardoso Pires, writer, to the narrators in which the writer represents himself, to the typographers, editors and booksellers, from the critics to the readers, from the professors to the students, we are still, in a certain way, under the control of this lagoon.')

[43] The film had more than 10,000 spectators in the first week, a very good result in a country where a film with 200,000 spectators is a blockbuster (see www.medeiafilmes.pt/noticias/arquivo_2002.htm).

novel. But it is told through the famed multi-vocal narrative, which results from the crossing of rumours from the village bar, legends and historical documents concerning the Palma Bravos with prudent reflections, meticulous testimonies and reports of cinematographic detail by the narrator.

According to Dietrich Briesemeister, the novel's narrative technique bears witness to both theory and practice of the French *nouveau roman* since it breaks away from conventional fiction by questioning the role of the omniscient narrator through a constant oscillation between times and spaces. The author argues that this might confuse the readers, but offers them the opportunity to analyse the disorder of dates and voices, and thus to encounter a fresh comprehension of the story's events. Prado Coelho defends, in contrast, that the novel is enigmatic throughout its narrative, which makes the demystifying style not only mystifying, but expresses skepticism in relation to future changes. The author remembers that Pires himself called *The Dauphin* an enigmatic novel and, by citing Karl Marx, suggests that this occurs 'possivelmente porque a desmitificação que eles pretendem executar é ainda feita com a linguagem do mito'[44] (Prado Coelho 2002: 28).

Apart from the challenging polyphony of voices that instigates the readers to construct meaning, the end of the narrative presents, in fact, the resolution of the riddle in an explanation that demonstrates a relation of cause and effect between the crime and the despotic attitude of Tomás Palma Bravo: Maria das Mercês became the victim of her desire of inscription. She tried to find affirmation in the adulterous relationship with the servant Domingos, because her husband who never had any sexual relationship with her had suppressed her desire.

Her passionate encounter with the African servant killed the young man who suffered from a heart problem and was already weakened after an attack by a colonial war veteran. Gafeira serves in this episode as an allegory of the Portuguese dictatorship to address its status as an empire, unwilling to let go of its colonies. Domingos' death led to Maria das Mercês' suicide, and her husband simply ran away from the spectacle.

The true crime that the narrator is trying to unveil throughout the narrative

---

[44] ('possibly because the demythification that they are trying to execute still takes place in the language of myth')

is, however, the non-inscription of the characters, which results from the values and repressive practices of the hegemonic identity represented by the aristocracy. But the deaths of Maria das Mercês and Domingos, and the subsequent disappearance of Palma Bravo demonstrate that the patriarchal-aristocratic order actually destructed itself. It is not by chance that the narrator notes at the end that a new epoch is beginning: 'este ano é uma data especial e tudo mudou na Gafeira'[45] (Pires 1999: 263).

Magalhães and Briesemeister both identify the novel's potential to make the reader participate intellectually in lifting of the fog through the reconstruction of the presumed crime.[46] Prado Coelho's reading of the novel lacks the belief that it is possible to lift the fog of non-inscription. The author suggests (or projects) that it is unlikely that the readers can escape their own imprisonment in the repressive mechanisms. In the same line, Cabral notes that the frustrations and sublimations with regard to the power structure are paramount and do not offer much hope for political change.[47] What seems to be at stake here is whether the reader is seen to be capable to inscribe him or herself into the novel by participating in the solution of the 'crime'. While it will depend entirely on the reader if this inscription – which is one of comprehension and not of political action – can be accomplished, the narrator/author is definitely successful in this task.

---

[45] ('This year is a special date and everything has changed in Gafeira.')

[46] Briesemeister (1997: 402) says that the reader is instigated 'zum scharfsinnigen Mitdenken bei der Rekonstruktion des Falles' ('to participate with astute thinking in the reconstruction of the case').

[47] Cabral (1999: 56) parts in his argument from an essay, *Memória Descritiva*, written by Pires on his novel, and sustains that Portuguese society has been deeply marked by the absence of political and social inscription: 'Aliás, todo o texto ensaístico é uma dissertação sobre as desfigurações e as desfocagens, que presidem à constituição da diegese do romance *O Delfim*, visto que o enunciado narrativo é atravessado pela convicção de que, na sociedade portuguesa, "o que importa está ausente mas real" (AJ: 172) como resultado da ausência de realização política e social numa sociedade em estado de censura.' ('The entire essay is a dissertation on the disfigurations and lack of focus that are responsible for the constitution of the diegese of the novel *The Dauphin*, given that the narrative enunciation is informed by the conviction that "what matters in Portuguese society is absent but real" (AJ: 172) due to the absence of political and social action in a society under censorship.'

Given the opposing interpretations regarding the possible impact of the novel on its readership, it seems worthwhile to discuss its ambiguous ending. There is, indeed, no straightforward idea on what will happen in the new situation of freedom from the former archaic rule. In actual fact, instead of causing euphoria, it makes the narrator sleepy. But the last words of the novel 'Pensa na manhã e espera. Espera. Espera o sono. O sono. Sono...'[48] (Pires 1999: 264) do not necessarily indicate a perpetuation of the frustrations and sublimations, as Cabral (1999: 56) suggests, but can be read as an anxiety in view of the challenges that the change of paradigm is producing and that require a rested mind and fresh awakening. There is no doubt that tomorrow will be the time to take action.

In contrast to the book, the film begins in the year in which the writer (Rui Morrision) makes the acquaintance of the Palma Bravos and develops chronologically with only two flashbacks. The first flashback is still part of the introduction of the characters and the conflict, whereas the second flashback tells details about Maria das Mercês' (Alexandra Lencastre) and Tomás' (Rogério Samora) relationship in a linear fashion, from their first encounter with the narrator/writer until the 'crime'. The closure is, therefore, the continuation of the second flashback, helping as such to develop the impression that the film has basically a linear narrative.

Coherence is also expressed on the cinematographic level. The film uses all the conventions of classic narrative cinema, in the sense that it constructs continuity through image and sound editing. The overall tone is sober, that is, the irony established by the commentaries of the narrator disappears together with his central position in the novel. The narrator becomes, actually, a much more optimistic character, but also more conservative. His subjective voice, which leads through the meanders of the novel, is reduced to two short voice-overs that are employed for brief explanations, but they are not use to construct a subjective perspective. Without this voice of consciousness, his resistance identity almost disappears. It is passed on to another character, the ambivalent and unsympathetic old village servant (José Pinto), who attests persistently the approaching end of the local aristocracy.

---

[48] ('Think about tomorrow and wait. Wait. Wait for the sleep to come. The sleep. Sleep...')

Figure 2: Rogério Sampaio and Alexandra Lencastre in *The Dauphin* (Courtesy: Madragoa Filmes)

There are a few narrative strategies that manifest a stronger dialogue with the novel's style and Lopes' own voice as an author. The first shots fly over the Gafeira lagoon and establish its emblematic character. The narrator's voice-over explains that this allegorical place intertwines the history of Gafeira with that of the Palma Bravos. The long-established power relationship between the aristocracy and the village becomes evident in the following sequence. We hear the *Missa Solemnis* by Hector Berlioz while the camera introduces with a diagonal crane movement the details of the ancient church square. The shot passes over the cross in the centre of the square, where a lizard is sitting next to a date inscribed in stone, 1636. In a bird's eyeshot, reminiscent of the aerial and omniscient shots over the lagoon, we see the churchgoers leaving the church. The crane movement of the camera now continues and follows the aristocratic couple getting into their Jaguar, escorted by Domingos (Milton Lopes) who holds a big black dog. This continuous movement of the camera relates the square, church and couple, serving as such as a visual metaphor for the durability of the ancient place and its patriarchal-aristocratic order.

While the novel reveals by means of the polyphony of voices that the author-itarian hegemonic identity is rooted in the history of the region, the film uses this kind of shot to unveil the power of tradition. The camera frequently pans over landscapes, walls, ancient objects and people, or uses inserts that con-template material solidity. These visual strategies have two functions: first, they are leftovers from the self-referential disruptions in the novel that make the spectators aware that they are watching a fiction film; and second, they register carefully the rigid structure that sustains non-inscription. The repeat-ed insert of shots that show Palma Bravo's dog barking ferociously, for ex-ample, underline its inherent violence.

As in *A Bee in the Rain*, the creative and critical reading of the original be-comes most apparent in sequences that are not part of the novel. These se-quences either emphasize the problem of non-inscription or interpret the social changes hoped for prior to the Revolution. The evaluation of the fac-tual changes is not exceedingly positive and the new identity envisioned in the novel does not take shape.[49] On the contrary, the new times maintain old costumes, as the added sequence on the first hunt after the disappearance of the *fidalgo* demonstrates. The hunt is organized thanks to the effort of a co-operative and grants the villagers for the first time access to the lagoon. Dur-ing the hunt, the governor of the region, the *regedor* (Alexandre de Sousa), who has gained in authority after the end of the feudal rule, bluntly guaran-tees the writer the privileges he had when he was a guest of Palma Bravo for the future. The concession of these rights is received without protest, in con-trast to the growing consciousness in the novel.

Another additional sequence shows the festive activities that close the hunt-ing season. A dreamlike shot in which a girl dressed as an angel and the colonial war veteran who injured Domingos cross in front of a bonfire ex-plores the clash of past and future. It demonstrates that the transition period in which Portugal encountered itself in 2001, the year of the making of the film, still has to negotiate the tension between the phantoms of the authori-tarian past, represented by the war veteran, and the vague expectations for

---

[49] Apart from the critical perspective of the narrator, the brief appearance of a young huntress, who also makes a short appearance in the novel, gives at least a glimpse at the possibility of a redefinition of gender roles.

the future, represented by the girl.

In order to highlight the novel's proposal that non-inscription can best be observed in the repression of the feminine, the film adds two sequences that focus on Maria das Mercês. In the first, Maria comments her status as almost prisoner on the telephone to a girl friend who has an active social and professional life as a recognized poet. In the second, Maria expresses her repressed sexual desire by masturbating. The two sequences are close to the novel's spirit and participate in directing the plot towards the aristocratic couple's conflict so as to expose the patriarchal power of repression.

The additional sequences display differences between the original text and the film: where the novel confirms the factual change in Gafeira after the self-destruction of the former rule, in the sense that a new epoch is beginning (with many challenges and problems), the film foregrounds that the hegemonic identity persists after the effective change of political paradigm. Only the actors have changed. Thus being, Lopes' reading confirms Prado Coelho and Cabral's analyses that non-inscription does not come to a closure in the novel. I would, however, argue that this is not a result of Lopes' interpretation of the novel's ambiguities since they are eliminated in the adaptation. The reason is that the novel has become a canonical text.

Cardoso Pires foresaw in his novel the self-destruction of Portuguese authoritarianism and revealed how it operated: by means of a historically inscribed right to keep others from acting. His political action as a writer consisted in the revelation of this *opus moderandi* in an avant-garde style. After the authoritarian rule, exercised in the book by the allegoric aristocratic character, it was not clear how a country used to repression would react, although there was no doubt about the need of political action. Lopes, for his part, knows that Portugal has missed so far – in 2001 – its chance to construct a new identity. Instead of focusing on the potential of inscription (the resistance identity of the main character or the polyphonic voices), he therefore challenges the very possibility of inscription under the new circumstances.

Seen under this perspective, the conventionalism of the narrative gains a deeper meaning. The coherent illusionist aesthetic – apart from a few moments that offer moments of reflection on the despotic order and its long tradition – express the continuity of the hegemonic identity before and after the disappearance of its actors, the Palma Bravos. It is through the linearity of the narrative that Lopes reminds the spectator of the perpetuation of non-inscription during democracy. The literary adaptation thus maintains the spirit of the novel, but resists devotion towards the original text and its current cultural status as a text of inscription.

Comparison and conclusion

The analyses of the two literary adaptations by Fernando Lopes demonstrate that while the filmmaker chose for each film a different aesthetic strategy, he remained true to a similar methodology. *A Bee in the Rain* from dictatorial times is characterized by a vanguard style based on an innovative yet symbolic neo-realist text that is reluctant about the likelihood of political change. Whereas the novel's author Carlos de Oliveira calls attention to the mechanisms of repression and the difficulties in acquiring a resistance identity, Lopes enhances this critique, assumes the resistance identity and takes action as a filmmaker.

Thirty years later and after the Carnation Revolution from 1974, the filmmaker chooses *The Dauphin* by Cardoso Pires, which already offers a resistance identity and the desire of inscription incorporated into Lopes' earlier adaptation. Enquiring again the power of tradition, the later film opts for a linear and more conventional narrative style. But instead of affirming the book's resistance identity, Lopes now demonstrates that the hegemonic identity survived democracy. The film's seemingly classic narrative displays that there is no reason for celebration. Given the persistence of the problem of non-inscription, it focuses on the unveiling of its mechanisms by addressing a larger audience. This audience needs to be reminded that the canonization of both the Revolution and the books that foresaw or desired the change of political paradigm might, actually, conceal this fact.

Lopes' presents diverging points of view regarding the possibility of an artist to take action. During the dictatorship, the young filmmaker desires to participate in overthrowing the regime in *A Bee in the Rain*. To do so he expands the style of the original novel and radicalizes its ideas by using the potential of the cinema. Paradoxically, by spelling out the resistance identity only hoped for in the novel, Lopes makes inscription possible and creates a masterwork. When adapting *The Dauphin*, the narrator/writer of the book loses his challenging voice and retreats behind the characters that live the drama of non-inscription. His resistance identity and the anticipated construction of a new identity outlined in the original text are both eliminated.

Instead, Lopes highlights the continuity of the repressive power mechanisms of the patriarchal-aristocratic order under the rule of an elected government. While Lopes' film is outstanding in its audacity to ignore the glamour of Cardos Pires' book and in its timeliness with regard to Portuguese society, his bravery will not be rewarded with the immortalization of the film. Even though driven by a similar anxiety of influence, Lopes does not present the young democracy with the outlook of being someone else. He simply throws it back on what it is: plagued by the old habit of non-inscription.

In both cases Fernando Lopes' literary adaptations recognize but do not rely on the cultural value of the canonical books on which they are based. Lopes has no interest in benefiting from their reputation as dissidents or in participating in their canonization through fidelity. Had the filmmaker chosen fidelity, he would not have turned perceptible and acted against the mechanisms of non-inscription revealed in both novels. Indeed, he would have obscured them by taking advantage of their status of rebellious or canonical texts. In the case of *The Dauphin* he would even have suggested that Portugal no longer has to deal with the legacy of its authoritarian past.

The change of political paradigm is not accompanied by an adjustment of the filmmaker's attitude, but rather by a changed understanding of political action. Under dictatorial rule, Lopes believed that non-inscription could be put to a halt. In democracy, he reveals the insight that political action is still contaminated and that it takes more than abolishing a dictatorship or freezing of a frame that depicts the representatives of the dictatorial order.

The critical comparison of his adaptations of immortal novels on Portuguese authoritarianism lays bare the limits of canonical texts as imaginary substitutes for historical and social processes of inscription. Harold Bloom (1994: 30–1) is aware of this limit in his idea that aesthetics are an individual issue:

> If we read the Western Canon in order to form our social, political, or personal moral values, I firmly believe we will become monsters of selfishness and exploitation. To read in the service of any ideology is not, in my judgment, to read at all. The reception of aesthetic power enables us to learn how to talk to ourselves and how to endure ourselves.

Fernando Lopes' second adaptation reveals, then again, a fresh perspective on the power of 'conventional' aesthetics and on the unexpected directions that anxiety of influence can take. Even though it will cost his film canonization, his art remains unsatisfied with the idea that we should simply endure and not improve ourselves.

Attempts to decolonize the mind: The representation of the African colonial war in Portuguese cinema[50]

Introduction

At the First International Conference *A Guerra Colonial - Realidade e Ficção* (The Colonial War: Reality and Fiction) held in Lisbon in 2001, the filmmaker Alberto Seixas Santos (2001: 498) observed that Portuguese cinema had so far failed to discuss the Portuguese colonial war that took place in the African countries Angola, Guinea-Bissau and Mozambique between 1961 and 1974. The filmmaker stressed that this was difficult to understand, since the war not only ended almost fifty years of dictatorship but also the mythic idea of a Fifth Empire. João Botelho (2001: 493) defended a similar position but invested the war with even greater historical significance, suggesting that the profound national distress that accompanied its end reflected the conclusion of 500 years of history. Both filmmakers emphasized that the colonial war had to be addressed with more consistency in Portuguese cinema if there is to be any coming to terms with this powerful trauma.[51]

From the scarce research on films that engage with the war (Matos-Cruz 2001, Ribeiro 2001), it becomes evident that the few films that represent it do so through the homecoming genre. From 1965 onwards filmmakers have told stories about soldiers returning from the battlefield.[52] During the dicta-

---

[50] This chapter is a revised version of an article published as 'Decolonizing the Mind? The Representation of the African Colonial War in Portuguese Cinema'. *Studies in European Cinema*, 2.3 (2005): 227–40. Reprinted by permission of Intellect.

[51] João de Melo (1997: 496), novelist and investigator of the colonial war, goes as far as to suggest that literature was perhaps the only part of Portuguese society that does not accept the taboo of a past that marked a whole generation.

[52] Films within the homecoming genre are: *Um Cão e Dois Destinos* (1965), *29 Irmãos* (29 Brothers, 1965), *Mudar de Vida* (1966), *Uma Vontade Maior* (1967), *Grande, Grande era a Cidade* (1971), *Os Caminhos da Verdade* (1972, unfinished). Films that question the dominant ideology are extremely rare: *O Mal-Amado* (1972-1974), *Perdido por Cem* (1972). *Deixem-me ao Menos Subir às Palmeiras* (1972) is about colonialism's violence and exploitation in Africa and was banned by censorship.

torship, these films defended, typically for pro-war films, nationalism and the values of the colonizer in order to encourage support for the soldiers.[53] Documentaries depicted, at the same time, the importance of the colonies, highlighting Portugal's economic interests and colonialism's 'civilising' dimension.[54] The few films that spoke up against colonialism were censored. After the war, documentaries openly criticized Portugal's colonial history,[55] while feature films preserved a domestic point of view by focusing again on the post-war situation of the home comer, his personal traumas, feelings of guilt and difficulties to adapt to society.[56] Any confrontations in battle are usually reduced to short flashbacks.

Since the Revolution in 1974 only five Portuguese feature films can be considered films on the colonial war[57], next to one African production that engages with its dimension as a war of independence: *Mortu Nega/Those Whom Death Refused* (1988) by the internationally much respected Guinean Flora Gomes. Presently, the first Luso-African co-production on the war is in post-production: Zezé Gamboa's film *O Grande Kilapy/The Great Kilapy*.

The first Portuguese director to engage with the colonial war was João Botelho, one of the key filmmakers of Portugal's '*escola portuguesa*', in *Um*

---

[53] Another way of representing Africa within the given framework of colonialist values was through comedies or melodramas in which it is used as an exotic setting for strong feelings: *A Voz do Sangue* (1965), *Estrada da Vida* (1968), *Limpopo* (1970) are examples of melodrama and *O Amor desceu de Pára-quedas* (1968), *O Zé do Burro* (1971), *O Vendedor* (1974) of comedy.

[54] See *Angola - na Guerra e no Progresso* (1971), *Esplendor Selvagem* (1972), *Miss Moçambique* (1972). Anti-colonialist documentaries are *Catembe* (1964) and *Índia* (72-75). António Faria provides an interesting description of the last film.

[55] See *Deus, Pátria, Autoridade* (1975), *Os Demónios de Alcácer-Quibir* (1975), *Actos dos Feitos da Guiné* (1980), *Gestos & Fragmentos* (1982).

[56] *Adeus, até ao meu Regresso* (1974), *O Último Soldado* (1979), *La Vitta é Bella* (1979), *A Culpa* (1980), *Antes a sorte que tal morte* (1981), *Matar Saudades* (1987), *A Idade Maior/Alex* (1990), *Ao Sul* (1993) and *Os Imortais* (2003). Television productions have only very recently taken up the subject and equally concentrate on the traumas of former soldiers. *Era uma Vez um Alferes* (RTP, 1987), *Inferno* (SIC, 1999) and *Monsanto* (SIC, 2000).

[57] Botelho (2001: 21) declared that *Farewell* was actually not a war film but a film about a family and their memory. He had chosen *If Memory Existed* as the film's first title.

Adeus Português/A Portuguese Farewell (1985). Five years later, Manoel de Oliveira, Portugal's internationally most recognized *auteur* and the dominant figure of its cinema, also addressed the trauma in *NON ou a Vã Glória de Mandar/No or the Vain Glory of Command* (1990). Just in time for the commemorations of the thirtieth anniversary of the Carnation Revolution, *Preto e Branco/Black and White* (2003) by film and television producer/director José Carlos de Oliveira and *A Costa dos Murmúrios/The Murmuring Coast* (2004), an adaptation of Lydia Jorge's famous novel by former documentary filmmaker Margarida Gil, took up the challenge to deal with the subject. The most recent production is *20, 13* (2006) by filmmaker Joaquim Leitão who explores queer issues within the war setting.

The small number of films on the war cannot be explained by the minute size of Portugal's annual film production or budgets alone, and different reasons have been named.[58] The anthropologist José Ribeiro (2001: 289) argues that the war is still related to the colonialist idea of belonging and the unwillingness to narrate its events results as much from a sense of humiliation as from the incapacity to admit mistakes. Portugal finds it difficult to recognize the failure of colonialism and the failure of anti-colonialism serves as a pretext to affirm its values.

Portugal was the last European country to give up its African colonies, which only gained independence in 1975.[59] I already cited the philosopher José Gil in the previous chapter who stresses that there was no serious confrontation with the country's history of authoritarianism. This obviously includes the colonial war.

The sociologist Boaventura Sousa Santos (2001: 40-2) advocates that Portugal has generally difficulties to think in post-colonial terms. The author explains that Portugal's relationship with its colonies was always characterized

---

[58] The filmmakers themselves argue with the lack of personal involvement. Both Botelho and Seixas Santos stress that they did not participate in the war and have no proper experiences to draw on. Additionally, Botelho (2001: 493) and Manoel de Oliveira (qtd. in de Bacque 1999: 184) express their dislike of spectacular cinema, which they associate with the war film genre.

[59] The transition from ancient empire to democratic European state was complicated. It took eighteen turbulent months in which three heads of state, two presidents and six provisional governments struggled with the new situation.

by hybridization, as well as by inter-identities. By drawing on the Shake-spearean characters Prospero and Caliban from *The Tempest*, he defines the concept. Throughout its colonial history, Portugal oscillated between being a prosperized Caliban in Europe, due to its backwardness compared with the technically and economically more developed European north, and a cali-banized Prospero, who partly assimilated to and mixed with the colonized. The country's semi-peripheral position in the modern capitalist system from the seventeenth century onwards, and its dependence on other nations, first Spain and then Great Britain, thus made it more difficult for the colonized countries to express their emancipation. They always lived in a pre-post-colonial situation, while running the risk to be colonialist in their anti-colonialist movements. The scholar claims that the Revolution in 1974 and the adherence to the European Community in 1986 are the moments when the negotiation of these inter-identities was finally decided in favour of Prospero. Paradoxically, at the beginning of Portugal's consciousness of anti-colonialism and decolonization, the rather incompetent and ineffective colonizer tried to assume a hegemonic position within Europe.

Following the arguments of these scholars, this chapter will examine how *A Portuguese Farewell* (Botelho, 1985) and *No or the Vain Glory of Command* (Oliveira, 1990), the first two feature films that stage the war, articulate heg-emonic and counter-hegemonic influences common to post-coloniality. Bor-rowing the expression from Ngugi Wa Thiong'o's book *Decolonising the Mind: The Politics of Language in African Literature* (1986), here the author discusses the struggle between two mutually opposed forces in Africa – the imperialist tradition on one hand, and the resistance tradition on the other – I will ask if the films[60] not only address the historical trauma but also decolo-nize the mind. In other words, do the films' representations of the war re-configure power relations and modes of representation or re-affirm them? In comparison with the previous chapter, what will be at stake here is not the lack of self-affirmation through non-inscription (Gil) described in the now canonical novels, but its other: how to avoid the idealization of national identity in the context of the colonial war?

---

[60] Since *No or the Vain glory of Command* is historically more complex and helps to contextualise the colonial war and Portuguese colonialism in general, I will first analyse this later film.

History

No or the Vain Glory of Command has become one of the most discussed films in Manoel de Oliveira's filmography. I will return once again to my discussion of the film in the chapter on Manoel de Oliveira since it is part of a series of six films on Portuguese and European expansion politics. The film's title joins two famous and contradictory phrases from Portugal's cultural history. On the one hand, Padre António Vieira's 'What a terrible word is a No' and, on the other, the old man from the Restelo's denunciation of the ambition and pride of Vasco da Gama's desire to discover the sea-route to India, in Luís de Camões epic *The Lusiads*.

Vieira's phrase is taken from a sermon (*Sermão da Terceira Quarta-feira da Quaresma*) in which the priest discusses what it means when a worldly sovereign is denied his desires and comes to the conclusion that mankind has to accept God's almighty power of choice. The Jesuit priest and missionary is one of the most outstanding figures of Portuguese culture. Eduardo Lourenço (1999a: 21) affirms that he shaped Portugal's imaginary for good when he developed, shortly after the country regained independence from the Spanish crown, his idea of a Fifth Empire. Based on Sebastianism, described in the preceding chapter, his prophecy suggests that the second return of Christ was related to the return of a Portuguese king and that it would lead to an empire with the Portuguese king as its sovereign, the Pope as its priest and the Roman Catholic Faith as its only belief. Viera's utopia advocates that God chose Portugal and its sovereign and he himself was elected to prophesize the country's future:

> Não há na cultura portuguesa discurso mais alucinatório e sublime que o de António Vieira. É a síntese arrebatada, mas simbolicamente coerente, de cinco séculos de vida colectiva vividos com a convicção arreigada – mas também culturalmente cultivada – de que a própria existência de Portugal é da ordem não só do *milagre*, como da *profecia*. Pela sua pública fidelidade crística, Portugal profetiza.[61] (Lourenço 1999a: 21)

---

[61] ('There is no other discourse as hallucinatory and subtle than that of António Vieira in Portuguese culture. It is the hot-tempered but symbolically coherent synthesis of five centuries of collective life that had been lived with the enrooted – and culturally refined – conviction that the proper existence of Portugal not only has

The most original idea of the Fifth Empire is that its mythical centre would not be Portugal, but rather Brazil, 'a anticipada certeza de perenidade e grandeza'[62] (Lourenço 1999a: 22).

As cited in the previous chapter, the inaugural text of this empire is *The Lusiads*. Lourenço (1999a: 17) highlights the poem's function in the construction of the nation's identity, which began to consider itself as significant: 'Camões, que conferiu à nova idade de Portugal a sua maxima expressão simbólica e épica, (...) Como se de súbito nos tivéssemos transformado numa autêntica "grande nação"'.[63] The only negative voice that appears in the canonical text is Oliveira's second reference for the title. In its forth song, the old man from Restelo refers to the vain glory of command when Vasco da Gama is leaving for his voyage of discovery.[64] This man of venerable appearance and astute opinion came to stand in for pessimistic and conservative viewpoints, since he did not believe in the success of finding a maritime passage to India. In Oliveira's film, his reputation is redefined as prophet of the failures portrayed by the filmmaker.

Even though the two phrase fragments cited in *No* suggest an affirmation of the old man from Restelo's critical perspective on discovery and Viera's pointing out of the insignificance of worldly power, I will show in this chapter that the title is misleading: Oliveira not only goes in line with the significance of the fragments, but with the ideas referred to by Lourenço.

There is of course a critical perspective and *No or the Vain Glory of Command* proves the constant denials of Portugal's imperialist drive. To achieve this, the film is structured by the dialectical confrontation of scenes set during the colonial war with flashback episodes from Portugal's history. While the war narrative tells the story of soldiers (Diogo Dória, Miguel Guilherme,

---

the status of a miracle but of a prophecy. Given its public Christian faith, Portugal prophesises.')

[62] ('the anticipated certainty of eternity and greatness')

[63] ('Camões bestowed Portugal with the highest symbolic and epic expression of this age (...) As though, from one moment to the other, we had transformed into an authentic "great nation"')

[64] As Randal Johnson (2007: 63) observes, Oliveira's film title is in fact a variation of the first line of the stanza.

Luís Lucas, Carlos Gomes, António S. Lopes) who are travelling on a military jeep to their base, the historical flashbacks result from their discussions with the Second Lieutenant (Luís Miguel Cintra), a former history student who relates and acts, together with the soldiers, in five historical episodes that question Portugal's heroic past.

The first flashback centres on the history of Viriato (Luís Miguel Cintra), the warrior-chieftain of the Lusitanians – a tribal confederation, and the alleged origin of Portugal as a nation – who fought unsuccessfully against Roman colonization. Although the history books present Viriato as the first Portuguese hero, Oliveira concentrates in his scenes on Viriato's assassination that led to the invasion by the Romans. In the final scene of the flashback, the Lusitanians look incredulously at the remains of their leader during his funeral. A close up of the ashes serves as a visual metaphor for the first devastating negation of a heroic identity.

The second episode stages an even more ridiculous failure: the battle of Toro (1476) lost by Afonso V (Luís Mascarenhas) against Spain when trying to expand the Portuguese territory and conquer the throne of Castile. Central to its scenes are the historically reported efforts to save the Portuguese flag in the face of defeat. But when the banner holder, the famous *Decepado* (the Mutilated) *dom* Duarte de Almeida (Luís Mascarenhas) tries to secure the flag although his hands are cut off one after the other, and this is by no means shown to be heroic. Rather, the outrageousness of the attempt to hold on to the symbol of patriotism becomes apparent when, in the end, the character only holds it with his teeth.

The third flashback demystifies yet another episode. It illustrates a subsequent aspiration to form, now peacefully, an Iberian Empire by marrying *dom* Afonso (Raúl Fraire), Afonso V's grandson, to the Spanish heir Isabel de Aragon (Lola Forner). The marriage ceremony is pompous, filmed in fixed, static shots. Its visual, political and religious dimension is then contrasted with scenes that concentrate on the royal family's human scale. These scenes demonstrate how the crown prince destroys the aspiration of supremacy by dying ridiculously during an improvised horse race. After his death, any hopes of a Luso-Hispanic empire are lost. King João II's (Luís Miguel Cintra) point-of-view shot of the Portuguese banner once again exposes the flag as a symbol of defeat.

After these demoralizing negations, the Lieutenant's narration moves on to a positive episode: the Discoveries. This flashback is based on 'The Isle of Love', the IX Song from *The Lusiads*. It is the only part of the epic that is not based on historic events and envisions the compensation of Vasco da Gama's navigators by the gods. Oliveira's adaptation is an idyllic version of Camões' splendorous description, but it remains true to its spirit: there is no critique or ambivalence in the representation of the most glorious chapter of Portuguese literature and the affirmation of its messianic vision. Moreover, the soldiers in Africa unanimously confirm the discoveries as 'um grande passo para a humanidade'[65] in the following scene.[66] Indeed, within the film's critical analysis of Portugal's history, the choice of 'The Isle of Love' and the confirmation of its celebratory tone is a remythifyng counterpoint to the deconstruction of other historic enterprises.

It is, however, not the concluding statement. The Lieutenant contrasts the affirmative event with the most traumatic episode of Portugal's history. As mentioned above, the young *dom* Sebastião disappeared while trying to defeat the 'disbelievers'.[67] The myth of his expected return is not encouraged by Oliveira's King (Mateus Lorena), an aggressive and maniac despot who orders the soldiers to keep on praying when the Moroccan attack starts. On the contrary, the bizarre images of soldiers who fall like skittles when hit by canon balls reveal the absurdity of his religious project.

The battle scenes of Alcácar-Quibir are finally juxtaposed with Portugal's last battle in Africa. The soldiers are attacked in an ambush and the Lieutenant kills an African guerrilla fighter. Reflecting on what he just did, he stands for a moment lost in his thoughts and is also shot. His sense of guilt is

---

[65] ('a great step for humanity')

[66] Oliveira approves of this interpretation (qtd. in Baecque 1999: 76): 'O que é importante no episódio da Ilha dos Amores, é que os deuses, que são representações do bem, recompensam os marinheiros das Descobertas, porque essas Descobertas são um legado oferecido ao mundo. É o que se valoriza, e não as façanhas dos guerreiros.' ('What is central in the "Isle of Love" is the fact that the gods, who represent goodness, compensate the sailors of the Discoveries, because the Discoveries are a legacy offered to humankind. This and not the heroic acts of the warriors is evaluated'.)

[67] Oliveira (qtd. in Baecque 1999: 187) stresses that he used Moroccan chronicles as research for the battle scenes, in order to avoid the accusation that he was favouring the Portuguese position.

further explored through the sudden appearance of a badly wounded guerrilla fighter (un-credited), shrieking in agony, which interrupts the soldiers' shooting. However, this fighter's agony does not appeal to either the soldiers or the spectators on a human level.[68] Rather, the grotesque scene and his exaggerated cries are used to draw attention to the changing historical situation, finally dawning on the soldiers who react with complete silence.

Figure 3: *No or the Vain Glory of Command* (Courtesy Madragoa Filmes)

The Lieutenant is taken to the hospital and, in a delirious state, experiences the prophesied return of *dom* Sebastião. But the mythical King does not bring a glorious future and much less the Fifth Empire. When he presses the sword in his hands until they bleed, the Lieutenant vomits blood. It is clearly

---

[68] Contrary to my analysis, João Bérnard da Costa (qtd. in Ribeiro 2001: 191) argues that this image is one of the strongest he has ever seen in films on war.

the belief in the Fifth Empire that brings his death, exactly on the historical 25 April 1974, the day of the Revolution, as the doctor notes in his book. Thus, the scene not only questions the myth of the Fifth Empire, it also uses the Lieutenant's death as a symbolic end to Portugal's endeavour of expansion and its fantasies of empires.

But does it end imperialist/colonialist discourse as well? Is it really possible to describe the film's synthesis of Portugal's history with Oliveira's famous observation (qtd. in Baecqu 1999: 188) that *No* is almost the contrary of *The Lusiads*? The filmmaker is convinced that his film breaks with the imperial mentality, as Portugal questioned it more resolutely than any other European nation: 'NON consiste em pegar nos *Lusíadas* do avesso. É o momento em que se desarma a festa. (...). É uma mudança de mentalidade completa, cujo eco ressoou por toda a parte na Europa. Nenhum país procedeu desta forma'.[69] This comment has become almost a standard interpretation of the film. It is not difficult to understand that Oliveira uses *The Lusiads* to stress his critical attitude towards the persistent Portuguese dream of a universal empire. But what about the citation of the founding text of national imperial identity? Does not the very episode 'The Isle of Love' confirm, partly, the messianic spirit? Even though many literary critics, such as Calafate Ribeiro (2004: 40), observe that the epic possesses 'uma subtil ambiguidade/duplicidade'[70], I would suggest that Oliveira's affirmation can be seen as symptomatic of a double consciousness: the colonialist/imperialist discourse in relation to the discoveries is co-exists with the questioning of the expansion ideology of the Fifth Empire, since their relationship is not acknowledged. This contradiction is, according to João de Melo (1997: 478), as old as Portugal's colonialism and misinterprets power relations as cross-cultural relations. Portuguese colonialism was, in fact, a result of the discoveries and the oversee expansion, but it used rhetorical and doubtlessly euphemistic explications to substitute its economic interests with the implementation of a civilizational process.

The problematic power relations are usually not considered in the film's

---

[69] ('*No* consists in turning *The Lusiads* upside down. It is the moment in which the party is dismantled. (...) It is a complete change of mentality whose echo sounded all over Europe. No other country proceeded this way.')
[70] ('a subtle discursive ambiguity/duplicity')

analysis. Randal Johnson, who is responsible for the first comprehensive study of the filmmaker's work in English, is aware of the contradiction but suggests that Oliveira puts them into perspective, since 'the voyages of discovery have a transcendent meaning. Those who are rewarded on the 'Isle of Love' are the voyagers, the explorers, the discoverers, not the warriors; the actors who play soldiers are not present in the sequence. The gift of discovery is being praised, not the desire for conquest' (Johnson 2007: 66). Brandlmeier (2010: 114) goes even further by suggesting that Oliveira's film is not about Portuguese history, but rather an allegorical portray of a 'a war of symbols and male rituals'. Both authors propose that the film focuses the blessings of culture as a counter draft to violence. This is exactly the point and post-colonialism's aim has been to show that, as Melo states, colonialism's violence cannot be separated from its cultural production.

The closure of *No* is less contradictory by being more ambiguous about Portugal's prospective identity. Portugal's future, always at the heart of any obsessive empire project, is left open. This is represented by means of a patient in the military hospital who is bandaged from head till toe with only one eye visible. The filmmaker uses various shots of this anonymous man during the Lieutenant's agony and a close up of his eye that observes, panic stricken, the Lieutenant's symbolic death. The uneasiness is double-fold, it results from the anxious desire of an end but also from the uncertain future of a body deeply traumatized and marked by the imperial endeavour. *The Lusiads* as reference for a new identity are insufficient in this moment of shock. All things considered, anxiety and doubt co-exist with the affirmation that Portugal was chosen to depart on the discoveries and remap the world.

Memory

João Botelho's approach to history is quite different in *A Portuguese Farewell*, the title of which is inspired in Alexandre O'Neill's homonymous autobiographical poem. It depicts the leave-taking of the poet's French lover who could not bear the misery and general apathy during the dictatorship.[71]

---

[71] The poem depicts unhappiness as typical of Portuguese identity: 'Não podias ficar presa comigo / à pequena dor que cada um de nós/traz docemente pela mão / a esta pequena dor à portuguesa/tão mansa quase vegetal' ('You could not be stuck with

The film aims to let go of this mentality and of the past by examining the suppressed collective memory for the last time. Wendy Everett (1996: 107) affirms, 'the nature of filmic discourse equips it to deal with current notions of memory as process, and essentially – as change', and the film stages the colonial war precisely to change the apathy – José Gil would say 'non-inscription' – that is considered responsible for the silence surrounding this event.

Farewell is also structured around two intertwined but less dialectic narratives. In the style of news footage of the war, black and white flashbacks of a group of soldiers are contrasted with the contemporary life of a traditional Portuguese couple, Piedade (Isabel de Castro) and Raul (Ruy Furtado), who lost their son Jorge (João Perry) thirteen years ago in the war. The contemporary narrative results from the journey of this elderly couple to Lisbon where they visit their widowed daughter in law, Laura (Maria Cabral), and their youngest son, Alexander (Fernando Reitor). Their encounters, depicted in long silent scenes, reveal their inability to come to terms with and address the son's death. The flashback narrative is slightly more dramatic due to the imminent dangers of the war and the announced death of the son.

The son is never singled out from the group of soldiers. The film begins with the image of a soldier on guard duty. The first shot is a close up of his opening eyes. A close up of his ear, a point-of-view shot of the bush and a close up of his gun further develop the construction of his body. The images define him not as an individual but as a soldier in combat, by revealing, simultaneously, his senses and their function within the situation: attention to the sight and sound of enemies and the possibility to shoot. He belongs to a group whose fate is described by a voice-over that stresses the collective situation, the soldier's tasks and feelings: they have been in the war for twelve years, on this specific mission for twenty-two months, and have developed a strong sense of brotherhood and mutual trust in each other. The narrator's individuality is neither significant in this sequence nor in the five following flashbacks, where a series of medium close-ups of the different soldiers indicates that the voice could be anyone's. Analysing the film's goal, Marc Chevrie (1987: 16) emphasises this scene and argues that while

---

me / with the small sorrow which each of us / carries sweetly by the hand/with this small sorrow in the Portuguese way/so gentle almost vegetal.')

the first shots aim to sharpen the senses of the spectator, the film redefines cinema as an adventure of perception. While I quite agree with the general analysis, I would say that the initial sequence serves primarily to construct a sense of colectivity, essential to the film's addressing of collective memory.

Figure 4: Poster of *A Portuguese Farewell* (Courtesy Madragoa Filmes)

Although the war is presented as a chain of dangerous and depressing events, all the flashbacks have in common that they highlight the harmony between the soldiers as a group, which includes various African soldiers. The presence of black soldiers reflects the historical reality that Portugal had hardly any young men left to draft at the end of the war. Pinto (2001: 59) notes that from 1966 onwards the recruitment of African soldiers reached 42 per cent in Angola, more than 50 per cent in Mozambique and 21 per cent in Guinea. But *Farewell's* suggestion of brotherhood across racial borders overlooks not only the fact that colonialism forced the Africans to take Portugal's side, but ignores the reason for the war: the anti-colonialist struggle.

In the family narrative, the colonial legacy has also few negative nuances. It is strongly visualized, be it through African immigrants or references to its tropicalized landscape. But the assumed multiculturalism and modernization do not ease the pain of the loss of loved ones and the characters are portrayed as incapable of living a normal life. They are silent, estranged, and sad. Laura, an independent modern woman who works at an airline company and has found a new partner, is, on the other hand, encouraged by the visit to finally cope with the loss of her husband.

Contrary to Laura whose profession proves her adjustment to society's changes, her brother's character reflects a darker side of the new freedom. Instead of working in his learned profession as a journalist, Alexander has to earn his living writing pornographic stories. But even though Alexander is incapable of communicating this or other issues to his parents, he opens up to his girl friend Rosa (Cristina Hauser) and tells her that his brother died in the colonial war.

The older generation, however, makes little or no progress in their suffering. A scene, in which Laura and Piedade attend a mass where the communion is offered, indicates why. The ritual's meaning of forgiveness does not give comfort but leads to a breakdown of the mother. While Laura and Alexander transform grief into mourning and by remembering and accepting the past can leave behind death and war, the mother is reminded of her son's sacrifice for the nation. Her breakdown also comments on the unacknowledged relationship between the Portuguese Church and the authoritarian regime.

How to carry on after the war is also the theme of the last flashback in which the surviving soldiers discuss their future in a military camp. As one soldier is teaching African children how to read, another one says that one-day they will talk about this with pride. There is, after all, a positive aspect to colonialism and this is its civilizational dimension. This paternalistic argument was already questioned during the war by the anti-colonialist guerrilla fighter and political theoretician Amílcar Cabral (1979: 18–9) who challenged Portugal's so called 'historical right to be in Africa' by arguing that it concealed the realities and results of colonialism. Cabral put it quite clear that Portugal was not at all superior to its African colonies: 'this [civilizing] process is being carried out by an underdeveloped country, with a lower national income than, for example, Ghana, and which has not as yet been able to solve its own problems' (Cabral 1979: 19). Botelho fails to include this anti-colonialist critique. He is only sensitive to Portugal's post-colonial domestic problems, the silencing of the war and the silent suffering of the people it affected. Like Oliveira, Botelho reveals a double consciousness, because the continuity that he establishes between past and present implies a fairly positive evaluation of colonialism. As a result, the film is essentially a collective memory of *personal* losses for which nobody is held responsible and that preserve aspects of colonialist discourse.

Comparison: Flashbacks and the African Other

Both films employ flashback as a powerful narrative device for cinematic representation of memory and history. Past events are employed in *No* to confront the trauma of the lost empire and in *Farewell* to confront the trauma of war itself. Healing the traumas is considered possible because flashback is a double-edged code that bridges past and present: it doubly positions the spectator in time without disrupting the narrative logic (Turim 1989: 17). Susan Hayward (1996: 123) explains that flashback's double nature makes it possible to represent the past as subjective story and factual history: 'part of this naturalizing process can be pointed at by the fact that the spectator is rarely in a position, thanks to the seamless codes, to question whose subjectivity the flashback might represent, whose truth it is and whether or not it is truth'. It is a powerful and, somewhat, treacherous device.

This is evidenced in *No*, where the historical episodes told by the Lieutenant are presented as the correct way to remember history. The historian Luis Reis Torgal (2001: 18) detects correctly that 'Não se trata neste caso de contar propriamente a história de Portugal, mas sim o episódio de um alferes que (...) conta aos seus subordinados a 'sua história de Portugal' de uma

forma descomprometida e quase anedótica'.[72] However, Torgal fails to observe that this is obscured by the flashback technique and the construction of
the Lieutenant as an authority by the soldiers who recognize and applaud his
interpretations as hard facts. In *Farewell* the individual perspective is
acknowledged more strongly through the voice-over and the use of one
family. The war experience is, nevertheless, equally constructed as a collective experience that downplays the subjectivity of perspectives.

Part of the naturalizing process in *No* relies in the suggestion that the Lieutenant's version of history provides a cure from the ideology of the Fifth
Empire. His encounter with Sebastian is not easily decoded as a personal
delirium because of the earlier flashback structure. Thus, it appears as part of
the 'collective imaginary' that finally comes true, even though very unlike to
how it was expected. It is necessary to turn the narrator's death into a symbolic sacrifice that frees Portugal of its former imperial identity. In comparison, *Farewell* focuses more on making this process conscious and demonstrates that the act of remembering results, partly, in coming to terms with
the past. The healing process is only impossible for some characters: the
mother does not overcome her grief and falls ill; the father does not express
his feelings but visits his son's grave for the first time; Laura is able to enjoy
a new relationship; and Alexander learns to acknowledge the death of his
brother.

Since flashback is a mimetic representation of thought processes looking at
the past, the spectator is usually as much witness as protoanalyst of the narrative (Turim 1989). In *No*, the Lieutenant is clearly the analyst until the end
of the flashbacks. It is his task to situate the soldiers and the spectator in a
position that enables them to understand the failures of Portugal's hegemonic dreams. *Farewell* offers a wider range of identification by engaging as
much with the soldiers as with its effects on the family members. The spectator can thus shift between analysand, who experiences first the grief and
then the mourning and analyst, who understands that ignoring the war causes
suffering.

The trauma of the colonial war is a strictly national issue, and a contextual-

---

[72] ('It is not about telling the history of Portugal, but rather the episodes of a
Lieutenant (...) who tells the lower ranked soldiers 'his history of Portugal' in a
disengaged and anecdotic way.')

ization of the colonized African countries is omitted from both films, with Africa featuring only as scenic backdrop to the events concerning the Portuguese protagonists.[73] Moreover, both films downplay cruelty or racism against indigenous people, even though novels and documentaries have accused the Portuguese military of being responsible for genocides and numerous massacres of the civil population during the civil war, not to mention the atrocities committed during colonialism. Franz Fanon's (2001: 13) famous observation that 'violence in the colonies does not only have for its aim the keeping of these enslaved men at arm's length; it seeks to dehumanize them' is also valid for the Portuguese colonies.

The fact that colonialism is still seen as inspired by a Christian and humanitarian vision, is symptomatic of the reluctance to assume a more critical position. That this reflects the continuity of hegemonic discourses becomes clear when confronted with Salazar's luso-tropicalist speech of 1959. Just before the colonial war started, the dictator defended that Portugal tried to achieve 'uma nação composita euro-africana e euro-asiática [que], estendendo-se por espaços livres ou desaproveitados, pretendeu imprimir aos povos conceitos muito diversos dos que depois caracterizaram outros tipos de colonização' (qtd. in Pinto 2001: 45).[74]

The concept of luso-tropicalism goes back to the Brazilian anthropologist Gilberto Freyre (n.d.: 10) who suggested that the Portuguese, because of their European and Moorish roots, stand out among other European colonizers as an essentially trans-national people capable of and willing to adapt to the tropics: 'O português é grande por esta sua singularidade magnífica: a de ser um povo lusotropical. (...) na realização de uma vocação que fixa o destino de toda uma civilização transnacional: a lusotropical, de que o Brasil faz

---

[73] In *No* the opening scene in which one uninterrupted travelling shot of an African tree lasts for almost five minutes is a peculiar example worth analysing in more detail. In *Farewell*, visual links to Africa are more complex. Yet, Botelho's (2001: 494) observation that 'to see the city centre of Lisbon like an African city makes me a little bit proud', hints at the omission of the contradictory effects of colonialism.

[74] ('A composed euro-African and euro-Asiatic nation that pretended, since it extends itself through free or disused spaces, to imprint on the people very different concepts than those which later characterised other kinds of colonization.')

parte.'[75]

Margarida Calafate Ribeiro (2004: 152) cites Caeiro da Mata to demonstrate that luso-tropicalism consists, in reality, of euphemisms: It turned five centuries of colonialism into five centuries of relationships between different cultures and people, the colonial society into a multi-racial society, the imperial nation into a multi-continental nation and the civilizational religious mission into Portugal's integration into the tropics. Sousa Santos (2001: 54) calls luso-tropicalism a comforting discourse for the colonizer by an underdeveloped and incompetent Prospero (deemed benevolent by Freyre). The discourse co-exists with more critical perspectives, such as Cabral's or Charles Boxer's, that make Portugal responsible for creating the underdevelopment of the colonized.

The films demonstrate that the belief in a 'better' luso-tropicalist colonization survived the end of colonialism as a myth. In relation to critical perspectives on colonialism, *No* only suggests a break with the past but cannot prove this, while *Farewell* is careful to show the presence of African immigrants in Portugal. And yet, their presence is potentially threatening to Portuguese identity, as shown by the African character that violently interrupts a woman singing *fado*, one of the strongest symbols of national identity.[76] It would seem, then, that the Other remains a problem for Portugal's post-colonial identity.

Conclusion

Undeniably, *A Portuguese Farewell* and *No or the Vain Glory of Command* set out to interrogate hegemonic memories and assumptions about the Portuguese colonial war. But the analyses and comparisons of the films also suggest that, as cultural critics suspect in more general terms, the first films on the subject do not free themselves completely from colonialist/imperialist

---

[75] ('The Portuguese is great because of his magnificent singularity: he is a lusotropical people. (...) his vocation is to be a transnational civilisation of which Brazil is part.')

[76] This scene corresponds to an earlier one in which the African is asked to turn down the radio that plays African music. The African character is, however, much more aggressive.

discourses. Although Oliveira exposes the continuous failures to construct a messianic imperial identity, his a-historical view of the discoveries fails to recognize their relation with colonialism and transfers the discussion to an affirmation of a shared cultural history. And while Botelho proposes that the war needs to be remembered to overcome suffering, he omits its negative sides by painting a friendly picture of inter-cultural harmony.

Nonetheless, both films try to come to terms with the unpleasant past: *Farewell* turns grief into mourning and *No*'s intellectual Lieutenant takes on the guilt, his death symbolizing the closing of the chapter on imperialism. Here lies the main difference between the two films: Oliveira believes that the imperialist mentality dies with the Revolution and only the cultural achievements survive, whereas Botelho does not think that his characters, soldiers and family, ever represented it.

Flashbacks as narrative technique in both films are essential to providing a healing from the past. They help to establish the idea that history is remembered in an impersonal and correct way, instead of being the result of a particular character's point of views. The flashbacks' function not only consists in coming to terms with the loss of loved ones or national imperial identity, but in offering a more affirmative image of the colonial war with the help of sympathetic characters, the affirmation of the cultural importance of the discoveries and the civilizing aspect of colonialism.

The war remains a domestic affair where the Other is of little importance and, at the most, identical or grotesque. Africans are either represented in a naïve way that overlooks historical realities (Botelho) or have a specific function that reveals something about the own position (Oliveira). Neither film acknowledges anti-colonialist positions. On the contrary, both defend the idea that colonization brought cultural benefits. Since the Other is not considered an addressee of reconciliation, the barriers between colonized and colonizer persist.

Given the ambiguities in relation to colonialist/imperialist discourses and the representation of the Other present in both films, it is not possible to speak of a decolonization of the mind. The films are still too preoccupied with national issues. *NO* and *Farewell* can be seen as important first steps in the representation of the war and the reshaping of its imaginary: Botelho illustrates that the upsetting memory needs to be addressed and Oliveira shows five years later that everybody, even the positive Lieutenant, has to be held responsible for the war. Consequently, the films describe a development in terms of re-configuring power relations and modes of representation. It is noteworthy that the earlier film by Botelho concentrates on personal reasons for the silencing of the Colonial War (the collective incapacity to mourn), while Oliveira sets out for a more complex, historical and cultural analysis (the collective dream of a universal empire).

The discovery of paradox: the European expansion in six films by Manoel de Oliveira[77]

Introduction

Historically, Portugal is an exceptional European country. It has remained in its boarders ever since it started out in the twelfth century as a small monarchy, when the Iberian Peninsula was divided by the Islamic invasion. It survived, as Eduardo Lourenço (1999a: 11) remarks, 'por insólito milagre'[78] and few countries sacralized its origins in the way Portugal did. By writing history as mythology it came to consider itself as 'povo de Cristo, e não meramente cristão (...) numa constância e num fechamento sobre si mesmo de que só encontramos símil no povo judaico'[79] (Lourenço 1999a: 12). As a frontier of Christianity and by fighting against Islam, the country assumed right from the beginning a militant religious self-image that was never abolished.

The Portuguese discoveries were nothing but a prolongation of this logic, fuelled by the idea of continuing the *reconquista* (Reconquista) and the desire to convert the Muslim population in the previously Christian Northern Africa. Initiated in 1415 with the conquest of Ceuta, they were promoted by *dom* João I and his son Henrique, *o Navegador* (Henry the Navigator). The following exploration of the African coast was a continuation of the Reconquista with other means, but the religious reasons were promptly substituted by economic necessities, above all by the commerce of spices with Asia. It is important to remember that the conquest of Constantinople by the Turks in

---

[77] This is an extended and revised version of an earlier text, published as 'Heterodox/Paradox – Manoel de Oliveira's Representation of the "Fifth Empire"'. *Dekalog2. On Manoel de Oliveira.* Ed. Carolin Overhoff Ferreira. London: Wallflower Press, 2008, pp. 60–88. It can be read in a slightly different version in Portuguese: 'Os Descobrimentos do Paradoxo: A Expansão Europeia nos Filmes de Manoel de Oliveira'. *Manoel de Oliveira: Uma Presença.* Ed. Renata Junqueira. São Paulo: Editora Perspectiva, 2010, pp. 117–46.

[78] ('miraculously')

[79] ('Christ's nation, and not just Christian (...) with a consistency and by being self-sufficient only comparable to the Jewish people')

1453 had made the European passage to India by sea impossible, prompting the search for new routes.

Portugal's national project of maritime voyages began to extend further, leading to the discovery of the Islands of Madeira, the Azores, the Canary Islands and Cape Verde, a new passage to India, as well as to the 'Discovery of Brazil', until reaching China and Japan. The country's identity was changed significantly by the maritime expansion politics, since Portugal became unexpectedly the first and longest lasting European empire that remained in Africa until the Carnation Revolution in 1974 and in Asia until the devolution of Macau in 1999.

As demonstrated in the previous chapter, Manoel de Oliveira is not only the country's internationally most prominent filmmaker, but also a key figure in the reflection of its identity. Portugal has always been a subject in his films, from his discussion of the relation between tradition and modernity in his first short film, *Douro Faina Fluvial /Labor on the Douro River* (1931), until his last film, *Angélica* (2010), which joins his traditional theme of impossible love with a photographic exploration of Douro's vineyards. The explicit discussion of Portuguese history, related to the desire of expansion, colonization and the construction of a universal empire, began rather late, in the middle of the 1980s, with *The Satin Slipper* (1985). This film, an adaptation of Paul Claudel's colossal drama of the same title and one of Oliveira's masterworks, poses for the first time questions on the relationship between history, fatherland, memory and religious and political identities. These issues join the filmmaker's foremost concerns in earlier films: the contradictions and ironies of the human condition, the impossibility of bodily love, theosophical interrogations, and the problems of representation and filmmaking.

All in all, six films pick up on the topic of historical expansionist politics – be they Portuguese or European – or even suggest recent imperialist drives by the European Union and the United States of America. Set at the end of the sixteenth and the beginning of the seventeenth century, *The Satin Slipper* (1985) is dedicated to the earliest experiences of expansion that followed the discoveries. It was filmed ten years after the end of the Portuguese empire and one year before the country's adhesion to the European Community. *No or the Vain Glory of Command* from 1990, discussed in detail in the preceding chapter, uses the last days of the colonial war in Africa (1961-1974) as its starting point to examine the unsuccessful attempts to achieve national splendor through expansion of the country's domain. Oliveira's interest in the subject intensifies in the new millennium: in the year of the commemorations of the 500 years of the 'Discovery of Brazil', *Palavra e Utopia/Word and Utopia* (2000) discusses the colonization of Brazil and the prophecy of the Fifth Empire by reconstructing the life of its visionary, father António Vieira, through his writings; *Um Filme Falado/A Talking Picture* (2003) is a response to the terrorist attack on 11 September 2001 and demonstrates the dangers faced by self-indulgent contemporary European voyagers who think that there is nothing more to discover; and while *O Quinto Império – Ontem como Hoje/The Fifth Empire – Yesterday and Today* (2004) condemns the persistence of the wild dream of expansion in Northern Africa, *Cristovão Colon – O Enigma/Christopher Columbus – The Enigma* (2007) assumes a patriotic position by proposing that the discoveries of Columbus should be included in the list of Portugal's illustrious accomplishments.

Said (1994: 8) famously defined imperialism as 'the practice, the theory, and the attitudes of a dominating metropolitan centre ruling a distant territory', and colonialism, 'which is almost always a consequence of imperialism', as 'the implanting of settlements on distant territory'. It is not only the territorial domination that defines imperialism, but mainly its dissemination within culture and the realm of ideas. The aim is to root it firmly in the consciousness of both colonizer and colonized: 'For the enterprise of empire depends upon the idea of having an empire (...) and all kinds of preparations are made for it within a culture; then in turn imperialism acquires a kind of coherence, a set of experiences, and a presence of ruler and ruled alike within the culture' (Said 1994: 10).

We reencounter Said's argument on culture as an important tool in the formation of imperial attitudes and colonialist identity in Eduardo Lourenço's affirmation that Luís de Camões' epic *The Lusiads*, which – as mentioned in the two earlier chapters – consecrated Portugal's seafaring explorations, soon became a key reference for Portuguese identity. Especially, when the country was about to give up its territory by fleeing from the Napoleonic invasion to Brazil, dislocating the metropolitan centre of the empire out of Europe:

> É a este título que, com a maior naturalidade, Camões se torna objecto das nossas paixões nacionais, que são menos literárias ou culturais do que ideológicas, patrióticas, cívicas e por vezes partidárias. Se ainda hoje, um pouco por toda a parte, as associações de emigrantes portugueses se colocam sob a égide de Ca-

mões, isso deve-se a este incrível processo de mitificação e, pode mesmo dizer-se, de divinização do sentimento nacional que se dá no primeiro quartel do século XIX. O que até então mais não era do que um livro, entre todos glorioso, decerto, torna-se o Livro, o breviário do sentimento exaltado da nossa identidade num momento dramático da nossa história.[80] (Lourenço 1999a: 147)

Father António Vieira participated, as I quoted Lourenço (1999a: 21) in the second chapter, in eternalizing the 'aventura descobridora e missionária'[81] and in shaping Portugal's imaginary for centuries. Let me recall that Vieira's prophecy of the Fifth Century resulted from a complex synthesis of ideas drawn from the discoveries, the Bible and earlier Portuguese prophecies (Ribeiro 2004: 45). It expanded the Sebastianist tradition of messianic believes in the return of an *encoberto* ('hidden') savior king who would be the *desejado* ('desired one'), which had been prophesized by Gonçalo Anes (Bandarra 1500–1545).

Vieira actually suggested that *dom* João IV would be this resurrecting king, given that his death would put Portugal again in a situation of political uncertainty. But, according to political necessities, the priest changed the protagonist of this empire several times. José Eduardo Reis (n.d.) points out the rather bizarre and contradictory dimension of Vieira's prophecy, as well as his capacity of turning truth into illusion:

> The pathetic setbacks to these predictions (which were inspired by an enormous hope in the redeeming quality of the future dimension of time) in view of the sheer evidence of historical facts, the death of dom João IV, the overthrow of Afonso VI and the premature death of Prince João, did not inhibit but rather stimulated Vieira's fantastic dialectic and sophistic ability to reformulate his as-

---

[80] ('It is under these circumstances that Camões becomes almost naturally the object of our national passions, which are less literary or cultural than ideological, patriotical, civical and often partidarian. If until today and almost everywhere the Portuguese immigrant societies take shelter under Camões, this is due to this incredible process of mythification and, one can almost say, divinisation of the national feeling that occurs in the first quarter of the nineteenth century. What was nothing more than a book, even though one of the most glorious, became the Book, the prayer book of the exalted feeling of our identity in a dramatic moment of our history.')

[81] ('missionary and discovering adventure')

sertive judgments and rethink his predictions, adapting them to the new circumstances and to their historical determination. The psychological and hermeneutic mechanism he *used* was always the same, that of subordinating reality to idealism, the facts to dreams, the present to the future.

Margarida Calafate Ribeiro shares this opinion. While she recognizes that Vieira 'wrote back to the empire' from Brazil, by defending the Indians and Africans, and by accusing the Portuguese colonialists of exploitation and corruption, Ribeiro censures his flight from reality and his reluctance to act within this reality. This distinguishes Vieira also from Camões:

> Mas enquanto o discurso camoniano preenche a distância entre o ser e o desejo com os seus versos, onde narra a histórica epopeia portuguesa e, inerentemente, apela à acção, Vieira preenche esse espaço com o discurso excessivo e retórico de uma construção imperial mental que é já uma fuga de um espaço e de um tempo que mesmo as mais exuberantes representações vão adivinhando como esvaziado.[82] (Ribeiro 2004: 49)

Lourenço is equally aware of Vieira's role in the mythification of Portugal as a chosen nation, but he offers a more restrained opinion on the priest's inventiveness by proposing that it can only be understood and decoded by taking into account that he based his ideas on the biblical vision of humanity's paradoxical existence. The inconsistencies are not Vieira's mistake, but a fact of the real world:

> António Vieira não era um louco rematado, antes um sagaz observador do mundo, diplomata insigne com o seu quê de maquiavélico, entenda-se, ao serviço de causa em si boa, como é próprio de um eminente jesuíta. A sua visão, de forte inspiração bíblica, constitui um todo. Não há outro código para decifrar os aparentemente contraditórios e até perturbantes acontecimentos de um mundo

---

[82] ('But while Camões' discourse fills in the gap between being and desire with his verses, in which he tells the historical Portuguese epos and, by so doing, calls for action, Vieira fills this space with an excessive and rhetorical discourse on the construction of an imperial mentality which is already a flight from a certain time and space that even the most exuberant representations recognize as being void.')

criado por Deus e governado pela sua Providência além do texto bíblico.[83] (Lourenço 1999a: 20)

It cannot be overlooked that the Fifth Empire as cornerstone of the Portuguese identity as 'Christ's nation' also has an anti-Islamic side to it. Adma
Fadul Muhana (1994: XVII-IX) explains this attitude by the constant threat
that Islam represented to the Western Church, to which Portugal served as
the frontier on the Iberian Peninsula: 'Vieira apenas ecoa o temor geral de
que jamais será possível um reino cristão universal sem a extinção do
maometismo. A sua heterodoxia vem de ele supor que o maometismo, por
sua vez, extinguirá o que sobrou do império romano – para que a destruição
de ambos dê origem à nova era do Quinto Império'.[84] Based on the defeat
and eradication of other believes, this political, religious and nationalistic
project is far from being an ecumenical prophecy. But since it questioned
long hold believes by the Catholic Church that defended that the Fifth Empire would be the reign of the Anti-Christ, it resulted in Vieira's imprisonment, his accusation of heresy and his condemnation by the Portuguese Inquisition.

When looking at the factual colonialist past and Portugal's performance as
an empire, Boaventura Sousa Santos finds no traces of splendour. As cited in
the previous chapter, the country was rather unskilled, inefficient and almost
always enslaved by a much more powerful colonizer: the British Empire:

A subalternidade do colonialismo português é dupla, porque ocorre tanto no
domínio das práticas coloniais, como no dos discursos coloniais. No domínio das

---

[83] ('António Vieira was not a completely crazy man, rather a canny observer of the
world, an honourable diplomat with a touch of Maquiavel, serving, obviously, a
good cause, as any notable Jesuit. His vision, strongly influenced by the Bible, must
be seen as an entity. There is no other code with which the apparent contradictions
and even disturbing events of a world, created by God and governed by the
Providence, can be deciphered than by the biblical text.')
[84] ('Vieira only echoes the general fear that a universal Christian Reign would be
impossible without the extinction of Islam. His heterodoxy results from his
supposition that Islam, on the other hand, would extinguish the leftovers of the
Roman Empire – so that the destruction of both would originate in the new era of
the Fifth Empire.')

práticas, a subalternidade está no facto de Portugal, enquanto país semiperiféri-co, ter sido ele próprio, durante um longo período, um país dependente da Ingla-terra, em certos momentos, quase uma 'colônia informal' da Inglaterra. (...) Nos domínio dos discursos coloniais, a subalternidade do colonialismo português re-side no facto de, a partir do século XVII, a história do colonialismo ter sido es-crita em inglês e não em português. Isto significa que o colonizador português tem um problema de auto-representação algo semelhante ao do colonizado pelo colonialismo britânico.[85] (Santos 2001: 26)

As we have seen in the chapter on the representation of the colonial war, one of the ways out of this dilemma is luso-tropicalist discourse. But instead of returning to idealized forms of self-representation, Lourenço suggests that Portugal should see itself now realistically and face the challenges of the European integration and of economic globalization:

Saído de ilusões da mesma ordem, povo missionário de um planeta que se mis-siona sozinho, confinado no modesto canto de onde saímos para ver e saber que há um só mundo, Portugal está agora em situação de se aceitar tal como foi e é, apenas um povo entre os povos. Que deu a volta ao mundo para tomar a medida da sua maravilhosa imperfeição.[86] (Lourenço1999a: 83)

Is this, then, Manoel de Oliviera's perspective in his films on the discover-ies, expansionist politics, colonization and imperialism, and the utopia of the Fifth Empire? Or does he repeat the double consciousness diagnosed in his discussion of the colonial war in *No or the Vain Glory of Command*? Char-

---

[85] ('Portugal's colonialism was doubly subaltern: as much in terms of its practice of colonialism, as in terms of its colonialist discourse. In terms of practice, the subalternity can be encountered in its semi-peripheral condition, since it was for a long time dependent on England, and in certain moments almost an unofficial English "colony". (...) In terms of colonial discourse, Portuguese subalternity resides in the fact that the history of colonialism was written in English and not in Portuguese. This means that the Portuguese colonialism has a problem of self-representation, which is similar to that of the colonized by British colonialism.')

[86] ('Leaving behind the same illusions, the missionary nation of a planet that is being missionized by itself, confined to the modest corner from which we departed to see and learn that there is only one world, Portugal is now in the situation to accept itself the way it is, a nation among other nations. A nation that surrounded the world in order to measure its marvellous imperfection.')

acteristic for Oliveira's critical stance and intellectual restlessness, none of
the films that tackle these issues repeat the same point of view or draw the
same conclusions, neither conceptually nor aesthetically. My main objective
in this chapter will be to trace the multifaceted route of Oliveira's embarkations and to study how his films position themselves towards the discourses
on Portuguese imperial identity. Thus, I aim to outline what kind of imaginary the filmmaker develops on the past, the present and the future of his
country.

The films

The Satin Slipper

It is no coincidence that *The Satin Slipper*, a co-production between Portugal, Germany and France, which was filmed in French, dubbed in German
and televised in both countries, but never commercially distributed in Portugal until this very day, was made one year before the country's adhesion to
the European Community. The story about the impossible love-story between the nobleman Rodrigue (Luís Miguel Sintra) and Prouhèze (Patricia
Barzyk), a noblewoman married to an elderly councillor, Don Peláge (Frank
Oger), of the Spanish King (Henri Serre), is an allegory on the failure of
constructing secular empires – historically or in contemporary times – as
well as a demonstration of the actual rivalries between the European nations.

The perdition of love is equivalent to that of the nation(s). The latter becomes apparent in the quarrels between the European countries (Spain, England, Austria and France) that dispute the dominion of the world. Divided
they fail to fight the Ottoman Turks that threaten them. On the world that is
the stage, greed makes fraternity – a functioning European alliance – impossible and humiliates those who try to equal themselves with God. Oliveira
follows Claudel's conviction that the real empire is to be found outside history or can only be achieved when serving God by renouncing symbolically
physical love and worldly power.

The protagonist Rodrigue is used as an exemplary figure to proof this case.
As a result of his rejection by Prouhèze, who offers her satin slipper to the
Virgin Mary so as to remain faithful to the holy sacrament of her weeding,
he accepts the Spanish King's offer to go as vice-king to South-America.
Power becomes a substitute of passion. At the end of play and film Rodrigue
returns under the reign of the new King (Jean-Yves Berteloot) from the New

World, crippled and without title or prestige. His situation worsens when he cannot persuade England to subject to Catholicism. But instead of insisting in Spain's national interests, Rodrigue acts according to his utopia of a Europe united in peace. When the English beats the Spanish Armada, he is sold as a slave and ends up serving at a monastery where he washes the visitors' feet. This deep fall in worldly affairs implies, at the same time, his rise in spiritual matters, since Rodrigue learns to devote himself entirely to God. His atonement is mainly the result of sacrificing sinful bodily love. Within the Christian logic, only after renouncing love are the characters able to expiate their sins: suffering and sacrifice are the way to salvation.

To tell this story, Oliveira follows during 400 minutes word by word of the original play written by the convinced Catholic Claudel. Beyond his faith to the original text, he is true to cinema as well. Ronald Balczuweit (2007: 190) argues that *The Satin Slipper* is a perfect cinematographic expression of the 'composição utópica claudeliana'[87].

The scenography consists of *tableaux* with a painted set as though it was a stage, filmed in long static shots, while the actors perform and speak frontally towards the camera, either getting closer when they are about to speak, or retracting when the second character framed in the shot is going to speak. With this device, the filmmaker substitutes the cinematographic conventions of focus and shot/reverse shot and displaces the cut out of the shot. Balczuweit (2007: 187–8) suggests that the main objective is to reproduce God's viewpoint with the camera:

> Assim, a superfície plana do ecrã marca, por um lado, o limite interior no qual o tema se materializa da ausência para a presença. No cinema de Oliveira, este ecrã mantém-se, ao mesmo tempo, como limite exterior que reflecte que o problema formal do drama (de leitura) claudeliano é constitutivo para o cinema. (...) A contradição entre a *omnivoyance*, a possibilidade de ver tudo, considerada uma especificidade do cinema desde os seus inícios, e a perspectiva implícita no sistema de óptica é assim dissolvida. Existe apenas um ponto de vista da câmara que, entretanto, não se deixa mais localizar: é aquele através do qual todos os aspectos do enquadramento são abolidos (...). A câmara e o projector, e o seu olhar é projectivo e criativo, não reprodutivo. Em perfeita sintonia com as intenções

---

[87] ('Claudel's utopian composition')

de Claudel, a câmara é, por assim dizer, o olhar de Deus.[88]

Only the last scene denounces this divine perspective and returns to the human look: the camera that just showed how Rodrigue was being sold as a slave to a nun dollies back to reveal the studio where the scene was filmed. Although the entire film was shot according to the vision of Claudel, it finally unveils the human scale of this very vision.

Oliveira expresses aesthetically the paradox of human existence, which is seen to be a consequence of the desires in the material world and the obligations of a spiritual, namely Christian, existence. After condemning human imperialist ambitions and European expansionist politics, two possible ways are pointed out to overcome the paradox: Rodrigue and Prouhèze will be compensated for their sacrifices of bodily love outside of history; while Prouhèze's daughter, Marie des Sept-Épées (Anne Consigny), rises above the dichotomy between love and earthly affairs. With the purpose of fighting the Ottoman Turks, she associates herself at the end with the Austrian King; and by engaging with a Catholic monarch in a religious project against Islam fulfills what play and film consider a divine mission.

It is worth remembering that, according to Vieira's prophecy, the world will convert to Catholicism after the end of the Ottoman Empire. Notwithstanding the film's critical stance against European imperialism and its disapproval of discoveries, expansionist politics and greed, it is rather surprising to detect these residues of the Fifth Empire. The affinity consists inoffensively in a Christian vision of the world an investigation of its paradoxes, but it reproduces the militant fight against the Turks as a form to serve God. The

---

[88] ('Thus, the plane surface of the screen demarcates, on the one hand, the interior limit where the issue materialises itself by passing from absence to presence. In Oliveira's cinema, this screen remains as much an exterior limit that reflects that the formal (reading) problem of the drama by Claudel is constitutive for cinema. (...) The contradiction between the *omnivoyance*, the possibility to see everything, which was considered cinema's specificity from its beginnings and the perspective implicit in the optical system is such dissolved. There is only one point of view of the camera and it cannot be pinned down: it is the one through which all the aspects of framing are abolished (...). The camera and the projector, and their view are projective and creative, but not reproductive. In perfect tune with Claudel's intentions, the camera is, so to speak, the eye of God.')

only added scene, which features Portugal and its occupation by Spain, is even more revealing in this sense, since it proposes that Portugal, which was central in the discovery of the New World that is now being disputed, was a victim in this key historic moment and did not participate in the worldly imperialist aspirations of the other European countries.

No or the Vain Glory of Command

Five years later, Portugal takes centre stage in *No or the Vain Glory of Command*. Since the film was discussed in great detail in the chapter on the representations of the colonial war, I will only recollect my findings in order to situate the film within the series of films on expansion. Focusing the last days of the colonial war in Africa, the film is constructed through flashbacks that single out some of Portugal's most important historical episodes of territorial extension, mainly projects designed to create an Iberian empire or to conquer North Africa. Suggesting that these initiatives were ludicrous and bizarre, the second film on expansionist politics recovers, simultaneously, ideas related to Vieira's prophecy of the Fifth Empire within the flashback episode dedicated to the Portuguese discoveries of Vasco da Gama and presents them as a cultural achievement. For the first time in Oliveira's feature films, the country's maritime adventures are singled out as a major step for humanity.

In my understanding, *No or the Vain Glory of Command* therefore reflects a double consciousness. Not only by acknowledging with this episode (which adapts the only fictitious part of Camões' *The Lusiads*, the 'Island of Love' of the XI Song) that colonialism's other are its cultural achievements, but also by generally ignoring the Africans as addressees of reconciliation in a film whose subject is a war in Africa. Portugal never ceases to be exceptional and a chosen nation in the film, remaining, even in the end, Christ's nation that will get back on its feet. Even though the film demonstrates that there were historical moments and Portuguese Kings (Afonso V, Sebastião, João I) who, like Rodrigue, had extreme ambitions and desires, these accompanied by the services carried out by the discoverers and recognized by (the) God(s).

In contrast to *The Satin Slipper*, where there is a clear connection between the discovery of the New World and the greedy European imperialist nations – above all Spain and England – *No or the Vain Glory of Command* does not recognize the same relationship between discoveries and expansionist politics when Portugal is the protagonist. The film encounters after the end of Portugal's empire not only failures but also compensation in the past. The maritime explorations are the nation's greatest accomplishment and, in view of the challenges of an uncertain future as former empire, recycled as key reference for the construction of a new cultural identity. Apart from offering the harshest critique of Portuguese expansionist politics towards Spain and Africa, the film is, paradoxically, explicitly patriotic, only rivaled by *Word and Utopia*, *A Talking Picture* and *Christopher Columbus*.

Word and Utopia

During the 1990s none of Oliveira's films takes an interest in the Portuguese discoveries or politics of expansion, even when they deal in one way or another with Portuguese identity, being *A Carta/The Letter* (1999) perhaps the only exception. In 2000, the year of the celebrations of the 500 years of the 'Discovery of Brazil', Oliveira returns to the issues by participating in the commemorative events with a co-production between Portugal, France, Brazil and Spain. But instead of offering a critical perspective on the colonization of Brazil, *Word and Utopia* develops an almost entirely positive vision by drawing again strongly on the imaginary of the Fifth Empire in the historical moment of its conception. This is only possible by ignoring the political aspect of the ideology and by turning one of the representatives of Portuguese colonialism, the missionary António Vieira, whose sermons, letters and other writings feature powerfully, into an anti-colonialist hero. The film is, indeed, a tribute to a great Portuguese and builds a cinematographic monument for what is already one of the most celebrated authors in the lusophone world.

Word and Utopia begins in 1663 with Vieira (Luís Miguel Cintra) being accused of heresy by the Portuguese Inquisition. From the first scene onwards, the priest appears as a victim of the intrigues of his country, orchestrated mainly by the Inquisition, but also by the representatives of the Church and the Portuguese empire in Brazil. After the introduction, a flashback takes the spectators back to the Brazil of 1625, where the young Vieira (Ricardo Trepa) vows during his ordination as a priest that he will dedicate himself to saving the native population.

During the narrative, which then follows chronologically the most important events in Vieira's life, the character is presented as following in Christ's footsteps and portrayed as a defender of the weak or marginalized, above all the Indians and African slaves in Brazil, and, later on in the European context, of the Jews or New Christians. Preacher, diplomat and missionary, he is true to his ideas and denounces corruption, slavery and abuse. His strength of character, courage, political attitude and powerful sermons are clearly superior to those of the villainous Inquisition, arrogant Portuguese noblemen and governors who only want to exploit Brazil, or the Portuguese clergymen who love plotting intrigues. The film underlines, on the other hand, Vieira's recognition by 'positive' rulers, especially Portugal's King John IV (Rogério Vieira), the converted Queen Christina (Leonor Silveira) from Sweden, the clergy in Rome and the Pope (João Bénard da Costa).

Given the effort of constructing an exemplary character, based on the importance attributed to the accusation of heresy as a result of the prophecy of the Fifth Empire, the film presents a rather messy perspective of the imaginary of Vieira's major ideology. One of the central sequences of the film, in which the accusation of heresy is developed, is quite revealing in terms of Oliveira's contradictory rhetoric. Firstly, a representative of the Inquisition reads the accusation, which consists of the main ideas of the Fifth Empire, exactly as they can be read in Vieira's *História do Futuro/History of the Future*. Oliveira uses a single medium shot with the Inquisition's representative in profile underneath a Christ on the Cross in the background. Vieira defends himself by saying that the Inquisition only resumed what they thought that he had said in a universal and vague manner and that he would have to reply extensively. The sequence concludes with Vieira's condemnation and, at the very end, a frontal shot of Christ on the Cross. To strengthen the positive characteristics of the film's hero and his position as victim, Vieira is then shown in his cell writing a letter in his defense. He accuses the Inquisition of being against the 'conservação, perpetuação e exaltação do reino de Portugal'[89] and of misinterpreting his ideas. Except, instead of misapprehending it, the powerful institution simply disagrees with his point of view, which has, on the other hand, divine approval through the image of the Christ on the cross. This image makes, metaphorically, its way from the background – where the Inquisition places it since it does not act in accordance to true Christianity – to the foreground – after the wrong condemnation of a true Christian. While the Inquisition, and their interpretation by Vieira

---

[89] ('conservation, perpetuation and exaltation of the reign of Portugal')

question his prophecy of the Fifth Empire, the shots suggest that he is backed up by this divine presence. This makes the whole scene quite confusing, if not inconsistent, because the images say the opposite of the words: there is no judgment of the fact that Vieira actually denies his own prophecy (only detectable for the spectators who have knowledge of the Fifth Empire), but the heavenly approval of his words.

Sentenced twice by his country to give up his active voice, the priest is redeemed at the end of the film by a letter of the pope that he receives on his deathbed. This scene is emblematic, since the whole film not only portrays Vieira's life and words but also consists in a rehabilitation and appreciation of his person. The fact that Vieira participated actively in the colonization process is completely overlooked. On the contrary, colonization is seen from a paternalistic and luso-tropicalist viewpoint. In this view the Church and courts men are villains and Vieira the only true Portuguese patriot who tries to save Indians and Africans, not only from the colonizers but also from their native religions. It is worth noting that, at the beginning of the film, they are briefly portrayed practicing their indigenous rituals, but rapidly turn into a willing and speechless audience to Vieira's sermons, desirous but not allowed to enter the churches. They never achieve the status of characters and are only seen as a docile and obedient spectatorship that accepts the authority of the priest's words.

As referred earlier, this luso-tropicalist idea of a harmonious co-existence of composite and eventually mixed cultures and races has been challenged in recent years by various scholars (Couto et al. 1997; Feldman-Bianco 2001), not to mention the vast bibliographic production of post-colonial studies that has foregrounded the oppression of other cultures and the impediment of their self-affirmation by the colonizers (Fanon 2001, Said 1994, Shoat and Stam 1994, etc.). Given these critical perspectives, it is difficult to accept the simplifying view of Oliveira's film, according to which the expansionist politics are only immoral when they are not practiced with a humanistic and truly Christian vision. The economic interests are condemned in the case of the Portuguese noblemen, indicted for corruption and exploration in the sermons of Vieira. The relation between religious and economic interests, as well as between catechism and colonization, word and action are not taken into consideration.

In his book *Message*, Fernando Pessoa famously called Vieira the emperor of the Portuguese language. In *Word and Utopia* neither the emperor nor his empire of words are suspect, because both are considered inspired by divine insight. Within Oliveira's work, the film thus once again affirms the enormous importance and power that the filmmaker attributes to the word. As he himself puts it, the four constituting elements of cinema – image, word, sound and music – are all equally important, but 'a palavra pode ser, em certas situações, o elemento mais forte e o mais enriquecedor, e, também, em muitas circunstâncias, o mais rápido e o mais eficaz para chegar às idéias como aos sentimentos, ou para os aprofundar'[90] (Oliveira qtd. in Baecque 1999: 171–2). While this is certainly a rare view in contemporary visual culture, it is also a celebration of logo-centrism, in the sense that it attributes to the word the capacity of capturing the truth, a metaphysic quality that has been scrutinized by linguistic and literary theory during the last century.

Figure 5: Luís Miguel Cintra in *Word and Utopia* (Courtesy Madragoa Filmes)

---

[90] ('The word, in certain situations, is the strongest element and the most enriching, and the quickest and most efficient to get to ideas and feelings, or to deepen them.')

But there are moments in the film that indicate that even though Vieira's words are indisputably heroic, they only create an imaginary empire and had a hard time affirming themselves in Vieira's reality. It is one of Oliveira's ironies that the film ends with the retribution of Vieira's active and passive voice by the pope in the moment of his death. Still, this proves as much the fragility of his words as does it suggest their importance for the future.

Given the significance of words, *Word and Utopia* is almost purist in the simplicity of its *mise-en-scène* that consists mostly of geometrically composed shots, few camera movements, long takes, the repetitive use of inserts with inter-titles indicating the different locations, and shots of the sea that represent Vieira's transatlantic journeys. But, like in *The Satin Slipper*, Oliveira gives the original text – the letters and sermons of the priest – a voice; this time mainly by staging the acts of writing, reading and orating, as well as the acts of listening. Most scenes either show the three different actors of Vieira (Ricardo Trêpa, Luís Miguel Cintra, Lima Duarte) preaching, reading or writing letters – from the pulpit, in his rooms, in the prison cells – , or the various spectators – the representatives of the inquisition, the Indians, the African slaves, the kings and queens – paying attention to his words.

There is a constant dialectic between the speech acts and the acts of hearing, as well as between the speech acts and shots of cultural arte-facts – paintings, sculptures and parts of churches –, which either contextualize, contradict or illustrate the spoken word. Religious symbolism is frequent and suggests divine approval and protection of Vieira's acts and words. In the first third of the picture this mythical side of the Catholic Faith manifests itself primarily through shots of Christ on the cross, while the Holy Spirit represented by a white pidgin is invoked when Vieira is arrested. The aesthetic purism of the film also constructs an impression of cool rationality around the priest's words that underscores the authority of his ideas and downplays their more fragile and irrational side.

A Talking Picture

Shot only three years later, but after the profound shock of the terrorist attack on 11 September 2001 in New York, *A Talking Picture* returns to the topics of discoveries and imperialism by concentrating mainly on the conflict between cultures and religions. Resembling *No or the Vain Glory of Command*, a Portuguese historian, Rosa Maria (Leonor Silveira), serves as a guide through the narrative. She is travelling accompanied by her daughter,

Maria Joana (Filipa de Almeida), on a cruise ship towards Mumbai in India, where they will meet her husband, an airline pilot. This journey of leisure, during which the historian aims to explain the rise and fall of ancient cultures around the Mediterranean to her daughter, ends tragically so as to address Manoel de Oliveira's worries regarding the future of Europe.

The cruise ship takes the route that another Portuguese, Vasco da Gama, avoided, which led to Portugal's discovery of the maritime passage to India. This had an important economic impact since it ended the Republic of Venice's commercial monopoly with Asia, which it was holding thanks to its domination of the routes that initiated in the Mediterranean. Already during their departure from Lisbon in the dust, Rosa Maria gives details to her little daughter about the peculiarities of the ancient Mediterranean empires and cultures on their way, remembering at first the mythical promise of *dom* Sebastião's return. Their short visits to what are now crowded touristic sites on their route include the harbour in Marseille, the ruins of Pompeii, the Acropolis in Athens, the Egyptian pyramids in Suez and the *Hagia Sophia* in Istanbul. Contrary to Vasco da Gama's trip around Africa that brought wealth and power to their country, this journey on the old European route ends fatally for the contemporary Portuguese tourists. They become the victims of a bomb, deposited by Islamic terrorists during their stop in Aden, Egypt.

The news of the bomb interrupts abruptly a dinner party to which Rosa Maria and Maria João were invited by the American captain (John Malkowitch). They join for the first time his illustrious table where he unites each evening three famous ladies. All characters are allegorical: the captain from the USA is a son of Polish immigrants and commands them; the words and music of the Greek singer (Irene Papas) are the basis of European culture; the French business woman (Catherine Deneuve) represents entrepreneurship and emancipation; and the Italian model and actress (Stefania Sandrelli) stands in for beauty. Rosa Maria is clearly an outsider. While they all understand each other speaking their respective languages, she has to speak in English in order to be understood. She is also the only one who remains reserved and does not flirt with the captain.

The brutal end to the harmonious encounter of these cultivated characters from different Western countries travelling to the Orient is equally allegorical: Oliveira draws a parallel between the European Union, united with its American patron, and the construction of the tower of Babel in times of religious conflicts. The conversations at the table that discuss European history and culture, the relationship between the Arabian and the Western world, or the lives of the three famous women – who, due to their dedication to either business, beauty or the arts did not have children – resemble the construction of the famous tower that was built to glorify humankind in disrespect of God. Only that today the table, that is, the world of vanity and Western alliances, is not destroyed by divine punishment but by Islamic fundamentalists who express the displeasure of the Muslim world with the lack of Occidental values.

Figure 6: John Malkowitch, Irene Papas, Catherine Deneuve and Stefania Sandrelli in *A Talking Picture* (Courtesy Madragoa Filmes)

It comes as a surprise that the characters who are sacrificed in this religiously inspired castigation are the historian and her little daughter. The Portuguese women are the only characters who cannot flee on the lifeboats from the ship and die during the explosion of the bomb. The reason is once more allegorical: the little girl, dressed in an Oriental outfit her mother bought at the bazaar in Aden, received an Arabian doll as a gift from the captain. When everybody is leaving the cruise ship in a rush, she returns to her cabin with the purpose of saving the doll. The result can be contemplated a few moments later in a close-up shot of the captain's horrified face, who sees the two women standing on the ship looking for rescue. In the moment of the explosion, Oliveira freeze frames the image and does not let us hear his cry of desperation and impotence.

During the narrative, the historian and her daughter are used to counterpoint the sympathetic but mundane European women, and to develop an alternative idea of Europe: while Maria Joana is a symbol of children's purity and curiosity, Rosa Maria is an exemplary woman and the only mother, behaving always in a serious and intellectual fashion, disinterested in pleasing the captain. While the main characters highlight at first the unjust marginalization and insignificance of Portugal in the Babylonian Europe – perfectly perceptible when nobody at the table understands Portuguese – the ending reverts this position by attributing to them the power of sacrifice. Only the possible shock of losing the true Christian values represented by the Portuguese characters – knowledge, curiosity, preservation of history and tradition, tolerance of religion, motherhood, etc. – which is stamped into the face of the captain, might make the West wake up from its selfish dreams of splendour.

Although the reason for the current political situation and the tension between East and West, Muslims and Christians is obvious to Oliveira, he presents history itself as much harder to comprehend. In the course of the film there are numerous moments that show the difficulties in understanding the paradoxical conflicts between the nations from a historiographical point of view; and the film's aesthetic renders visible how tricky it is to make sense of the past. As minimalist as *Word and Utopia*, the most recurrent aesthetic feature in *A Talking Picture* implies that history cannot be seen: words have the power to recreate it, but they are also limited in their capacity of explanation. In Marseille, for instance, the two main characters hardly notice the plate that indicates the foundation of the city by the Greeks, and Oliveira uses a shot of their skirts in front of the plate to further obstruct the vision of the site. The long take of a book in which Pompeii is recreated when its pages are turned over is another example with which the filmmaker visualizes the gap between what we see and what would be its explanation.

The characters can only try to encode the visual world, and they do so with references to myths and legends, but these are equally no secure source of information. There are recurrent motifs on the visual and oral level, like symbols of protection (the mosaic of a dog or the disappeared stature of a goddess), references to conflicts between cultures and religions (in Istanbul and Gizeh), and to wisdom (prophets, goddesses or other mythical figures like Moses, Athena or the *Hagia Sophia*), but there is no unifying idea or explanation. Unlike *The Satin Slipper*, the camera does not offer a general view, a godly vision, but merely fragments of civilizations' remains that make characters and spectators wonder about their meaning and why those who created them came to be extinct.

The only certainty is that Europe's modern civilization will also come to its end, because it subscribed to the American values of success, power and a nostalgic relation to its cultural patrimony. While Rosa Maria and Maria Joana actually die in the film, the other Europeans who have been 'Americanized' will simply die out. For that reason, Oliveira suggests that the importance of Portugal as a guardian of the humanistic values that will guarantee a harmonious coexistence with the Orient must be rediscovered.

This is to say that even though Oliveira acknowledges the complex relationship between cultures and the inexplicability of their downfalls by showing that it is impossible to answer Maria Joana's questions about changing cultures and religious tensions, the film does offer a solution. This solution, however, does not engage deeper with Muslim culture. A more complex exploration of the lack of values that threaten the existence of Europe would be needed to avoid the newly stated dichotomy between a negative view of political and economic systems of expansion, such as the European Union, and Portugal's potential of revitalizing its values with the aim of ending Islamic terrorism. What remains unspoken is how the Muslim and the Christian world would engage after such a renewal in the future, since the allegory of the little girl protecting the doll is as paternalistic as the idea of saving the native and African slaves in *Word and Utopia*.

Similar to the earlier films, Portugal occupies in *A Talking Picture* again a singular role, which consists in its historical mission as unifier of the world. The comparison between the journey to the Orient of the Portuguese historian on the ancient European route and that of Vasco da Gama – who appears portrayed in a glorifying fashion in a painting in the cruise ship's dining room – underlines the contrast between the times of the discoveries and the present day, at the same time that it puts forward the idea that the earlier voyage was not inspired by the selfish interests of the contemporary Western world. The fact that modern-day Muslim culture is ignored and its most stereotyped image, the veiled woman, is protected by Portugal, displays the Christian inspiration of the film, as does the sacrifice of the two women that serves as a wakeup call to save Europe. Thus, the film simply renews the mythology of the humanistic discoveries, as well as that of Portugal's Christian mission put forward in the prophecy of the Fifth Empire.

Comparable to *The Satin Slipper* and *No or the Vain Glory of Command*, the vision of the earlier Portuguese journeys of expansion is affirmative and lacks a critical assessment of the commercial ambitions that, in fact, propelled the search of the maritime passage to India. What is more, *A Talking Picture* proposes a positive self-image of Portugal as a post-colonial country that not only preserved Europe's true values, but is capable of bridging the millenary cultural conflicts it participated to create over centuries. Albeit its astute analysis of the contemporary conflict between Orient and Occident, *A Talking Picture* is a return to patriotic and paternalistic values that take Camões' glorification of the discoveries and Vieira's idea of Portugal's role in uniting all religions under Portuguese Christianity at its basis, and considers them capable of saving the Western Tower of Babel from destruction.

The Fifth Empire – Yesterday and Today

The Fifth Empire – Yesterday and Today (2004), an adaptation of the play *El-Rei Sebastião/King Sebastian* by José Régio, returns to a straight-forward discussion of Portugal's political and historical ideologies, offering a more ambivalent perspective on the contemporary imperialist ambitions of the West and their religious inspiration. While the narrative recoils to the sixteenth century, the change of the title not only stresses the continuity and validity of the imaginary of the Fifth Empire, but uses it as a contemporary synonym of Sebastianism.

Regio's play and Oliveira's adaptation both focus on a single night in which *dom* Sebastião contemplates the decision to invade Morocco with the purpose of fighting the 'unfaithful', disseminate Catholicism in Africa and bring Portugal immortal glory. The irony is that the King will disappear in the battle of Alcácer Quibir and inaugurate the myth of Sebastianism – the belief in the return of the 'desired one'.

Contrary to *No or the Vain Glory of Command*, Sebastião is not sketched as a maniac despot. His characterization is initially built, in accordance with Regio's play, from the point of view of his court and people who do not take him serious and rather consider him a confused freak. But Sebastião's final decision to take his army to Morocco, even though his country cannot afford it and does not desire the enterprise, is not the choice of a mad man. The King is a tragic figure who opts for the self-destructive and unrealistic endeavour out of diverse reasons: he was taught to look towards Africa in terms of conquest and to think of himself as the 'desired one', a savior figure and political successor of the great Portuguese Kings. His incapacity to distinguish between unrealistic dreams and reality due to the messianic encouragement are part of his heritage, as is the self-destructive idea of sacrifice.

Although his court criticizes him, it is partly responsible for his decision because of its submissiveness and willingness to obey authoritarianism. While Shakespeare's Hamlet is tragic for encountering himself at the threshold of the era of reason and is incapable of relying on traditional values such as revenge, Régio's and Oliveira's Sebastião is tragic for not being able to escape the wild dreams of an irrational nationalistic Catholicism. In fact, Sebastião does not desire this unobtainable objective; he simply does not have a choice between being and not being sacrificed to 'serve' his country.

Against the portrayal of an either venerated Christ-like figure or disapproved maniac, play and film stress Sebastião's awareness that he will become the immortal hero of this self-destructive ideology, which is perpetuated by his religious tutors, the court's noblemen and his servants. Simon the shoemaker (Luís Miguel Sintra), inspired in the prophet Bandarra, is especially interesting since he reveals to the King, on the one hand, the relation between fantasy and ideology and persuades him, on the other, to accept his fate and to sacrifice himself.[91]

---

[91] The deconstruction of the relation between the imaginary world of the main character and the manipulated (political) reality is as much a common topic in Oliveira's work as is his heterodox perspective of certain 'wrong beliefs' or authoritarian stances by the Catholic Church. Films in which he challenges erroneous interpretations of Christianity are: *O Acto da Primavera/Rite of Spring* (1963), where he tries to recover the true meaning of Christ's passion; *O Passado e o Presente/Past and Present* (1972), in which he develops a critical perspective on bourgeois marriage; *Benilde ou a Virgem Mãe/Benilde or The Virgin Mother* (1975), where he shows that the incapacity to deal with sexuality results in irrational ideas; *O Convento/The Monastary* (1995), in which he questions the dichotomy of good and bad; and *Espelho Mágico/Magic Mirror* (2005), where a wealthy woman's obsession with the apparition of the Virgin Mary is used to reflect on the

In Regio's play the matter of fate remains ambivalent throughout, since the question if the King should engage with the mission to fight Islam and his condition as the 'desired one' who receives a call from God is not answered. Oliveira pronounces Sebastião's relation with divinity differently in a sequence in which the previous Kings ask the sleeping Sebastião what he is going to contribute to Portugal's greatness. When Alfonso V (João Pedro Vaz) criticizes the Fifth Empire and asks his grandson to transcend it, the filmmaker shows in a medium shot an image of Christ (unidentified) carrying the cross. Christ then turns towards the camera and looks directly at the spectator. This interpellation is an even more evident sign of Christ's presence in Portugal's political affairs and of his approval of the idea of transcending the Fifth Empire in a peaceful way than the many images of Christ on the cross in *Word and Utopia*.

Comparable to *The Satin Slipper*, also based on a play, Oliveira uses again the theatrical device of a fixed camera to which the characters act most of the time frontally. However, it lacks the earlier film's artificiality due to its more realistic acting, the detailed recreation of sixteenth century costumes and the usage of original settings in the Convent of the Order of Christ in Tomar. It is in terms of place and time the most restrictive of the six films, but this is compensated by shots of the convent's abundant Manueline style, which preceded Baroque by incorporating exuberant maritime elements and representations of the discoveries. In its formal simplicity, the film is aesthetically closest to *Word and Utopia*, except that through its dark tone it develops the former film's strictly rational look.

In accordance with the ambivalence of José Regio's play, which leaves in the open whether the conversations really take place or if they are the expression of the King's unconscious (as dreams or deliriums) – that is, whether he was chosen by God or not – Oliveira creates a fantasmagorical atmos-

---

contemporary need of religion. Moreover, Oliveira explores the question of guilt in *Aniki-Bóbó* (1942) and *A Divina Comédia/The Divine Comedy* (1991) from a less moral than humanistic point of view. Nonetheless, Oliveira is a profoundly Christian filmmaker and the idea of following Christ's life as an example is taken serious in *The Satin Slipper*, *A Carta/The Letter* (1999), where a young woman becomes a missionary instead of following her passion, and in *Word and Utopia*, in which Vieira confronts the dogmas of the Inquisition by sacrificing his freedom.

phere through lighting that oscillates between light and shadow. The *mise-en-scène* thus gives Regio's play a voice, in the sense that it pays visually tribute to the playwright's journey into the tormented soul of *dom* Sebastião. Notwithstanding the sophistication of the lightning, the film is, like most of the filmmaker's most recent films, of a formal minimalism (the referred frontality of the shots, the view cuts, the concentration in terms of space, etc.) that attributes some rationality to the irrational setting.

Figure 7: Ricardo Trêpa and Luís Miguel Cintra in *The Fifth Empire* (Courtesy Madragoa Filmes)

Whereas Oliveira reveals in *Word and Utopia* his appreciation of Vieira's prophecy of the Fifth Empire as an ecumenical and pacific project, *The Fifth Empire*, filmed only four years later, presents a far more critical perspective. The film hints in its title at the fact that all desires of greatness are belliger-ent and lead to warfare. This is probably a result of the filmmaker's reflec-tions after the attacks of 11 September 2001. The parallelism between the invasion of Morocco by Sebastião and the invasion of Iraq by the United

States and Great Britain in 2003 is obvious. More importantly, in contrast to *A Talking Picture*, Oliveira chose an already existing text, an outstanding play whose ambiguity stems from a far more complex worldview on the possibility of political manipulation and religious doubt. Apart from the fact that his reading of the text underlines similarities with the present situation – when the conflict between cultures and religions has reached extreme and global dimensions – the filmmaker adds the sequence in which the ancient Portuguese Kings debate Sebastião's role, distinguishing again Portugal's glorious past and deeds as discoverers and the possibility to transcend the politically inspired expansion. Thus, the film ends less ambivalent than Regio's play. Bright sunshine awakes the King who is keen to embrace his fate, take his sword and lead the attack against the 'unfaithful'. The historical Sebastianist episode now seems to be an integral part of God's ways, which are incomprehensible to humankind, than a condemnation of the King's choice and historical wrongdoing.

Still, *The Fifth Empire* is the darkest of the six films under analysis, not only in terms of time, place and lighting, but also in terms of its negative vision of the politics of expansion. In no other film Oliveira criticizes or demonstrates so clearly the irrational reasons (the perpetuation of a glorious past, the desire for eternal prestige, dreams of greatness that go beyond the economic reality of the country, the instrumentalization of religion) that are responsible for the invasion of a Muslim country. As a result and in agreement with the filmmaker's intentions, various film critics associated *dom* Sebastião with George W. Bush and his invasion of Iraque. Oliveira himself noted that Bush had a Sebastianist inclination when he expressed his desire to disseminate democracy and liberty throughout the world and thus manifested a viewpoint similar to that of the Fifth Empire (see Johnson 2007: 131). But according to his Christian worldview, the filmmaker does not portray the prophetic ideology of the Fifth Empire as wrong in itself. It has again a potential, which lies in its Christian principles.

Christopher Columbus – The Enigma

At the age of ninety-eight, Manoel de Oliveira made his last film on the Portuguese expansions. In *Christopher Columbus – The Enigma* (2007) he focuses exclusively on the discoveries, particularly those realized by Columbus, and leaves out any references to Sebastianism or the Fifth Empire. Portuguese history and its identity take centre stage in all their splendor, very much in line with the source from which the film takes its cue: the book

Cristóvão Colón era Português/*Christopher Columbus was Portuguese*, written by the physicist Manuel Luciano da Silva and his wife Silvia Jorge da Silva, that assembled proofs that the Genovese navigator was in fact Portuguese.

The film consists of two parts. The first shows the young Manuel Luciano da Silva (Ricardo Trêpa) parting with his brother (Jorge Trêpa) from post-war Lisbon in 1946 on a transatlantic ship to the United States of America. Shots that present the two brothers discussing their journey in front of a statue of *dom* João I establish a link between the Portuguese migrants and the Portuguese navigators of the fourteenth and fifteenth century. Their arrival in the United States spotlight positive and negative details, such as their fascination with the country's technology, the solidarity between the compatriots and the deception with the rude treatment at the migration office. Most scenes are set in the fog, which creates a phantasmagorical and eerie atmosphere for the land of liberty. The characters' expectation to encounter a nation superior to their own country appears to be an illusion. Notwithstanding, many shots pay homage to the American cinema that portrayed the dim years before and during the Second World War: silent movies and *film noires* from the 1930s and 40s.

The dark ambience changes when da Silva has managed to establish himself as a practitioner and starts getting interested in his lifelong passion, the true identity of Columbus. He returns from Massachusetts, where he lives and works, to Portugal to marry Silvia (Leonor Baldaque). During their honeymoon the da Silvas start to collect evidence on Columbus' origin and parentage. They drive from Oporto to the Alentejo where they visit the church of Cuba (the probable birthplace of Columbus), the museum of the castle in Beija (to visit the sepulcher of this supposed father, João Gonçalves Zarco, a Portuguese nobleman who served Henrique, *o navigador*, as colonizer of the Islands of Madeira) and the mythical 'Escola de Sagres' (Sagres School), created by the prince and regarded as the starting point of the Portuguese maritime discoveries.

The second part of the film moves forward in time and reaches the present, and the investigations are now conducted and finalized with Manoel de Oliveira and his wife Maria Isabel performing the parts of Manuel and Silvia. They visit the Columbus monument in New York, make a boat trip to the Statue of Liberty, travel to Dighton Rock State Park and take a plane to Porto Santo, on Madeira, where they visit Columbus' house.

Oliveira uses an angel (Lourença Baldaque), a young woman dressed in the colours of the Portuguese flag, red and green, wearing a sword in her hand, who accompanies the couple throughout the film as an unambiguous patriotic sign that serves to bridge the temporal ellipsis. The angel is introduced as the custodian angel of the kingdom and protector of the kings of Portugal during the visit to the church of Cuba, from where it disappeared, and mentioned again in the dialogue during the New York visit to Columbus' monument, where a similar angel can be found on the pedestal. The angel obviously disappeared from Cuba to protect the investigations on Columbus' identity and to help rediscover Portugal's lost son.

While the first part of the narrative traces Manuel da Silva's biography and establishes the topics of his investigation, its main objective is to set up the relationship between the migration to the United Sates and the discoveries, dignifying as such the negative image of the uncultured and poor Portuguese migrants who spread across the world in the nineteenth and twentieth century. Another important issue is the demythification of the United States, whose identity as welcoming nation that evokes hopes of unlimited possibilities is called into question. The second part deepens the argument on Columbus' Portuguese identity by offering, simultaneously, more thoughts on the United States and its unfulfilled promise as the country of liberty and an anchorage point for the exiled.

This critique is translated into sound and image. In the sequence of the boat trip to the Statue of Liberty, for instance, Oliveira shows the American flag blowing in the foreground and the Statue of Liberty in the background, as if the national symbol could wipe away the promise of the Statue. Looking at *Miss Liberty*, Silvia sings and Manuel recites the Sonnet *The New Colossus*[92] by Emma Lazarus, inscribed on the Statue. They comment that these verses

---

[92] The poem goes: 'Not like the brazen giant of Greek fame, / With conquering limbs astride from land to land; / Here at our sea-washed, sunset gates shall stand / A mighty woman with a torch, whose flame / Is the imprisoned lightning, and her name / Mother of Exiles. From her beacon-hand / Glows world-wide welcome; her mild eyes command / The air-bridged harbour that twin cities frame. / "Keep ancient lands, your storied pomp!" cries she / With silent lips. 'Give me your tired, your poor, / Your huddled masses yearning to breathe free, / The wretched refuse of your teeming shore. / Send these, the homeless, tempest-tost to me, / I lift my lamp beside the golden door!''

rather express a desire than an accomplishment. What is more, claiming yet another individual for Portugal, Oliveira has Silvia reveal that the poet, born in New York, was in fact a Sephardic Jew of Portuguese descent. Albeit her diasporic lineage, the blame for migration is first put on Europe – by means of the poem's lyrics – and then on the USA for not fulfilling its promise, but never on Portugal, where Jews were forced to convert to Catholicism and persecuted for centuries.

The questioning of America's hegemony in *Christopher Columbus* is an understated continuation of the same task in *A Talking Picture* and *The Fifth Empire*. However, a new and surprising perspective is added. Sharing the evocation and glorification of the discoveries as cultural achievement present in *No or the Vain Glory of Command*, Oliveira not only assigns a divine dimension to the Portuguese maritime adventures by employing the guardian angel and assures the spectator of the celestial patronage of both the characters and their country (comparable to the visual references to Christ in *Word and Utopia* and *The Fifth Empire*). Including Columbus in the list of the great Portuguese navigators when the investigators visit the Dighton Rock State Park is also only part of the story. Portugal becomes, in fact, responsible for all the modern maritime discoveries. The enigma in the title is only rhetoric: besides giving the world numerous islands, the passage to India and Brazil, it gave access to the powerful and imperfect north of America.

There is a stunning scene that suggests poetically and ideologically Portugal's direct responsibility for the existence and the creation of the United States of America. When Silvia and Manuel finish their visit to the School of Sagres, the cradle of the Portuguese maritime discoveries, they go outside and walk to a high cliff over the Atlantic Ocean. There they recite, after a shot in which the angel looks frontally at the spectators, reassuring them of her divine presence, the famous first verse of *The Lusiads*:

> As armas e os Barões assinalados / Que da Ocidental praia Lusitana/Por mares nunca de antes navegados / Passaram ainda além da Taprobana,/ Em perigos e guerras esforçados / Mais do que prometia a força humana,/E entre gente remota edificaram / Novo Reino, que tanto sublimara.[93] (Camões 1997: 7)

---

[93] ('Arms and the Heroes, who from Lisbon's shore, / Thro' seas where sail was never spread before, / Beyond where Ceylon lifts her spicy breast, / And waves her

This is followed by a subjective shot of the Atlantic Ocean that expands until the shores of the United States, extending as such the 'Novo Reino' ('fair kingdoms of the rising day') of the Song. What is more, the verse is recited as if it were a wedding vow, echoing the earlier nuptial ceremony between the couple before they part on their honeymoon. A symbolic analogy is delineated between the vow of the couple and their promise to recover Columbus, between them and the 'matrimony' of the Portuguese with the sea. The different bonds express nothing less than the nation's pledge to discover the world, first pronounced –as we already know – by Camões.

The main characters' foremost objective is to argue in favour of the Portuguese identity of Columbus and to critically assess the American promise to be the Promised Land, since it rivals with Portugal's task as 'Christ's nations'. Beyond this affirmation of the nation's hegemony, the film also brings the little attention given to the central historical sites of the discoveries, as well as their degraded state to the spectators' awareness. This occurs during the visit to the 'School of Sagres' and in Porto Santos in the house where Columbus lived the last years of his life. The film not only tries to rewrite national history, it also calls attention to the lack of preservation of the memory of Portugal's great deeds.

No other film by Manoel de Oliveira is at once so unpretentious and utterly patriotic. There is no greater paradox than that between the simplicity and beauty of its visual narrative and the power of the idea that Portugal is the greatest and most exceptional nation on the planet, because it gave the modern world both Americas. The most amazing idea is that since Portugal is the mother of the New World, the unfulfilled promises of the United States must be associated with the failure of the Portuguese dreams of grandeur cited in *The Lusiads*. They are, as always in Oliviera, a result of the human limitations, on which God, and the representative of His chosen nation, Manoel de Oliveira, look with sympathy.

---

woods above the wat'ry waste, / With prowess more than human forc'd their way / To the fair kingdoms of the rising day.')

Conclusion

Between 1985 and 2007 Manoel de Oliveira accomplished his personal cir-
cumnavigation of the Portuguese discoveries in relation to the country's
identity. With the European Community at sight and in a moment in which
Portugal had lost any kind of leadership after five hundred years of imperial
identity, he embarked in *The Satin Slipper* on an assessment of Europe's
imperialism during the first centuries of maritime expansions. Before long,
he changed his course in *No or the Vain Glory of Command* and crossed the
centuries in search of the failed national initiatives to extend Portugal's
boarders in the name of Sebastianism. His disapproval of this ideology offered the filmmaker the chance to idealize the discoveries as a cultural contribution to the History of mankind by detaching them from any involvement
with colonialism.

A decade of silence on the subject followed. In the year of the commemorations of the 500 years of Portugal's 'Discovery of Brazil ', Oliveira hoisted
again the sails to rediscover António Vieira, consecrating his writings and
his prophecy of the Fifth Empire in *Word and Utopia*, sightless for any critical judgment of the priest's inconsistent ideology. After this celebratory
transatlantic back and forth between Portugal and Brazil, the filmmaker remembered the European route to Asia and crossed the Mediterranean on the
lookout for explanations of the terrorist attack on the World Trade Centre in
New York in 2001. Disenchanted with the contemporary European expansion towards the Orient, the Portuguese discoveries – namely Vasco da Gama's route to India – idealize once more present-day Portuguese values to
the point of considering them an alternative to the mundane European Baby-
lonia in *A Talking Picture*. It is the shock therapy of the possible loss of these values with which the filmmaker hopes to change Europe's course towards disaster.

In due course Oliveira returned to Portugal. The adaptation of an outstanding
play by José Régio on *dom* Sebastião in *The Fifth Empire* offered him the
basis for a less patriotic and more profound interpretation of the motives of
political expansion. But while Régio knew that military expansionist politics
– past, present an future – are by nature abominable nationalistic dreams,
Oliveira still believes that a Christian transgression of the Fifth Empire is
still possible.

After revisiting the ancient Portuguese routes of expansion – first to South

America and the North of Africa, then to Africa and to India, followed by the sea route to Brazil, once again to India and a second time to the North of Africa – the filmmaker encountered a route that he had not navigated before and that he now claims to be Portuguese as well: Christopher Columbus' discovery of America. The last finding, that Columbus belongs to Portugal and that all the modern maritime discoveries have been accomplished by Portuguese navigators annul the erratic routes of expansion in the unifying idea of Portugal's exceptionality.

Manoel de Oliveira is a filmmaker moved by doubts and the certainty that the human condition is paradoxical. The world in his movies is far from perfect and reflects, as Fausto Cruchinho (2003: 9) proposes, his profound Christian humanism: 'a sua tão conhecida perversidade não é senão um desejo insensato de melhor compreender o mundo tal qual Deus o criou'[94]. In his dialogue with the great myths that have come to structure the Portuguese imaginary as a chosen nation, he tries to unmask the reasons behind the consecration of the imperialist and religious expansionist politics that have driven Portugal, Europe and the United States of America. But even though he presents, at times, perspectives close to the contemporary critical views on Portugal's colonialism, they are always unconditionally Portuguese and Christian. As a result, his embarkations in the national imaginary offer paradoxical discoveries: not only of the paradox of human existence, but also of the paradoxical, but unquestionable mission and difference of the Portuguese people. On the lookout for demythification, the filmmaker ends up remythifying Portuguese identity, because the discoveries of the maritime routes cannot be anything else but of divine origin. As the 'filmmaker of Christ', Oliveira does not encounter any other solution than to reaffirm, in the tradition of Luís de Camões and António Vieira, if not the splendor of Portugal, at least its exceptionality.

---

[94] ('His famous perversity is nothing more than an unwise desire to understand the world that God created.')

The adolescent as post-colonial allegory: Strategies of inter-subjectivity in Portuguese films of the 1990s[95]

Introduction

Some of the most interesting Portuguese feature films of the 1990s engage with the representation of adolescents and the way in which they try to construct their subjectivity. Of the 104 films produced in the last decade of the twentieth century at least nineteen narratives[96] focus on an adolescent main character. This interest can be found among filmmakers of an older generation, like João César Monteiro, Alberto Seixas Santos and António Pedro

---

[95] This chapter is a revised version of an article published under the same title in 2005 in *Camera Obscura*, 59.20.2: 34–71. Reprinted by permission of Duke University Press.

[96] The films are *Filha da Mãe* de João Canijo (Portugal, 1990); *Na Pele do Urso* de Anne and Eduardo Guedes (Portugal, 1990); *O Sangue* by Pedro Costa (Portugal, 1990); *Nuvem* by Ana Luísa Guimarães (Portugal, 1991); *Adeus Princesa* by Jorge Paixão da Costa (Portugal/France/Spain, 1992); *Paraíso Perdido* by Alberto Seixas Santos (Portugal, 1992); *Das Tripas Coração* by Joapquim Pinto (Portugal/France, 1992); *O último mergulho* by João César Monteiro (Portugal/France, 1992); *Xavier* by Manuel Mozos (Portugal, 1992); *Longe Daqui* by João Guerra (Portugal, 1993); *O Miradouro da Lua* by Jorge António (Portugal/Angola, 1993); *Sinais de Fogo* by Luis Filipe Rocha (Portugal/Spain/France, 1995); *Corte de Cabelo* by Joaquim Sapinho (Portugal, 1995); *Comédia Infantil* by Solveig Nordlund (Sweden/ Portugal/Mozambique, 1997); *Ossos/Bones* by Pedro Costa (Portugal/ France/Denmark, 1997); *Três Irmãos* by Teresa Villaverde (Portugal/France, 1997); *Os Mutantes* by Teresa Villaverde (Portugal/France 1998); *Jaime* by António Pedro Vasconcelos (Portugal/Brazil/Luxembourg, 1999); *Glória* by Manuela Viegas (Portugal, 1999). *Zona J* by Leonel Vieira (Portugal, 2000); *Noites* by Claudia Tomaz (Portugal, 2000); *Peixe Lua* by José Álvaro de Morais (Portugal/France/ Spain, 2000); *António, Rapaz de Lisboa* by Jorge Silva Melo (Portugal, 2001); *Duplo exílio* by Artur Ribeiro (Portugal, 2001), *Frágil como o Mundo* (Portugal, 2001) by Rita Azevedo Gomes, *Rasganço* by Raquel Freire (Portugal/France, 2001), *O Gotejar da Luz* by Fernando Vendrell (Portugal/ Mozambique, 2001); *A Selva* by Leonel Vieira (Portugal/Brazil/Spain, 2002); *O Rapaz do Trapézio Voador* (Portugal/Spain, 2002); *A Passagem da Noite* by Luís Felipe Rocha (Portugal, 2003); *Sem Ela* by Ana de Palma (Portugal, 2003); *André Valente* by Catarina Ruivo (Portugal, 2003) demonstrate that this trend is going on.

Vasconcelos, as well as among a newer crop of directors like Pedro Costa, Teresa Villaverde and Manuela Viegas. It is also noticeable that some authors, like Teresa Villaverde and Pedro Costa, dedicate several of their films of the 1990s to adolescent characters.

These films are not merely about the troubles of growing up and the common conflicts of family, first love, sexual experimentation, or the trying out of limits. Rather, they show the adolescent's complicated transitional identity faced with crises of family, unemployment, and migration. The characters featured in these films come from the notably marginalized population, like the African ghettos in Lisbon, as well as the more middle and working class homes in Lisbon and Oporto, the interior of the country, or they were born in the former colonies.[97] Undoubtedly, the difficulties in constructing subjectivity are as much marked by the hegemony of Portugal's identity as an empire as by the modernization which results from Portugal's adhesion to the European Community in 1986.

The question of identity was firmly put on Portugal's agenda in 1974 when the Carnation Revolution shattered 500 years of Portuguese self-image as a colonial power. Eduardo Lourenço (1999a: 77–83) observes that the profound identity crises that followed the reinstallation of democracy after the end of the Salazar dictatorship left the former empire without a clear idea of how to relate to its historical experiences and shared cultural codes. He argues that Portugal's membership in the European Union, with its capitalist imperatives, further amplified the Portuguese identity crises. This occurred after twelve years with a nominally socialist, but, following the collapse of imperial power, severely depressed economy: 'obscuramente, no meio de orgias pagas com o dinheiro dos outros, pela primeira vez, Portugal não sabe bem o que é. Não sabe bem o que é como destino'[98] (Lourenço 1999a: 68). A necessary cultural revolution has not taken place because the young de-

---

[97] The films with narratives directly related to the hegemony of Portugal's former colonies are: *Paraíso Perdido, Comédia Infantil/Nelio's Story, Longe Daqui, O Miradouro da Lua, Corte de Cabelo/Hair Cut, Ossos/Bones, Os Mutantes/The Mutants* and *Zona J/J Zone.*

[98] ('strangely, in the middle of the orgies paid with the other's money, for the first time, Portugal does not quite know who it is. It does not quite know what is its destiny.')

mocracy had not been prepared for the deconstruction of 'uma ideologia estruturalmente imperial sem império, militante, hagiográfica, ultranacional-ista, aberta ou inocentemente hostil à inspiração democrática, sem a qual não era viável superar meio século de "pensamento único"' [99] (Lourenço 1999a: 79–80).

The interest in adolescent characters as allegory for the identity crises in Portuguese Cinema seems easily explained, given that adolescents, per definition, find themselves in a situation in which they have no final identity. Furthermore, adolescence is nowadays usually referred to as a moment of discontinuity, rupture, perturbation and conflict, since anxieties towards its destructive or transgressive potential have grown. Suicide, drug abuse, early motherhood, delinquency and anorexia are some of the phenomena that encourage fantasies of adolescents' pathological dangers. Does this mean that the allegory of the adolescent in Portuguese film necessarily contains a pessimistic view of a troubled post-colonial Portugal incapable of growing up?

The allegory reveals itself as more complex when linked to the contemporary view of identity as neither essential nor final. Identity is now understood as a temporary positioning within an identity process. It results from the articulation of the subject into already existing discursive practices: 'identities are such points of temporary attachment to the subject positions which discursive practices construct for us' (Hall 1996: 6). In order to clarify this process, Stuart Hall explains, with reference to Stephen Heath's discussion of the concept *suture* within the context of identification in film, that identities are representations constructed across the division from the place of the Other. While taking up its position, the subject is not only hailed – in the sense of being spoken – but also invests into discourses and practices – in the sense of subjects that can be spoken – in a process through which subjectivities are produced. Hall's use of the term identification indicates the general instability of identity formation as a result of the delicate balance between self and other, as well as of the complex inter-dependence between text and reader/spectator, which makes the construction of identity representations possible.

---

[99] ('a structurally imperial ideology without empire. Militant, hagiographic, ultra-nationalist, openly and innocently hostile to democratic inspirations, it was not possible to overcome half a century of "single thinking"')

The balance or tension between self and other is particularly significant for the identity formation of the adolescent since it is marked by transition. This lack of stability has a negative connotation, and the adolescents' potential for identity construction have given way to an anxiety-ridden view of adolescence and its transgressions. The constant breakdown of the dependence between self and other is interpreted as a threatening failure.

But is this really the case? The psychologist Jessica Benjamin (1995: 14), by introducing the concept of inter-subjectivity, defends that the subject learns early and takes pleasure in recognizing the Other as subject. This capacity is maintained even when the subject starts to take a greater interest in affirming its own self. Inter-subjective theory departs from the assumption that if the characteristics of the Other have been interiorized through loving identification, the human being is capable of relationships that are characterized more strongly by love of the Other than by his/her negation. Resolving the tension between these impulses has generally been considered essential for identity formation; and its breakdown, which occurs when the subject is not capable of seeing the Other as an equivalent centre of experience, as pathological. Benjamin suggests the contrary: fantasy only takes over when the tension is permanently resolved, because then idealization or objectification is the result.

The collapse of balance is only temporary because the subject is always trapped in a contradictory dependence on the Other and a tension between self-affirmation and recognition of this other:

> In its encounter with the Other, the self wishes to affirm its absolute independence, even though its need for the Other and the Other's similar wish undercut that affirmation. (...) The need for recognition entails this fundamental paradox: at the very moment of realising our own independent will, we are dependent upon another to recognize it. At the very moment we come to understand the meaning of *I, myself*, we are forced to see the limitations of that self. At the moment when we understand that separate minds can share similar feelings, we begin to learn that these minds can also disagree. (Benjamin 1995)

How does the breakdown occur and what is its potential for the subject? Benjamin suggests that destruction/negation is actually a way of engaging with the Other beyond intra-psychic processes like symbolic identification or projection. The important discovery that the self makes is the reality of the

Other as subject, which actually informs the discovery of its own reality:

> Destruction makes possible the transition from relating (intra-psychic) to using the object, to carrying on a relationship with an other who is objectively perceived as existing outside the self, an entity in her own right. (...) If she (another entity) survives without retaliating or withdrawing under the attack, then we know her to exist outside ourselves, not just as our mental product. (Benjamin 1995)

The intra-psychic side of this process is equally important in the development of mutual recognition, given that there is no such thing as a normative ideal of balance that equates breakdown with failure and the phenomena of internalization, fantasy, aggression that come along with it, with pathology:

> If the clash of two wills is an inherent part of inter-subjective relations, then no perfect environment can take the sting from the encounter with otherness. The question becomes how inevitable elements of negation are processed. (...) A relational psychoanalysis should leave room for that messy, intra-psychic side of creativity and aggression; it is the contribution of the inter-subjective view that may give these elements a more hopeful cast, showing destruction to be the Other of recognition. (Benjamin 1995)

The capacity to relate to the Other and to oneself as a reality results from this negation, but also from the survival of the Other. The intra-psychic mechanisms, which are a constant symbolic digestion process and part of the cycle of exchange between the individual and the outside, only become a problem when the Other does not come into view as a reality. It is only then that the symbolic identification can turn the Other into an object, and submission to (idealization, feeling inadequate) or contempt for the Other (demonization, aggression) may be the outcome. But if the Other resists, the subject can go beyond symbolic identification and engage in emotional identification. Benjamin calls this cross-identification. It is 'the capacity to put oneself in the place of the Other based on emphatic understanding of similarities of inner experience' (Benjamin 1995). It is the key to establishing a shared reality and to recognize the other *and* the self.

This account of the constant return of tension between intra-psychic and relational aspects of identification, which enables the self to see the Other as subject and to *reflect* upon its relation to the Other, offers an innovative perspective within the discussion of identity formation. While Hall points out that identification belongs to the imaginary as well as to the symbolic, in the sense of the symbolic order/language, and argues that it is, always, partly constructed in fantasy[100], Benjamin's theory of inter-subjectivity does not differentiate between imaginary, real and symbolic, since she does not investigate cultural representations. But she offers an insight that is not entirely apparent in Hall's discussion. Departing equally from the iterabilty of the identification process, the tension between intra-psychic self-affirmation (symbolic identification) and recognition (as a result of emotional cross-identification), inter-subjective theory suggests that the imaginary *can enter* the field of reality, even if only temporarily.

To go beyond identity's assumed homogeneity, both Hall and Benjamin consider it central to examine identification. The potential of identification is encountered in its process and relational character. It offers not *one* identity, but a variety and diversity of identifications. Hall (1996: 16) not only stresses that both text and spectator invest in a relationship related to representation, but foregrounds, by citing Judith Butler (1993: 105), that as identification belongs to the imaginary, it can even indicate the limits of identity politics: 'Identifications are never fully and finally made; they are incessantly reconstituted, and, as such, are subject to the volatile logic of iterability. They are that which is constantly marshaled, consolidated, retrenched, contested and, on occasion, compelled to give way'.

Although this observation has led to much controversy, it is constructive in relation to the adolescent as allegory because it indicates a chance to deal with the Portuguese identity crises. Adolescents generally know no essential and fixed identity, since they always encounter themselves in a process of unstable identification. In relation to the post-colonial identity crisis, the adolescents represent the potential to change the situation. The capacity of recognizing the Other as subject is especially true for the adolescent because

---

[100] Hall (1996: 4) suggests that identities 'arise from the narrativisation of the self, but the necessarily fictional nature of this process in no way undermines its discursive, material or political effectiveness, even if the belongingness, the "suturing into the story" through which identities arise is, partly, in the imaginary (as well as the symbolic) and therefore, always, partly constructed in fantasy, or at least within a fantasmatic field'.

of the constant breakdown of the tension between self and other that defines his/her transitional identity.

The question of identification offers also a different theoretical approach towards spectator/text-relationships. As it is well known, Roland Barthes' differentiation between the closed *readerly* and the open *writerly* texts established that the *writerly* texts, by ignoring rules such as coherence, linearity or closure, open up the possibility of multiple meaning. Bertolt Brecht's much earlier concept of *distanciation*, which first appeared in 1926, likewise considers those texts more progressive that, instead of following dominant aesthetics, engage in anti-illusionist and self-reflective strategies by foregrounding the artistic process (see Knopf 1986: 93–141). A distanced position makes a critical view possible. The admiration of formal strategies leads to a hierarchization that favours avant-garde aesthetics for their critical potential in relation to ideology and distrust conventional texts for their possible emotional identification.

Given that identification can be defined as being intra-psychic *and* relational, the subject is not necessarily imprisoned in the imaginary or symbolic field, but might find access to other realities. If the spectator, while attaching him/herself to a text through identification is neither hailed into it (through symbolic identification) nor invests into it (through cross-identification), his/her relation to a text can also be described in inter-subjective terms. The relationship of the spectator with the text can be unstable, defined by moments of symbolic identification *and* moments of reflection on the Other. This perspective goes beyond a rejection of realist aesthetics and considers it possible that the text, as long as it is not closed in terms of either *positive* or *negative* essential identities, can encourage recognition of the Other.

By using inter-subjectivity as an additional framework to spectator/text-relationships, it becomes possible to explore whether the text promotes the recognition of the Other as a reality. This depends on the possibilities the text offers to identify with final or unstable identities. If the text only encourages intra-psychic mechanisms that work towards a dissolution of the tension between text and spectator through the suggestion of an *ideal* identification (that privileges the assertion of the spectator), it can be considered as establishing the idea of a final identity. If the text pursues complex strategies of identification and constantly re-establishes the tension between spectator and text, it can be considered as promoting the idea of unstable identities.

The theoretical framework developed above is useful for the understanding of the Portuguese films that feature adolescent main characters. It helps formulate questions that clarify the meaning of the allegory for the crises of national identity: Do the filmmakers simply denounce the incapacity of subjectivity formation in the young Portuguese democracy or do they offer solutions? Do their films intend to discuss the need and possibility of inter-subjectivity as a means of identity construction? In other words, do these films work towards the idea that Portugal is a helpless adolescent or do they encourage complex identifications with the most vulnerable in order to come to terms with the crises?

This chapter concentrates on Paulo Costa's *Ossos/Bones* from 1997, Joaquim Sapinho's *Corte de Cabelo/Hair Cut* from 1995 and Teresa Villaverde's *Os mutantes/The Mutants* from 1998, because their approaches to the adolescent's strategies of subjectivity construction demonstrate a yearning for inter-subjectivity in Portugal's post-colonial identity crises. I consider them the most interesting proposals in recent Portuguese films.

Using adolescents as allegories of post-coloniality, the films discussed in this chapter differ significantly from the films analysed in the previous chapters. Set during the dictatorship and/or imperialism, or even completed under the New State regime, it seems only logical that they focus on intra-psychic mechanisms and that they work towards a resolution of tension instead of re-establishing it. Tension is, however, created through avant-garde aesthetics to allow for a critical view of the symbolic identification related to an oppressive regime. Let me have a brief look at the films from the three earlier chapters within the theoretical framework just established, in order to set up their differences with the films on adolescent characters.

Filmed under a dictatorial regime, *A Bee in the Rain* operates with a negative view on the hegemonic identity of landowners and a self-reflexive avant-garde aesthetic. The fact that it was filmed during authoritarianism explains the valuation of the formal strategies that serve to reveal how even the representatives of the ruling class are imprisoned in non-inscription. The film neither idealizes the working class nor condemns the ruling class but points out that their shared imaginary can be imploded by the means of art, in the moment when its underlying intra-psychic mechanism becomes apparent. *The Dauphin* equally avoids positive or negative essential identities. Instead, it positions the spectator in a conflict that is mediated by time. The young democracy is still under the impact of the long history of authoritarianism and the tension between past and present is established through the chronology of the film's narrative time. The quality of both films consists in offering the spectator the possibility to discover him or herself as a subject of history that has a choice who to identify with. While the earlier film has been canonized for offering a resistance identity – political action through art – the latter film demonstrates that more conventional aesthetics do not imply emotional identification that foster idealization, but – since it does not offer an alternative – will probably never achieve immortality.

The colonial war as subject matter proves to be trickier in terms of identity politics, given that the film's other would have to be the colonized countries. João Botelho and Manoel de Oliveira only spotlight the question of national identity and end up resolving the tensions between love and negation of the fatherland: either through an idealization of the family bonds in *A Portuguese Farewell* or by demonizing the war and idealizing culture in *No or the Vain Glory of Command*. No narrative strategy is strong enough to re-establish tension with this kind of ideal identification.

In the case of Manoel de Oliveira's films, this chapter's theoretical framework helps to provide further evidence for his paradoxical strategies. *The Satin Slipper* is, essentially, a film about idealization: the intra-psychic mechanisms of Rodrigue and Prouhèze, as well as of the European nations. To use Gil's expression, they are classical examples of non-inscription. The avant-garde techniques constantly re-establish tension with the spectator, but – more often than not – they express Manoel de Oliveira's recognition of our limited understanding of God's ways than a step outside of the symbolic field established by the camera. *Word and Utopia*, *A Talking Picture* and *Christopher Columbus* face the same problem as *No or the Vain Glory of Command*. Neither the film on António Vieira nor on the History teacher and her daughter demonstrate recognition of indigenous or Muslim cultures, but rather contempt for others: the Inquisition, the colonizers or the European cultural and economic elite. Identification is neither varied nor diverse since both films idealize the values that their Portuguese main characters represent. It would, on the other hand, be interesting to include *The Fifth Empire* as an example of an adolescent character into the comparison of this chapter, since the tensions that Sebastião has to endure are politically more explicit than those of Costa's, Sapinho's and Villaverde's characters. Christ's literal presence in the film reminds, nonetheless, of the prospect of an ultimate symbolic identification that Sebastião embraces in the closure. I will try to show that the following examples are far more down to earth and that inter-subjectivity is, in fact, their utopia.

Absence of the Other

The Mutants started as a documentary project on so called 'difficult' adolescents who live in state run institutions. Since permission was not granted to film in these homes, Teresa Villaverde decided to write a feature inspired by some of the stories she had encountered during research. Without much space or opportunities to affirm their subjectivity, the three main characters, Andreia (Ana Moreira), Pedro (Alexandre Pinto), and Ricardo (Nelson Varela), try to survive in Lisbon's contemporary reality.

The film starts with Andreia's suicide attempt because she is pregnant. The adults in the hospital of her institutional home want to assist her by treating her like an equal but she runs away, trying first to find the father of her child, who is part of the African Diaspora, and then her own estranged mother. When she returns, she is expelled from the home due to her rebellious behavior and sent to a second home in the centre of the country from which she runs off again. She ends up giving birth all on her own in a gas station toilet. Leaving her child behind to be taken care of by worried adults, Andreia tries to go on alone but does not get far and faints in a nearby forest.

Her story is told in parallel to Pedro's and Ricardo's who escape from a different institutional home. The boys have a couple of adventures before they are caught and taken back by the police. After having been arrested, Pedro is allowed to visit his father (António Capello) who is an alcoholic. When he returns to Lisbon, because his father beat him up, his desire to stay with his social worker and her family is frustrated. Thus he returns to his father when he cannot find Ricardo in Lisbon.

It proves that Ricardo, a Luso-African,[101] is the more vulnerable of the two. He is almost violated during their first escapade in which they participate in

---

[101] The concept 'Luso-African' was introduced by F.L. Machado to denominate the first generation of Portuguese nationals born in African countries. Interestingly, Rosana Albuquerque (2004) applies the concept also to Africans born in Portugal, since they have a right to obtain the citizenship when their parents already posses it or when they become 18 years old.

the shooting of a German pedophile film in order to get some money. While Pedro is visiting his father, Ricardo has nowhere to go but runs away from the institution and lives on the streets. In need of money, he steals in a warehouse where he is caught and kicked violently to death by a group of men.

The film does not provide a closure. The narrative comes abruptly to an end: the adolescents and many others who are introduced in short sequences have no place where they can stay for long. They constantly try to position themselves somehow as adolescents: in relation to friends their age, family members and representatives of society. Andreia's strategy differs, nevertheless, from that of the boys, and not only because she does not have a companion. Where they look for freedom, also in terms of having a good time, she tries to find someone to share her responsibility with. She has turned into a woman before she had time to become one and she can barely comprehend her pregnancy.

The problem is that the adults consider Andreia, the boys and the other adolescent or child characters to be fully accountable for their acts, either giving them too much responsibility or by demonizing them. In a scene at the very beginning of the film, a ten-year-old black boy is dragged out of a police car as though he were a dangerous criminal. The treatment that the adolescents receive is obviously inappropriate to their emotional and physical maturity. But the characters do everything they can to avoid victimization and react against this false positioning.

The film shows that what is positive for the average adolescent, easily turns into a threat to them. After the German porno film shoot, Ricardo and Pedro try to enjoy themselves at an amusement park. Lacking money to go on the rides, they hide and smoke pot. On the next day, the owner of the ride calls the police. When they try to run away he sets its machine in motion to stop them. What is entertainment for the average teenager becomes a trap for Pedro and Ricardo. In fact, it is difficult for these marginalized adolescents to participate in any legal form of consumerism, since the leisure industry, strengthened by the economic development within the European Union, is a source of exploitation or danger.

Consumerism is not really what they are after. Villaverde stresses that family is the key aspect of their identity formation and the adolescents consider themselves as depending on it. Andreia and Pedro both make an effort, even if in vain, to return to their parents. Ricardo's situation is shown to be more

difficult and radicalized through the complete absence of a home. As a mulatto, neither black nor white, without parents his identity is even more fragile. His situation is translated visually when he and Pedro play a videogame
in an entertainment centre. Ricardo wins and the machine tells him: 'I am the
future.' The filmmaker then uses a close-up of Pedro's eyes looking straight
into the camera to insist on the irony of this meaning: Ricardo, like most of
the adolescents, does not have a chance at all. But it is the white boy Pedro
who challenges with his look the gaze of the spectator.

Besides constituting subjectivity, the gaze also occupies the dominant position, the position of power: 'The gaze is not necessarily male (literally), but
to own and activate the gaze, given our language and the structure of the
unconscious, is to be in the 'masculine position', as E. Ann Kaplan (1988:
30) notes. All adolescents in the film have difficulties in constituting their
subjectivity. But while Pedro is capable of occupying the position of the
gaze and hence of the 'male' subject for a brief moment, the Luso-African
Ricardo cannot even engage in this kind of tension with the spectator. Still,
he is never, except when he is killed, portrayed as an object or a victim.

The attention given to the specific situation of young Luso-Africans within
the discomforting portrayal of contemporary Portuguese teenagers is of singular importance. Racism is a sensitive topic in a society that has not yet
questioned thoroughly colonialism's discriminatory discourses and practices.
In contrast to the films discussed in the chapter on the representation of the
colonial war, Villaverde demonstrates that the luso-tropicalist discourse on
composed and eventually mixed cultures and races is a fairy tale.

The Luso-African generation born in Portugal rather confronts the common
problems of immigration such as unemployment, labor exploitation and discrimination, as the sociologist Rosana Albuquerque (2000) claims: 'the
equality given by law is taken away be inequality and disfavour faced in
daily life. (...) Luso-Africans, the old as well as the young generations, are
still seen as immigrants. Their blackness is a distinction mark that assigns
them the status of foreigners. These two characteristics underline the whole
context of inter-ethnic social relations'. *The Mutants* makes this perceptible.

Although Ricardo's character faces a more complicated situation than his
white friend Pedro, they have in common that their desire to participate in
the games of contemporary society is constantly frustrated. They are the very
opposite of Zygmunt Bauman's (1996: 31–2) player, one of four post-

modern projects of identity construction[102] trying to keep away from fixation:

> The worry of the player is that each game should indeed start from the beginning, from 'square one', as if no games were played before and none of the players has amassed wins or losses which would make mockery of the 'zero point' and transform what was to be a beginning into a continuation. (...) The mark of postmodern adulthood is the willingness to embrace the game wholeheartedly, as children do.

Even though they engage with the entertainment industry, Ricardo and Pedro try to avoid this postmodern lack of stability and continuity by reencountering those who are responsible for them, their parents. What is more, on the verge of adulthood, the available games endanger the lives of the adolescents, especially Ricardo's. But the other two characters also have to realize that they have no one to turn to. It is unclear why Andreia cannot stay with her mother, who mentions that custody of her daughter was taken away from her. She seems to be ill, perhaps an alcoholic like Pedro's father, who in the prior scene tried to beat him. The parents are incapable of participating in their children's upbringing because they have problems of their own, a fact that is understood by the youngsters. But the adolescent's project remains to be recognized and nurtured by their adult family members, who seem, in many ways, to be the real emotional children.

Within the logic of the film it is the adults who have to start recognizing the adolescents as what they are: young people in need of others. To render this visual, Villaverde employs divers cinematographic strategies. The adolescent characters have a presence on the screen that stands in for the withdrawal of the Other. Hardly ever is there a shot/reverse shot. Especially in the scenes when the characters ask others for help, the filmmaker shows their demand with an uninterrupted close-up of their faces while denials of support come from off screen. When Andreia visits her mother on the run from the second home, the mother does not engage at all emotionally with her. Not only does she ignore that she is pregnant, she is self-centreed. While she speaks vaguely about her illness, an uninterrupted close-up shows Andreia for 75 seconds listening to her mother. The length of the shot stands in

---

[102] Vagabond, stroller and tourist are the other three identity projects.

for her needs and demand for recognition. But Andreia is not victimized by the shot, rather resisting negation. She is clearly constructed as subject in this scene, vulnerable but with a separate and equivalent centre of self. Despite the fact that the shot is uncommon and thus perhaps uncomfortable because it lacks the shot/reverse-shot convention, the resulting tension offers the spectator as much the desire to withdraw, as the possibility of an empathetic understanding of Andreia's emotional needs.

The adolescents are not idealized. They are rebellious and have a strong need of self-affirmation. Their constant search for freedom brings Andreia, Ricardo, Pedro, and various other adolescents into more or less dangerous situations, captured in recurrent shots of moving vehicles or their hair flying in the wind. Their progression in space seems to make them feel closer to a sense of themselves.

Almost every time when they are enjoying themselves, this feeling is reversed and either the dangers or the limits inherent in their condition are revealed. One example is a sequence, quite near the beginning of the film, in which a boy steals a handbag in a train station and escapes on a transport train. The camera accompanies the movement of the departing train and shows the tracks that he is leaving behind, indicating that the boy is out of danger of being caught. When the camera reveals him lying on his back, relaxing, it starts to move against the direction of the train until it shows the boy in a close-up. The tracks are now dangerously close to his head. His self-affirmation was only temporary. He is caught in the contradiction between his search for independence and self-affirmation and his relation to society. This constant tension is rendered visible by the sequence.

The film's narrative does not offer a conventional cinematographic discourse. The chronological stories are told through a structure that obeys a visual pattern and not a plot of cause and effect. This also results from the way Villaverde uses space. She rarely reveals where her characters are and, although they move all over Lisbon, they seem imprisoned within the frame of the shots. It is more important to be close to them than to tell an easily accessible and coherent realistic narrative. This technique produces a controversial effect: it distances the spectator from their story as well as confronts him/her with their emotions when their presence becomes most intense. There is a constant tension between experiences of difference and the recognition of similarity of emotions.

Another impressive example is the scene in which Andreia gives birth in the gas station's toilet. The filmmaker desynchronizes the sound and uses 48 images per second, which makes the highly emotional scene more discomforting, since the physical pain is extended by the slow motion. On the other hand, it becomes also bearable, because this artificial extension reveals difference by exposing the filmic apparatus. Since it is not constructed as a realistic scene, the spectator is distanced from the pain of the character; but it is so strong that it still invites emotional identification.

The filmmaker rarely offers occasions for the spectator to be stitched into the narrative through simple identification with the character's position. Point of view shots are almost completely avoided and occur only on two occasions in which they are distorted because the two characters, Ricardo and another Luso-African boy, are under the influence of drugs. First, one of the boys they are hanging out with on the streets at night has sniffed glue. The camera introduces the boy by observing him for some time as he is floating on the river in a tire. Then there is a cut to the other children and adolescents who rescue a dog from the river. Cut. The camera now captures the boy's point of view with an up-side-down shot that reflects the effect of the glue and shows the other adolescents on the pier. A shot in which one of the kids is playing soccer with a famous soccer player from the national team in slow motion follows. It gives a glance into the simple and common desire to identify with a hero but is interrupted by reality when a real ball hits the water next to the character.

The second sequence of point of view shots is equally discomforting. It is set within the amusement park and shows how the rides turn into a cacophony of lights and sounds for Ricardo. His world is at first upside down and then out of kilter. Since the subjective shots are juxtaposed with shots of the unsteady and slightly terrified Ricardo, his state and vision have nothing pleasant. There is no liberating effect from the drugs, only a feeling of sickness and confusion.

Villaverde offers, briefly, less anxiety-ridden identification with Andreia on three occasions: when she is trying to find her boyfriend, she takes shelter in a tree from which the camera shows the immensity of the sky; when she is expelled from the first home, the scene opens with a medium close up of the director who confronts her about the impossibility of staying in this institution; and when she goes to see a doctor and sees her fetus on the ultrasound screen. These subjective shots offer engagement with her feelings: her loneliness, her helplessness and her incapacity to understand her motherhood.

Figure 8: Ana Moreira in *The Mutants* (Courtesy Cinemateca Portuguesa)

There is yet another sequence worth describing in the context of the character's subjectivity. When the director in the hospital accompanies Andreia
after her suicide attempt, she disengages from his conversation and imagines
herself getting up to get cigarettes. A shot shows how her rebellious spirit
literally leaves her body. After walking through the hospital in search of
something to smoke, her double lies down next to her and the two girls share
a cigarette, pleased. Like the other two examples, this scene describes an
intra-psychic mechanism. It is the only one in which Andreia achieves a
sense of self-affirmation. In contrast to the boys, she accomplishes relief
from her uncomfortable situation through fantasy, while the drug consumption of the boys is portrayed as isolating and full of unpleasant physical side
effects.

A comparison of Andreia's and Ricardo's subjective shots and scenes exposes how gender and race affect the adolescents. Although Andreia is on her own, due to the marginalization and isolation of her unwanted mother-hood, she is capable of affirming herself. Ricardo is less successful. In the scene where he is almost raped no shot reveals his perspective and thus the aggressor, but an uninterrupted shot of him offers recognition of his situa-tion. Pedro, in contrast, is not only the object of these insistent shots but looks back at the spectator to confirm his reality as a subject. The only scene in which Ricardo's subjective position is accessible is out of joint. Given his vulnerability and death, race features as an even worse stigma than gender.

Due to the narrative strategies such as the open end, the general lack of cause and effect, long close-ups, glances into the subjectivity of various characters across gender and race, as well as the evasion of shot/reverse-shot, the film's spectator/text-relationship is complex and unstable. The spectator is invited to shift between emotional involvement and distance. It is easy to sympathize with the characters' needs and desires, but also to dis-tance oneself from them and from the narrative, to feel uneasy about certain shots or to be challenged to make sense out of a sequence. The main visual feature is the characters almost unpleasant presence that obliges the spectator to perceive them as others in a tension that neither dismisses them nor lets them take over the emotions completely. They are there to be recognized as a reality.

Re-negotiation with the Other

Where Villaverde looks at the marginalized youth from Lisbon, Joaquim Sapinho's *Hair Cut*, from 1995, focuses on the lower middle class where a young woman rebels against the gender identity that is imposed on her. On the day of her wedding, the nineteen-year-old Rita is on her way to a hair-dresser in a shopping centre. Her good looks are highlighted when a man of African descent, who works in one of the other shops, grabs her and tells her about his desire. When arriving at the hairdresser, a girl suggests that Rita have her beautiful long haircut. Hoping to use this as a proof that her future husband Paulo loves her and not her looks, she accepts. In the perfume shop where she works, her colleagues are rather shocked about the new style and suspect male authority behind the change: 'It was Paulo who asked for the cut, right?' Rita only reveals her haircut to Paulo at the moment when the registrar asks him whether he wants to marry her. After some hesitation he says yes with no conviction. He does not like the new look, and it is obvious that it is difficult for him to accept an independent young woman instead of a love object. In the course of the narrative, Paulo will have to take her as she is and endure the tension between Rita's demand for recognition and his self-affirmation. For the time being, everything becomes a power play: where to sit in a restaurant or whose name is first on the answering machine. Even though they realize that it is the greatest fun doing things together, they do not bear the tension long. After making love, Paulo imposes himself again and cuts the hair of the sleeping Rita even shorter. As a reaction to this imposition, Rita leaves in the middle of the night and goes to her friend Teresa's apartment. But Teresa is busy throwing her boyfriend Lucas' belongings out of the window and does not let her in. Reconsidering, Rita walks off to the subway to find Paulo who is filming at a metro construction site. When she finally sees him and shouts his name, he cannot hear her. Her Luso-African admirer who has been following her helps Rita out of the site from the shopping centre. His interest in her has not altered because of her short hair. They end up having a good time, eating hot dogs and dancing to the rap music of other immigrants. In a video game shop their fun is turned into someone else's game: skinheads humiliate and chase them. Paulo equally has a bad night. When he gets home and finds his best friend Lucas in front of his apartment, they start arguing: Paulo learned after the wedding that his friend had become a heroin addict and reproaches him for that. Lucas accuses him of being insensitive to his problems and the friends separate after a fight. On the doorstep Paulo finds the sleeping Rita and takes her into bed. He undresses her and returns to objectifying her by filming her naked skin. When Rita finds the tape the next morning she is not preoccupied with Paulo's interest in her image. She pays more attention to other sequences that Paulo filmed the night before, especially those of a dog shown in a close-up. Not only Rita has changed her attitude: Paulo takes Rita to her work place and promises to pick her up later. It is a pledge for their relationship.

There is a certain naiveté about Paulo and Rita and their place in the world. Family ties only exist in photographs that Rita sometimes looks at. They are orphans within a dazzling post-modern world. Sapinho shows his characters repeatedly in moving cars and inserts frames of highways and subways into the narrative. But the accelerated rhythm of the rapidly developing commercial metropolis of Lisbon corrupts the relationships among the characters.

The film is pessimistic about this economical and technological evolution since it makes people unreliable and selfish. Lucas experiences this coldness when he becomes a heroin addict: his best friend and his girlfriend abandon him. Teresa does not even care about Rita's problems or bother to show up at her wedding. The photographer who takes her place as second witness exemplifies that the bonds in this society are interest related when he wants to be paid for his task.

Lisbon, which is being excavated so as to become faster and more modern, is a place of domination: Paulo does not want to let go of machismo and skinheads are the more extreme version of his chauvinism. Tension, so to speak, is constantly turned into fantasy and appears to be the other side of modernization. It is also not by coincidence that Paulo and Lucas work with video and that there is a reference to another profession that registers the surrounding world, the photographer. But while the photographer is one-dimensional as a character and as a professional – he shoots what he is paid for –, the video camera and the different people who operate it – Paulo, Lucas, and Rita – not only register fantasies that result from intra-psychic mechanisms, but also reveal their very construction.

The film presents counter-strategies against intra-psychic mechanisms: Rita, Lucas and the Luso-African resist against the identities that are being imposed on them. Rita realizes that her and Paulo's protest against a conventional wedding is only a pose because the gender roles are actually maintained. She knows very well that in order to be loved by Paulo he has to recognize her as who she is. This is why she changes not only her image, but also the way she positions herself towards him. A classic clash of wills is the result. But Rita's negation does not end in total withdrawal or retaliation. First, because she comes back; and second, because Paulo gets the point. The destruction carried on by Rita makes a new form of relationship possible: she becomes a reality outside himself.

Sapinho is less convinced about the inter-subjective skills of his male character. Paulo has not completely changed and he objectifies Rita again with the camera. But Rita's attitude towards Paulo's obsession is different and she is able to encounter other aspects in his filmmaking. It is, in fact, possible to speak of cross-identification between Rita and Paulo after their night of mutual attempts at annihilation, since the balance between destruction and recognition is re-established after its breakdown.

The other two characters are less important, but they illustrate the same principal: Lucas fights against the one-dimensional way in which Paulo is starting to see him and insists that he is a subject in his own right. He wants Paulo to understand and recognize his drug problem instead of being lectured by him.

The Luso-African character is a more complicated case, because Sapinho introduces him as a stereotype to illustrate Rita's attractiveness and a more sexualized machismo than Paulo's. Later in the narrative both he and Rita are presented as victims of racial or gender discrimination. And only Rita is recognized as subject. Sapinho is obviously more interested in the discrimination of women and the difficulties it poses to their identity formation, remaining ambivalent about the Luso-African character. The adult man does not really escape a typecast: he sings and dances with fellow Luso-Africans, and maintains his sexual interest that is physically violent in the beginning. He serves to demonstrate that within Portuguese society there is a relation between Paulo's machismo and racial discrimination in the scene when Rita is attacked by the skinheads for going out with a black man. But the character is too ambiguous to invite any form of emotional identification or recognition. His is a serving function, for example when he helps Rita to overcome objectification. She gets away from his pursuit at night because she sees him on the monitors of the surveillance cameras in the metro. After having been distressed by being filmed, Rita is finally able to make use of it and escapes the desiring look. Earlier subjective shots that fragmented her body disappear, even though the Luso-African character still manifests his desire to take her home. But apart from the fact that there is a moment of cross-identification between them, Rita does not even greet him on the next day, when he gazes at her again in the shopping centre.

The film is self-reflexive in terms of filmmaking throughout. The first images show an awkward Rita posing uncomfortably for Paulo's video camera. His objectifying gaze opens the film. This strategy of classical cinema usually 'equates the exemplary male subject with the gaze, and locates the male eye on the side of authority and the law, even when it is also a carrier of desire', as Kaja Silverman (1992: 131) puts it. When Rita arrives at the registry office, it is again Paulo's gaze through the camera that receives her. Sapinho questions this strategy during the film and proves that Paulo's look loses its capacity to constitute Rita's identity when she or others choose to negate it.

Paulo's video images assume various functions in the film, and they are used with different intentions. Lucas films the quarrelling couple on the wedding day against Paulo's will. Taking on Lucas' point of view, the camera eye exposes their crises and records Paulo's loss of control. In another scene Lucas' camera reveals that their relation actually does not follow role models: Rita provides the money since she has a stable job, and it is she who pays the photographer because Paulo is penniless. His insistence on being in charge in their relationship is clearly an imposition.

After Paulo cut Rita's hair, flashbacks of video images are inserted in the narrative and reveal his double morality: he kisses a trendy black girl with a shaved head. The images that depict his desire are then juxtaposed with others that he took of the longhaired Rita working in the shop. Whereas the later images testify to his desire through the gaze, the earlier images question its authority. The inserted images are all shot with a handheld camera. The video camera is constantly and literally being passed from one hand to another; or, in a scene in the apartment, pushed away by Rita when Paulo is positioning it to film them when they are making love. Since it is mobile it can be used by anyone and offer multiple viewpoints that question power structures.

As mentioned above, cameras are also useful to help Rita detect that the Luso-African character is following her. In the end of the film, when she looks at the images Paulo filmed the night before, she seems more capable to deal with the power that she herself had ascribed to the camera eye before. That Paulo again filmed her naked body has become less important, since she is now aware that she can react against Paulo's macho attitudes and obsession with her image. Her viewpoint now engages as much with her images as with other objects. While Paulo's point of view shots in the narrative are always questioned, subjective shots of Rita's perspective usually are affirmative in terms of identity construction. Her first point of view shot shows the haircut in a magazine that she decides on having. When they move into the new apartment and the atmosphere is unpleasant between her and Paulo, she plays with a mirror and the reflections of the light rays comfort her. In the subway, she is able to escape, and when she watches Paulo's recordings, she is content. Paulo has only the right to one more subjective shot after the deconstruction of his gaze. As he drives home from work at night, his views of the dark highway are shown. These shots function dramatically to take the character home but they also indicate his feelings.

In the beginning, Rita is rather ambivalent about her desire to be looked at.

In Paulo's video she feels exposed, but in the shopping centre world she constantly checks her image in the shop window's reflections. Her transformation is told through a narrative that neither follows rules of coherence in terms of cause and effect nor ends in closure. The semi-open end, the promise that dismisses the resolution of a happy end, is one of the many moments in the film where tension is re-established, as much between Rita and Paulo as between the spectator and the narrative. The spectator is constantly involved in a tension with the narrative that negates ideal identification since Rita and Lucas fight for their recognition as subjects. Moreover, Sapinho uses self-reflexive strategies that reflect on filmmaking: each time it offers a symbolic identification with the masculine gaze, it questions this identification through other images. In Paulo's case, it is the scenes filmed from the point of view of other characters that interrogate his intent to assume a dominant position. In the case of the Luso-African, it is the images from the surveillance camera that reveal his objectifying gaze. But he is a double agent, as much of the desiring male gaze as of racist objectification.

The intra-psychic mechanisms of machismo and racism as a way of fleeing into a fantasy world of demonization and domination are related. But the racial issues are only important to dramatize and highlight Rita's problems. In terms of gender the film's narrative constantly re-establishes tension and a closure where the characters engage in cross-identification. Whereas machismo is explored through Paulo's behavior towards Rita and Lucas and contradicted by their reactions, racism is simply shown to be a fact. What is more, the black character and Paulo maintain their desiring look to affirm their masculine identity. But while Paulo learns to engage and recognize the Other, the Luso-African character does not become a subject worthy of Rita's or the spectator's recognition.

Beyond identity

The presence of the second generation of immigrants, the young Luso-Africans in Portugal, is central to Pedro Costa's film *Bones* from 1997. Three characters of Lisbon's African immigrant district *Fontainhas*, which is called *Estrela d'África* (Star of Africa) in the film, develop very different strategies for how to live or survive in a culture that does not recognize them and still sees them as others. The film's beautiful photography earned it the prize for best cinematography at the Festival of Venice and it works against realist or neo-realist aesthetics. Neither a pure fiction film nor a documentary, Jean-Louis Comolli (qtd. in Lemière 2009: 107) has coined the expression 'mutant film' for this and other films that transgress genre boarders.

The problematic relationship that results from the colonial encounters is represented through the contemporary encounter between three young immigrants and one elderly nurse. The pains in overcoming the positions of ex-colonizer and ex-colonized is perceptible in the division of spaces between which these characters shift: the marginal and ghetto-like *Estrela d'Áfrïca* and the middle-class apartments of the city. The inhabitants of these spaces suffer, nonetheless, the same identity crises, be it the young immigrants Tina, Clotilde and the Father, or the representative of Portuguese society, the elderly nurse.

The characters in the immigrant ghetto obviously suffer more. Tina is a young girl who has just given birth. Her friend Clotilde picks her up from the hospital, since Tina's partner (the Father) deserted her on the way there. Back at home, Tina attempts to kill herself and the baby by opening the oven gas bottle, but it is not enough to kill them. Tina is the most endangered in terms of identity construction. Her motherhood makes it even more difficult for her to survive. When her boyfriend disappears with the baby, which he uses to beg for money, Tina's despairs and Clotilde traces the Father to the Nurse's apartment. The Nurse met him when he was begging on the street. Lonesome, she let him stay with her. Trying to get access to her apartment, Clotilde pretends that her daughter got hurt and takes her to the hospital. She offers her services to the Nurse who accepts and gives her the apartment key. Clotilde passes the key on to Tina who attempts her second suicide in a place that looks just like all the other apartments where second generation immigrants work for little money as cleaning personal. Here the gas supply in unlimited, but she is rescued by the Nurse. In the sequence with the nurse it becomes clear that Tina's wish for self-destruction is not her only response to reality. The nurse offers her to stay the night, but Tina refuses. She also hands back the money that she is offered. Although life does not seem worth living, she does not want to depend on charity and is unwilling to lose her self-respect.

Her boyfriend, and father of the child, approaches the question of dependence and subjectivity construction quite differently. Whereas Tina insists on her independence from the Nurse but relies on Clotilde and other friends from her community, the Father neglects those who depend on him and chooses the role of social victim. The Nurse is for him the very representation of help. He tries to sell her the baby, but, as she refuses, gives it to a former lover of his, a prostitute. The second woman he turns to becomes paradoxically, a mother figure by assuming the responsibility for the baby. Cutting off their sexual relationship, the prostitute assumes responsibility only for the new-born and not for the childlike father. Even though he behaves irresponsibly in relation to the women, his passivity and helplessness also deconstruct stereotyped characteristics of masculinity.

The problem of his complete lack of individuation might be explained by his social marginalization and his ethnicity. It is not clear why his rejects his paternal role. There are other characters, married black men, whose individuation is radicalized in their chauvinist behaviour towards women. Clotilde's husband, for example, uses her. She is responsible for everything: work, the children and the love life. Her husband behaves like a crude cliché of machismo when he first drags Clotilde from a party, flirts with Tina and then sleeps with the Nurse. He and other male characters with much darker skin than the Father are mainly characterized by their interest in sex. This suggests the Eurocentric racist idea about the lazy, womanizing African. The adolescent Father, in comparison, not only has no traces, but is also portrayed as a helpless, sad orphaned child who does not know how to relate to his role as a father. What he has in common with the other men is that they are generally incapable of reciprocal relationships or of empathy: but while the adolescent Father is shown as positioning himself as an object that depends on the charity of Portuguese society, Clotilde's husband bases his identity by denying the women their subjectivity.

Clotilde is the only character capable of shifting between the worlds of the Portuguese and the African immigrants. She has the keys to the identical looking apartments where she cleans during the day. All the same, this does not end in an approximation of any kind. Because of the way she is treated by her husband and her concern with Tina, Clotilde moves in with her friend. She also takes on a destructive attitude towards the Father as representative of machismo at the end of the narrative: she turns on the gas while he is sleeping in the Nurse's apartment. Her character reveals that intersubjectivity, the recognition of the Other, is not only restricted ethnically but, mainly, in terms of gender.

Although the Nurse is the immigrants' only link to mainstream society, the women do not engage with her. There is a reason why the Nurse is more receptive. Even though living in a situation of greater economical comfort, she is lonely and needs the Other: the child, the Father, Tina or Clotilde's husband. The relationships between her and the other characters are, however, defined through the exchange of objects: food, the baby as desired object, the key to her house; and the division of social functions: she saves the baby due to her profession and gives Clotilde and Tina low paid jobs. The character of the Nurse, that recalls luso-tropicalist discourse in terms of harmonic sociability between the races, is neither only giver nor taker since her apartment serves as an allegory for the real situation in which all the characters of the film find themselves: it is the meeting point and shared space of Portuguese middle class and marginalized immigrant.

Edward Said (xxix) observed that 'partly because of empire, all cultures are involved in one another; none is single and pure, all are hybrid, heterogeneous, extraordinarily differentiated, and monolithic'. This is true for the marginal Star of Africa, where 'a latitude rácica está a tal ponto diluída que não se distinguee bem onde tem início a epiderme do português do continente e a do falante da lingua portuguesa do ultramar'[103] (Jorge 2009: 157), but even more so for the apartment space where the different cultures enter in negotiation but prove incapable in defining a new identity, which could result from the recognition of this shared situation. The Father is trying to survive alone and at all costs, the Nurse and the mature men are interested in (sexual) self-affirmation. The only solution offered by Costa is Cape Verdean sisterhood, a cross-identification between the female characters, mainly Clotilde and Tina, but also between the many other female characters that are shown in short scenes – waiting for a bus, working or comforting Tina. But this means that Clotilde, Tina and other female characters end up negating the Other: the men of their community and the Nurse, the only representative of Portuguese society.

While this idea of Cape Verdean female solidarity is an invitation to symbolic identification, given that it puts forward the idea of an essential female identity, it is at the same time an offer to recognize the female immigrants as a reality. This suggestion is already present in the first shot of the film in

---

[103] ('the racial latitude is so deluded that it is impossible to distinguish the epidermis of the continental Portuguese from that of those who speak Portuguese from oversees')

which a sad young woman in shabby surroundings is looked at by the camera. The medium close up of her remains for 45 seconds. And during these long seconds there are brief moments in which her eyes start to wander and glimpse into the direction of the camera. Although the gaze of the camera is observing her, the spectator is confronted with her capacity to look back. This character is one of Tina's friends from *Estrela d'África*. Marginal to the story, she takes care of her in the worst moment of depression. She is not the only one who confronts the camera's gaze momentarily. The next scene shows Clotilde in her kitchen where she lights a cigarette at the gas cooker. A cut confronts the spectator with her face in a close-up and due to the darkness of the *mise-en-scène* her eyes can hardly be seen. The shot is equally 45 seconds long; and as Clotilde smokes, her eyes wander as well. In the darkness of the shot there are again moments in which she seems to be looking back. Yet another scene is worth mentioning. Two Cape Verdean women work in an industrial kitchen. When they hand the food through a framed sideboard, they look out from the restricted space in which they encounter themselves, almost crossing the eye line of the spectator.

In an analysis of Rainer Werner Fassbinder's films in order to discuss his 'aesthetics of pessimism', Kaja Silverman (1992: 125) differentiates between the gaze and the look. She argues that Fassbinder's characters are not capable of constituting their subjectivity, but are rather haunted by the gaze because the director refuses to affirm their psychic and social existence. His characters depend on the gaze, but cannot return it: 'What happens within Fassbinder's cinema is that both the gaze and the images which promote identity remain irreducibly exterior, stubbornly removed from the subject who depends upon them for its experience of 'self' (Silverman 1992: 127). This implies that 'no character within that cinema, male or female, is ever represented as possessing the gaze, regardless of how central his or her look happens to be to the articulation of the visual field' (Silverman 1992: 129). In contrast to classic cinema, the male desiring look is not equated with the gaze, but with loss of control. According to Silverman, Fassbinder therefore does not express the 'left-wing melancholy', a patronizing victimization and

representation of vulnerability that he was accused of[104], since the disloca-
tion of power is central to his aesthetic. His 'representational contestation'
(Silverman 1992: 154) does not simply give positive images of women,
blacks, gays or other marginalized groups and, accordingly, neither resub-
stantializes identity nor essentializes it. In relation to the male characters,
Silverman (1992: 155) suggests that Fassbinder bestows them with the capacity to become 'something other than what the male subject has classically
been – to slip out from under the phallic sign, away from the paternal function'.

Many critics compare his aesthetic approach with that of Robert Bresson's,[105] Andrei Tarkovsky or Carl Dreyer, but also point out his indebtedness to Raoul Walsh, and Jacques Tourneur (see Ranciére 2009: 61). Undoubtedly, his films also evoke an 'aesthetics of pessimism' and the question
of left-wing melancholy. His main characters do not possess the gaze and the
beauty of their suffering and isolation is explored in certain frames. Tina and
the Father, especially, are exposed in close ups, looking expressionlessly
into nothing. They also hardly communicate. In the first ten minutes of the
film there is no conversation at all. The only time a human voice is heard is
when Clotilde enters the apartment and announces that she arrived.

The *mise-en-scène* also highlights the character's desolate situation. The
urbanization *Estrela d'África* consists of narrow corridors and is only filmed
at night or the early morning twilight. The interiors are dark and contrast
with the bright light that enters the windows of the city apartments where
Clotilde works. Yet, this brightness gives way to the same darkness in the
apartment of the Nurse when her loneliness is exposed and the Father becomes a frequent visitor. The compositions of the shots indicate strongly the
character's seclusion and marginalization. When they are not shown in
close-ups or medium close-ups, the characters are usually positioned in the
background of the frame with the fixed camera gazing at them from another

---

[104] Silverman also mentions that the filmmaker related aesthetics with victimisation
and expressed that he considers victimised women as being more beautiful than
those who react.
[105] James Quandt (2009: 31) gives a list of aesthetic features that the filmmakers
share. And Jeff Wall (2009: 152) suggests that, due to the marginal situation of the
characters, Costa actually 'corrects' Bresson and takes his aesthetics further.

space, like a corridor or another room. The color gray predominates, but the cold blues or greens of props or clothes contribute an intentional beauty to the shots.

There are no shot/reverse shots. Usually two characters are framed together frontally in a fixed shot when they engage in any kind of communication. The only connection shot between two characters occurs when Clotilde picks up Tina at the hospital. No word falls between them but extreme close-ups of their eyes are juxtaposed. This indicates an understanding between the female characters that is restrictive and so deep that it operates on the level of the look.

The characters are generally incapable of getting in touch with the outer world so as to position themselves within a visual field that might serve to constitute their subjectivity. They are caught within the background of the rooms, the narrow spaces of buses or the corridors of their neighbourhood. What is more, there is not one single point of view shot that would encourage identification with them. The characters' world seems to be too remote from the spectator's view of the world to offer some form of engagement with it. The visual strategies concentrate on isolation and suffering and thus turn the characters into victims. And since their circumstances are not really explored, they often seem caught within the frame and not within their condition.

The visual strategies, the negative portrayal of the African men and the celebration of sisterhood all work towards a resolution of the tension between text and spectator in favour of symbolic identification. The characters are portrayed as being as powerless as Fassbinder's characters, but they are also turned into objects. What is more, the mature Cape Verdean men do posses the gaze, while the characters like Tina or the Father are not capable of looking. Cross-identification with them or their reality becomes almost impossible, only in those moments when they resist. But Costa's discussion of Portuguese' post-coloniality offers in brief moments a tension between text and spectator in order to encourage inter-subjectivity: some of the female characters do, for seconds, occupy the position of the gaze from which they glance at the spectator.

As mentioned before, Silverman argues that the look is within desire and functions as an erotic yearning, and the gaze that triumphs over the look, stands outside desire. However, by freeing the look from the sexual connotation of object theory, it can also be described as standing in for a yearning for recognition when directed straightforwardly at the spectator. From an inter-subjective point of view, the marginalized women in Costa's film are saying: 'Recognize my intent.'

The nurse's apartment also indicates that the descendants from former colonized countries are a presence that cannot be reduced to the object status formerly ascribed to them. However, at the end of the narrative, Costa, unfortunately, opts for a negation of their partners by his female characters, which results in a permanent resolution of tension through fixed identity. *During* the film there are more complex strategies – especially the looks of immigrant characters that for seconds cross the gaze of the spectator and therefore establish a tension with the spectator – and that offer the possibility to recognize some of the characters as subjects.

Conclusion

In the three films analyzed, the allegory of the adolescent clearly indicates that the filmmakers did not see an easy solution for Portugal's identity crisis during the 1990s. The future of the adolescent characters is endangered as intra-psychic mechanisms of self-destruction are not the exception but the rule: Villaverde's Andreia tries to commit suicide, Sapinho's secondary character Lucas is a heroin addict, and Costa's Tina tries to kill herself twice. Intra-psychic mechanisms like objectification and aggression as consequences of the adhesion to the European Community and a long history of despotism and colonialism are depicted as well: the authorities constantly try to abuse the adolescents or want to get hold of them in *The Mutants*; Paulo tries to dominate Rita in *Hair Cut* and skinheads chase her and a character of African descent; *Bones* shows the social exclusion of the immigrants and the male chauvinism within its community.

But the characters try to find ways out of demonization and self-destruction. Villaverde's Andreia, Pedro and Ricardo reject the state institutions and set out for their families, even though their search for inter-subjectivity remains unsuccessful because the Other, the key element to their identity formation, is evasive. Only Sapinho's characters, Rita and Pedro, overcome objectification mechanisms after a long day and night of negation and engage, at least temporarily, in a reciprocal relationship that dismisses conventional gender identities. For Costa's Tina, Clotilde and the Father there is no such solution:

the Father affirms his position as object of charity; and even though Tina is saved by Clotilde's efforts to establish conditions for inter-subjectivity, these are exclusive and reaffirm the gender divide.

None of the films simply denounces the incapacity of identity construction or opts for an affirmation of a final identity through narrative closure. Although Costa uses the construction of an essential or *positive* identity as a survival strategy of his female characters, he challenges a simple text-spectator relationship by confronting the spectator with the look of the Cape Verdean women. But the male Luso-African characters have *negative* fixed identities: they are selfish and sex-obsessed caricatures. Since their behavior is not further contextualized, this could easily be seen as reminiscent of colonial discourse. Its discriminatory stance 'tells us more about the White erotic imaginary than about the objects of its fascination',[106] as Ella Shoat and Robert Stam (1994: 21) remark.

While Costa shows inter-subjectivity as gendered and gender identities as fixed, Sapinho foregrounds identity's construction. Rita and Pedro almost lose each other because of established role models they need to overcome. The filmmaker's aesthetic strategy deconstructs Paulo's intention to dominate the gaze, but is less successful in its discussion of racial discrimination. The Luso-African character remains a stereotype, even though he reveals the relation between machismo and racial discrimination. As self-reflexive as Sapinho's film, Villaverde's feature insists on the need of the Other through an aesthetic that shifts the spectator between distanciation and empathy: the adolescents' search for attention is exposed, sometimes radically, through their constant presence on screen or need of self-affirmation.

There is a cultural pessimism about Portugal's society in all the films discussed. *Hair Cut* and *The Mutants* show their characters lost in Lisbon's city centres, shopping malls, amusement parks or traffic system. Modernization, a result from the subsidies by the European Union (EU), complicates the identity construction of the young people because of the growing social problems and loss of values it conveys: drug abuse, consumerism, breaking apart of families, to name just a few. All parts of society are affected by this

---

[106] Research by Rosana Albuquerque (2004) has shown that the situation of female immigrants is actually more difficult due to patriarchal structures within the communities.

disorientation: in *Hair Cut* the adolescents are lower middle-class, in *The Mutants* they either come from lower middle-class or working-class backgrounds and in *Bones* they are exploited second-generation immigrants. Even though Costa gives less importance to Portugal's economic development, the difference in social standards is evidently responsible for the separation of the ghetto world from the comfortable life of the middle class homes. It is perhaps not surprising that *Hair Cut* is the most optimistic film, given that the characters are orphaned and family problems affect them less.

The films all recognize that Portugal is now a modern European nation that still has to resolve its historic legacy of colonialism and has no new identity to offer. The filmmakers would probably agree with David Morley and Kevin Robins (1995: 21) who argue that the European Union still follows the intra-subjective mechanism of rejecting the Other: 'in the new Europe, the same exclusionary principles continue to operate, and European identity is still constructed against those – without and within – who appear to be non-European or anti-European (…) Europe is 'Europe' against these Others'.

All films foreground that inter-subjectivity is most difficult to achieve for immigrants from the former colonies. Sapinho is sensitive to the problem although his African character is marginal to the narrative and remains a stereotype unworthy of recognition. Costa suggests the recognition of the immigrant women but is aggressive against the male African characters that are also stereotyped. Villaverde, on the other, believes that race takes a greater toll on identity construction than gender. Ricardo is the most endangered character, and his quest for inter-subjectivity ends tragically within a country where it is still possible to diagnose the effects of 'uma ideologia estuturalmente imperial sem império'[107] (Lourenço 1999a: 79-80). One wonders how the narrative would have turned out to be, if Andreia was part of the second-generation immigrants.

It is now possible to conclude that the films use the adolescent as post-colonial allegory because the end of dictatorship and colonialism has not improved the capacity to recognize the Other. But even though Pedro Costa, Joaquim Sapinho and Teresa Villaverde insist that the adolescents represent the identity crisis, they also encounter means to work against intra-psychic mechanisms. They consist in their character's unstable identities, their

---

[107] ('a structurally imperialist ideology without empire')

search for inter-subjectivity and capacity of cross-identification, as well as in the opportunities for complex strategies of identification that the self-reflexive narratives present to their spectators. Within the framework of inter-subjective theory it can be argued that *The Mutants*, *Hair Cut* and *Bones* constantly try to re-establish tension between intra-psychic *and* relational aspects of identification. While the films set out to do so in varying degree and with different approaches towards gender and race, they actually offer moments that make it possible for the spectator to engage with the position of the Other and to recognize him/her as a reality. In the hands of Costa, Sapinho and Villaverde, the allegory of the adolescent is a potent tool to communicate Portugal's need for inter-subjectivity in its uneasy transition between colonial legacy and uncertain European future.

Part II: Facing past and present from a transnational perspetive: between identity and difference

Ambivalent transnationality: Luso-African co-productions after independence (1988–2010)[108]

Introduction

In the sequence of its adhesion to the European Community in 1986 and in search for a place in an increasingly globalized film market, Portugal established a vast amount of trans-national cinematographic partnerships. Next to the economic reasons, the preference to sign agreements with the former colonies prior to treaties with European countries indicates another set of motives. Whereas the interest in collaborating with Brazil was formalized as early as 1981, Portugal set up official regulations for the funding of transnational films with Cape Verde in 1989, with Mozambique in 1990, with Angola in 1992 and with São Tomé and Principe in 1994 (see Matos-Cruz 2002: 17–20).

The partnerships have a symbolic meaning and their significance for both sides cannot be overemphasized. In fact, they have offered to Portuguese directors a more expressive engagement with the colonial past in Africa. As demonstrated in the first part of this book, the end of colonialism and empire has been an important issue in Portugal's national cinema – the colonial war, the expansion politics, the second generation immigrants from Africa – but it is more often than not a subtext. Joaquim Sapinho's *Hair Cut*, discussed in the last chapter on the national productions, serves as a typical example of how the colonial past is remembered by means of a secondary character that has a narrative function for the main characters but no life of his own. While returning soldiers or colonizers (*retornados*) are central to films such as *A Idade Maior* (1991) by Teresa Villaverde or *Paraíso Perdido* (1992) by Alberto Seixas Santos, colonizers in Africa or Brazil and immigrants feature more prominently in the trans-national-productions. With regard to the directors from the African countries with Portuguese as official language (PALOP), after years of stagnation the treaties made a return to film production possible and have allowed for a discussion of their colonial and post-colonial condition. In the case of Cape Verde, they turned the country finally

---

[108] This chapter has been published in a slightly different version with the same title in *Journal of African Cinemas*, (3/2), (2011): 231-55. Reprinted with permission of Intellect.

into a film-producing nation.

Like many other sub-Saharan cinemas the national cinemas in the PALOP still suffer from technical and financial deficiencies and face profound problems in terms of distribution and exhibition. Nonetheless, their cinemas' histories – told by Claire Andrade-Watkins (1995, 2003), Manthia Diawara (1992) and Frank Ukadike (1994), to name but the most relevant[109] – had a dissimilar start when compared to the anglophone or francophone African nations. The authors' accounts underline that in contrast to the British, French or Belgian colonizers, the Portuguese only set up a very restricted infrastructure for documentary production during the colonial period, which was of little help after the overdue independences in 1975.[110]

But unlike other colonies, the PALOP were already active in filmmaking during the armed fight against Portuguese colonialism between 1961 and 1974. The organizations involved in the liberation struggles – MPLA (Movement for the Liberation of Angola), PAIGC (African Party for the Independence in Guinea and Cape Verde) and FRELIMO (Liberation Front of Mozambique) – invited international filmmakers to accompany their wars of independence.[111] These initiatives and the films themselves have been regarded as key factors for opening up a new and important chapter within

---

[109] There is a number of publications available in Portuguese, published by the film institute of Angola (Instituto Angolano de Cinema, 1982), its archives (Cinemateca de Angola 1985), the Portuguese film archive (Cinemateca Portuguesa 1987), by Portuguese researchers Matos-Cruz e Abrantes (2002), as well as by the Portuguese Communist Party (Partido Comunista Português 1981).

[110] The first Portuguese production company was *S.A.R.L. Films Angola*, funded by the filmmaker António de Sousa in 1951 for the production of ethnographic documentaries (see Monteiro 1951: 9). While *Cinangola* was created in the last years of colonialism with the aim of producing propaganda and informational films, it was used for the creation of *Promocine*, the first Angolan film collective after independence (see Cinemateca de Angola 1985: 6).

[111] According to Diawara (1992: 89–91), the Yugoslavian filmmaker Dragutin Popovic and a film crew from the Netherlands were invited by FRELIMO, as well as filmmakers from the People's Republic of China and the American Robert Van Lierop who also filmed in Mozambique. Filmmakers from France, Italy, the United Kingdom, Cuba, Switzerland and the Netherlands were invited by PAIGC, while French filmmaker Sarah Maldoror, of Caribbean descent, filmed in Angola.

the history of African and World Cinema.

Most of the films were documentaries that informed about the wars' atrocities and the desire for self-governance, whose aim was to raise consciousness in local and international audiences. Besides demonstrating film's capacity to construct and represent a society, its identity and culture, the productions also offered the benefit of training local technicians and directors in filmmaking.

Not by chance, the socialist governments in Angola, Cape Verde and Guinea-Bissau, and Mozambique established film institutes in the first years of independence. Angola and Mozambique were particularly successful in setting off national cinemas in the late 1970s and the beginning of the 1980s and produced a reasonable amount of documentaries and some fiction films. Civil wars, economic crises, corruption, and the end of the cold war and the general lack of funding, infrastructure, equipment and qualified technicians soon brought an end to these promising beginnings.

The 1980s with their internal and external problems were followed by the end of the civil wars and mono-party regimes in the 1990s and early 2000s. The countries opened up politically and economically to an ambivalent future. In the wake of this change of paradigm, democratic elections became possible, but also the introduction of neo-liberal economic rules and other shortcomings of globalization. The treaties on cinematographic co-production are part of the ambivalent new situation, since they encourage filmmaking based on technical and financial dependency.

National and trans-national productions

When comparing the number of national films with the number of co-productions in the PALOP, it is more than evident that feature film production relies almost exclusively on trans-national alliances. Since independence, thirty-one fiction features were produced, of which 74 per cent (twenty-three films) were with the help of partners from other countries. Portugal clearly leads the list with twenty films, followed by France with seven films. Other European (Belgium, two films; Germany, Netherlands, Luxemburg, Sweden, Spain, one film each) or African countries (Morocco and Tunisia, one film each), or communist and former communist countries (Cuba, one film; Yugoslavia, one film) made only sporadic appearances as co-producers. Brazil (three films) has marked presence as a film partner only recently. The table below shows that only 26 per cent of the total feature film production (eight films) have been produced exclusively with national resources in the PALOP in the last thirty years.

Table 1: Relation between co-productions and national productions in lusophone African cinemas (1980–2010)

Country	N° feature films	Co-produ. (cp) with Portugal/ % of all cp	N° other cp	N° national prod.	Total of cp
Angola	9	6/67%	1	2	78%
Guinea-Bissau	6	3/50%	1	2	67%
Cape Verde	6	6/100%	0	0	100%
Mozambique	10	5/50%	1	4	60%
Total	31	20/66%	3	8	74%

Portugal's cinematographic participation in Cape Verde is with 100 per cent (six films) the highest among the PALOP. The country is completely dependent on the former colonizer.

Despite the fact that Angola had a promising start in the 1970s and 1980s, trans-national productions now reach 78 per cent of total feature film activity. Portugal was a partner in six of nine films (67 per cent), and Cuba co-produced one film, *Caravana/Convoy* (1992), directed by Rogélio Pais and Júlio César Rodrigues. The national films date from the late 1970s and 1980s: *Faz la Coragem, Camarada?/Be Brave, Comrade* 1977) and *Nelisita* (1982) by Ruy Duarte de Carvalho.[112]

In Guinea-Bissau, co-productions represent 67 per cent of total production. Three of six films (50 per cent) were produced with Portugal as partner and one feature, *Xime* (1994) de Sana Na N'Hada, with the Netherlands. The two

---

[112] In terms of trans-national documentary production, one feature film was produced by Mauritanian filmmaker Abderrahmane Sissako: *Rostov-Luanda* (1998, Angola/Mauritania).

national productions are from the 1980s: *Mortu Nega/Those whom Death Refused* (1988) by Flora Gomes and *N'tturudu/The Mask* (1986) by Umban U'kset.

Mozambique's numbers are more balanced, but more than half of all features produced in the country (60 per cent of films) are co-productions. Three out of seven (43 per cent) were produced with Portugal and one, *Vreme Leoparda* (1985) by Zdravko Velimirovi, with Yugoslavia. The list of national films is longer than that of any other country from the PALOP, but most of them are from the 1980s: *Mueda Memoria e Massacre/Mueda, Memory and Massacre* (1980) by Ruy Guerra, *Canta meu Irmão, Ajuda-me a Cantar* (1982) by José Cardoso, *O Vento Sopra do Norte/The Wind Blows from the North* (1987) by José Cardoso and *Desobediência* (2003), a television feature by Licínio de Azevedo, a Brazilian filmmaker.[113]

Transnationality

Cinema has always been a trans-national art or industry, but the lack of balance between national and trans-national productions in the PALOP, and the former colonizer Portugal as dominant partner, raise questions on the influence that the co-producing companies might exercise on the films under analysis.

There has been much interest in post-colonial co-productions in African and film studies and scholars have inquired the possible ideological input on narratives and identity construction in trans-national films. More often than not they have been discontent with the control exercised by previous European colonizers, especially by France. While trans-national anglophone or francophone film productions have been critically assessed (Diawara 1992, Gugler 2003, Russel 1998, Ukadike 1994, Diop 2004, Gardies 1989, Niang 1996, Sherzer 1996, Thackway 2003), lusophone films, apart from important articles (see Andrade-Watkins), mostly in the context of general accounts of African film history (Diawara 1992, Ukadike 1994), have not been subject to closer analysis.

The concept of transnationality offers itself as an important tool for this en-

---

[113] There are two feature documentaries to be mentioned: *Frontières Sanglantes/Boarders of Blood* (1987, Mozambique) and *Música, Mozambique!* (1980, Mozambique/Portugal) both directed by Mário Hernique Borgueth.

deavour. By proposing answers to questions on past and present of the globalized film market, it has taken centre stage in film criticism in recent years. Benedict Anderson (1983) famously started the academic discussion by suggesting that nations are nothing more than imaginary communities. When film studies realized that films and their study also participate in the construction of cultural boarders by establishing a restricted community of communication (see Schlesinger 2000: 29), transnationality seemed to offer an alternative.

Will Higbee and Song Hwee Lim (2010: 8) specify three different definitions or ways that transnationality is now being employed. The first is more strongly related to the European and North American academic world and tries to challenge the concept of national cinema; the second has a more historical outlook, acknowledging the presence of transnationality and cultural hybridization in film history; the third consists in a critical assessment of post-colonial or diasporic film productions.

Any new theoretical tool not only brings the chance of new insights. Transnationality's inflationary use and its often celebratory and Eurocentric tone point towards challenges and dangers of the concept. Higbee and Lim (2010: 9) identify a set of problems:

> (...) it also tends, for the most part, to be taken as a given – as shorthand for an international or supranational mode of film production whose impact and reach lies beyond the bounds of the national. The danger here is that the national simply becomes displaced or negated in such analysis, as if it ceases to exist, when in fact the national continues to exert the force of its presence even within transnational film-making practices. Moreover, the term 'transnational' is, on occasion, used simply to indicate international co-production or collaboration between technical and artistic personnel from across the world, without any real consideration of what the aesthetic, political or economic implications of such transnational collaboration might mean – employing a difference that, we might say, makes no difference at all. It is precisely this proliferation of the term 'transnational' as a potentially empty, floating signifier that has led some scholars to question whether we can profitably use, or indeed need, the term at all.

Due to the colonial history and the complex identity discourses, the Luso-African productions are not just another kind of international production. And even though it would seem that I am working within the framework of the third definition suggested by the authors, I would rather not engage with their definitions but look at the concept by remembering the discussion of Portugal's transnationality. I believe that this will make the question of the concept's rhetorical employment – with an either positive or negative conno-tation – less relevant and foreground its inherent ambivalence. This goes in line with Higbee and Lim's (2010: 18) proposal of a critical and discursive posture towards the concept:

> The concept of 'transnational cinema' cannot be merely descriptive because all border-crossing activities are necessarily fraught with issues of power; neither can it be purely prescriptive as this often amounts to nothing more than wishful thinking. Rather, we propose a critical, discursive stance towards the question of the transnational in film studies so that we are alert to the challenges and potenti-alities that greet each transnational trajectory: whether it takes place within a film's narrative and production process, across film industries, or indeed in aca-demia.

In this chapter transnationality's ambivalence is relevant for two reasons: first, because of the construction of hybrid identities within the films and second, because of the trans-national production mode. Let me remember that Portugal established its late colonial and post-colonial relationships based on the idea that it was more identical than different from the colo-nized. As mentioned earlier, Gilberto Freyre celebrated the Portuguese as a 'transnational' people, while the philosopher Agostinho da Silva, a distin-guished scholar and Portuguese emigrant to Brazil, used Fernando Pessoa's metaphor of 'A minha pátria é a minha língua'[114] in 1956 to reshape the no-tion of Portugal's identity in the Portuguese-speaking world (see Domingues 1998). The concept of lusophony turns Portugal's territory into that of all the countries that speak its language, bestowing on it again the 'magic dimen-sion of empire' (Feldman-Bianco 2001: 408–9), much in tune with Father António Vieira's idea of a Fifth Empire. I will return to the concept in more detail in the last chapter of this book.

The debates surrounding luso-tropicalism and lusophony cited so far, as well as my analysis of national films, confirm that they are understatements at the expense of the identity of the Other – colonized, immigrants, African free-dom fighters, Arabs etc. There are, however, films that feature characters

---

[114] ('My country is the Portuguese language.')

searching for inter-subjectivity and that demonstrate that transnationality is neither good nor bad, but simply an encounter. And any encounter, as Jessica Benjamin (1995) suggests with her concept of inter-subjectivity, involves ambivalent, that is, simultaneous and conflicting experiences. It is again a question of holding the tension between self-affirmation and recognition of the Other.

The studies on anglophone and francophone co-productions mentioned above have explored the question of the trans-national production mode and suggested that – in Benjamin's framework – self-affirmation by the European producers is the rule in trans-national cinematographic enterprises. Nobody is on a philanthropic mission. Transnational productions are job opportunities for European production companies, laboratories, technicians and directors, and offer profit. And they present a chance to polish up the ex-colonizer's image stained by colonialism, or to get credit for 'fostering' the talent of African filmmakers.

What can we expect from Luso-African productions? In a situation where treaties guarantee continuous film production between Portugal and its ex-colonies, there is probably room for neo-colonial self, but given the growing awareness and critical debate of traditional discourses on colonialism, there should also be space for post-colonial inter-subjectivity and challenging perspectives – already detected in the Portuguese films on the adolescent as allegory.

Since two of the twenty co-produced films are still in post-production and another two have not been launched on DVD, I will concentrate my following analysis on sixteen films and make only brief comments on the others. In contrast to the earlier chapters but according to the necessity to give a general overview of the trans-national feature film landscape, instead of presenting in-depth analysis the films will be discussed individually in a resumed fashion within the context of the four co-producing PALOP. Given my understanding of transnationality as ambivalent, I will try to comprehend how the co-productions negotiate the elements of national and transnational identity. Are they capable of holding the post-colonial tensions? Are new and multilateral perspectives that confront out-dated discourses the exception or the rule?

The lusophone co-productions

The table below lists all twenty Luso-African feature films produced between 1988 and 2010.[115]

Table 2: Luso-African co-productions (1988–2010)

Country	Year	Filmmaker	Title	Co-Production
Angola	1988	Ruy Duarte de Carvalho	*Moía ou O Recado das Ilhas* (The message from the islands)	Angola(A)/ France/ Portugal (P)
	1993	José António	*O Miradouro da Lua* (The watchtower of the moon)	A/P
	2004	Zezé Gamboa	*O Herói/The Hero*	A/France/P
	2004	Maria João Ganga	*Na Cidade Vazia/ Hollow City*	A/Portugal
	2004	O. Fortunato de Oliveira	*Comboio da Canhoca/ Canhoca Train*	A/ Morocco/ P/Tunisia
	2010	Zezé Gamboa	*O Grande Kilapy/ The Great Kilapy*	A/Brazil(B)/P
Cape Verde	1988	António Faria	*Os Flagelados do Vento Leste/*(The victims of the East wind)	Cape Verde (CV)/ P

---

[115] As can be noted, many films were financed not only by Portugal and the PALOP, but also with the assistance of financial bodies or co-producers from other nations. However, the films are only considered national productions by Portugal and the respective African nations in the official publications (ICAM, ICA). There are two more productions that received funding from an African country, namely Mozambique. But both films by José Carlos de Oliveira, *Preto e Branco* (Black and white, 2003) and *Um Rio* (A River, 2005) were produced exclusively by Portuguese production companies.

	1996	Leão Lopes	*Ilhéu da Contenda/* *Isle of Contempt*	Belgium/CV /France/P
	1997	Francisco Manso	*O Testamento do Senhor Napumoceno* *Napumoceno's Will*	Belgium/B/ CV/France/P
	1998	Fernando Vendrell	*Fintar o Destino/* *Dribbling Fate*	CV/P
	2007	Ana Ramos Lisboa	*Cabo Verde – nha Cretcheu/Cape Verde* *My Beloved*	CV/P
	2008	Francisco Manso	*A Ilha dos Escravos* */Slaves' Island*	B/CV/P Spain
Guinea Bissau	1992	Flora Gomes	*Udji Azui de Yonta/* *The Blue Eyes of Yonta*	Guinea-Bissau (GB)/P
	1996	Flora Gomes	*Po di Sangui/* *Tree of Blood*	France/GB/ P/Tunisia
	2002	Flora Gomes	*Nha Fala/My Voice*	France/ P Luxemburg
Mozambique	1998	Solveig Nordlund	*Comédia Infantil/* *Nelio's Story*	Mozambique (M)/ P/Sweden
	2002	Fernando Vendrell	*O Gotejar da Luz/* *A Drop of Light*	M/ Portugal
	2007	Teresa Prata	*Terra Sonambula/* *Sleepwalking Land*	Germany/ M/Portugal
	2009	João Ribeiro	*O Último Vôo do Flamingo/The Last Fight of the Flamingo*	M/P Portugal
	2010	José Carlos de Oliveira	*Quero Ser uma Estrela /I Want To Be a Star*	M/P

When looking at the involvement of filmmakers in the co-productions, a balance between the number of directors from Portugal and from the PALOP can be observed. This implies, at least statistically, equal opportunities of expression. Eight directors from the PALOP (four from Angola, two from Cape Verde, one from Guinea-Bissau and one from Mozambique) were responsible for ten films, while the remaining ten productions were directed by six filmmakers from Portugal, being one of them a Swede who has been a Portuguese resident for more than three decades and one a Portuguese who spent her childhood and youth in Mozambique and Brazil.

Two other interesting points can be singled out. First, all films engage with African reality. Their main characters make only sporadic trips to Europe, in most cases to Portugal. Second, there is a great variety of issues related to the historical and cultural specificities of the country where the film is set or in relation to the origin of the filmmaker. Four major topics can be identified: Portugal's colonial history, the civil wars in Angola, Guinea-Bissau and Mozambique, migration to Europe (Portugal and France), and the encounter of African and European traditions, values and customs.

Angola

A small film renaissance took place in Angola when after the end of twenty-seven years of civil war (1985–2002) three co-productions directed by Angolan directors were distributed in 2004. Zezé Gamboa directed his first fiction feature *The Hero* (2004). The film engages with Angola's difficult post-war reality through a multi-narrative in realist style. It tells the story of the war hero Vitorio (Oumar Makena Diop) who lost a leg in combat and is now trying to reintegrate into Angolan society. His story crosses with those of the adolescent Manu (Milton Santo Coelho) and the prostitute Maria Bárbara (Maria Ceiça) who desire to reunite with their families separated during the war.

The troubled identities of the characters and the touching narrative on the splitting up of families represents the reality of a population that is facing more than half a million deadly war victims and tens of thousands of injured or dislocated people. The happy ending in which the characters reaffirm their identity and live the bliss of a non-biological family with a secure professional future reflects, on the other hand, rather the yearning for a recomposed national identity than the hard comings of most of the population.

This genuine desire underscores the need of solidarity and respect for the former soldiers of the civil war, whose fight is compared to the anti-colonial resistance in the 1960s and 70s. The film thus suggests that the anti-colonial values are still shared by all Angolans and could help to construct a stable post-war identity, as well as conduct the country towards reconciliation. This hope for national unity is apparent in the surrogate family and the reintegration of the hero. His missing leg ends up mobilizing different parts of the society and enables him to transgress due to an act of solidarity the common social obstacles pointed out in the film: corruption (among politicians) and neo-colonialism (among Portuguese firms). Throughout the films the diverse tensions of Angola's post-war situation are explored as being strongly related to colonialism. The new identity is only possible through recognition by the fellow Angolans and should be inspired by a common cause like the war for independence. Zezé Gamboa's next film, *The Great Kilapy* (2010), shot in Brazil, Portugal and Angola after an interval of five years without feature film production, will engage with the colonial war.

Figure 9: Oumar Makena Diop and Maria Ceiça in *The Hero* (Courtesy David & Golias)

While Gamboa's film focuses on the post-war period, 's *Hollow City* (2004) is set during the civil war. Her project dated from 1991 but, given the political situation, could not be turned into reality until after the end of the war. The story focuses on a little orphan, N'dala (João Roldan), who is brought from a refugee camp into the city in order to be saved from the battles that intensified after the first democratic elections. His flight from a group of children under the guidance of a Portuguese nun (Ana Bustorff) is a rereading of the novel *As Aventuras de Ngunga/'Ngunga's Adventures: A Story from Angola* (1972)written during the colonial war by Angolan writer of Portuguese descent Pepetela.

Since the film adapts the original text to the time of the civil war, it inverts almost everything that happens in the book: while Ngunga lost his parents during a massacre by the Portuguese military and becomes a hero fighting them, N'dala's parents were assassinated by Angolan guerrilla fighters and he himself ends up dying tragically. The inter-textual references are established through a character named Zé (Domingos Fernandes Fonseca), who plays Ngunga in a school theatre production. Zé is also the only person to assist N'dala in the empty city. The emptiness referred to in the title stems from the obligatory retreat at night, but serves at the same time as a metaphor for the complete lack of values in Angola's society. Most of the adults that N'dala meets are merely interested in money, alcohol and sex. Except for a fisherman (Francisco Custodio) who represents the traditional cultural identity to which N'dala would like to return.

The boy develops no interest what so ever in the urban culture to which he is introduced by Zé and that consists of action movies, dance music and parties with prostitutes. His life in the rural area is remembered in short flashbacks that show a festivity in his village, interrupted by the arrival of guerrilla fighters. A return to his former life is therefore as utopian as his possible salvation by the Catholic nun who is trying to find him in the city. During an assault in which N'dala is being used by adults since he is small, he shoots a man just as Ngunga did in Pepetela's book. But in contrast to Ngunga, who assumes his identity as an African man by killing the head of the PIDE (Portugal's secrete police), this homicide is stripped bare of any sense or function. In the closure, in which N'dala ends up dying through the same weapon, the film leaves no doubt that the times have changed profoundly since the colonial war.

Hollow City shows a young boy's loss of innocence that stands in for the disillusion of an entire country, just as the original Ngunga stood in for the national hopes thirty years earlier. In contrast to *The Hero*, the film demonstrates that the values that supported the anti-colonial fight have been corrupted and that it is now impossible to construct a mature adult identity modelled on the past. By staging the civil war instead of looking at the quest for a new identity, her film is rather a testimony of the self-destruction that is coming to an end. The nation will have to contemplate this past and start from scratch.

The project for *Canhoca Train* (2004) by Orlando Fortunato de Oliveira dates from 1986 and suffered the same fate as *Hollow City*: it was only shot after the political stabilization in 2002. The film is set during colonial times and tries to clarify the reasons for the civil war through the story of a group of fifty Angolans who were arrested arbitrarily. This occurred after the revolt of a black cleaning man whose wife had been violated by a Portuguese soldier.

The ignorance and aggression of the colonizers is highlighted in the narrative, as well as the divergences between the representatives of the many different Angolan identities. The disagreements are linked to Portugal's violence and lack of values, making colonialism indirectly responsible for the outbreak of the civil war. A wide range of factors is pointed out persuasively in the discussions that take place while the group of Angolans – consisting of revolutionaries, apolitical farmers and submissive administrators of mixed race – are waiting for rescue inside a boxcar on a deserted rail track.

The ethnic and political diversity and the clashes between the various subsequent identities, the influence of theories on assimilation, the revolt against the colonizers, as well as the utopia of a society based on racial mixture are stirred up in this inhuman condition. Although the Portuguese characters – mostly militaries or PIDE agents – are stereotyped, there is one man working at the train station who demonstrates compassion and a humanist attitude. This helps to make the compelling argument that colonial repression and the complex tensions they created exploded in Angola's civil war even more credible. Much of the film is dedicated to debates between the different positions. They help to assess the colonial past, as well as the civil war. By showing colonialism's effect on Angola's identities, the film offers the most complex account of the past. It does not glorify the anti-colonial struggle like *The Hero*, or dismiss it like *Hollow City*. Instead, it considers it worthy of a profound examination in order to learn lessons from its violence.

Before this small film renaissance, two co-productions had been produced at the end of the 1980s and the beginning of the 1990s. The first production dates from 1988 and was directed by Ruy Duarte de Carvalho, a Portuguese writer who holds an Angolan passport since he decided in the country after it gained independence. *The Message From the Island* (1988) is set in Cape Verde and tells the story of an Angolan woman of Creole descent, Moía (Edmea Brigham), who makes a first visit to her mother's home country. Travelling around Cape Verde's different islands, she tries to understand her mixed cultural and racial identity. The film suggests in a highly inter-textual and self-referential aesthetic that the encounter between Africans and Portuguese created an original identity of rare beauty.

Moia demonstrates the complexity of this identity through the participation of the character in manifold popular celebrations, such as the carnival, or religious festivities of Portuguese origin (the *comemoração da bandeira*[commemoration of the flag]), as well as through its music (the most famous Cape Verdean singer, Cesária Évora, performs a *morna*) and traditions. But Moía is also confronted with the colonial past in scenes that incorporate literary references, mainly *The Tempest* by William Shakespeare, so as to investigate the creation of Cape Verdes cultural hybridity. As a result, the Creole identity is interpreted as a violent and creative fusion of African and European cultures. In the end, the young woman is proud to be part of this culture that managed to find a way to hold the tension between so many different cultural elements with grace. Problems like poverty and mass migration as the other side of Cape Verde's hybridity are left out in this celebratory film.

Though it also suggests luso-tropical hybridity, the discourse in *O Miradouro da Lua* (1993) by Portuguese filmmaker Jorge António is, in contrast, extremely simplistic and discards problematic aspects of colonialism with great ease. The film narrates incoherently the story of a young Portuguese man, João Araújo (João Cabral), who travels to Angola in search of his father who stayed in Angola after the end of colonialism. It is his father's death, discovered by João at the end of the narrative, that serves as a metaphor for the end of colonial identity. It is aimed to set the main character (as well as his generation) free from any feelings of guilt or association with Portugal's colonial history.

The film is eager to suggest that there are no cultural differences whatsoever between the young Portuguese and the Angolan youth that integrates him with delight. Both share a preference for urban globalized culture such as commercial cinema, fashion shows and discotheques. Not only is João a welcome newcomer to the urban crowd (the women constantly dispute his attention), he even becomes a part of Angola when he discovers his half-brother. The blood bond substitutes the earlier colonial relationship and is pointed out as a clear sign for the still existing linage between Portugal and Angola. Possible tensions or unpleasant legacies are wiped out and replaced by the right to remain in the country on the basis of brotherhood.

Cape Verde

The first Cape Verdean feature film ever to be produced was a co-production directed by Portuguese television director António Faria in 1988. The film, spoken entirely in Portuguese, is a superficial adaptation of one of Cape Verdes most famous novels, *The Victims of the East Wind* (Manuel Lopes 1960). While the novel depicts the struggle for survival of a Creole family during one of the terrible but common droughts on the Island Santo Antão in 1943, the homonymous film reduces the conflict between the population and the merciless nature to an enumeration of events without paying any attention to the characters' threat of losing first their identity and then their lives.

The hopelessness to cultivate the land, the impossibility to go to school because of hunger and desperation, the adults' loss of religious faith due to the tragic events of the drought, as well as the cultural impoverishment, especially music, one of the last remedies against the devastation, are only glanced at. In addition, the subtle references to the exploitation of the population by the Portuguese colonizers in the original text vanish altogether in this fuzzy and poorly narrated adaptation.

The country's second feature was directed by Cape Verdean director Leão Lopes in 1996 and used another famous novel as its source: *Isle of Contempt* (Teixeira de Sousa 1972). The book is set in the 1960s and describes with restrained irony the decadence of one of the dominant Portuguese families on the Fire Island, the only island with renowned racial separatism. The family's fall is accompanied by the ascension of a new class of Creole upstarts – returned immigrants, landowners and professionals with higher education like the local doctor.

The ambivalent character of Eusébio (João Lourenço) and his desire to maintain some of the former glory of his family serves as the story's motor. But while the romance reveals his egoistic and opportunistic personality, the homonymous film offers only a shy critique of the racist attitudes of the ridiculous Felisberto (Camacho Costa), a cousin of Eusébio. In the tradition of luso-tropicalist discourse, it closes with the harmonious coexistence between the two social classes.

In contrast to its title, the film about this island of contempt underscores mainly the hybrid identity of the island's inhabitants. Eusébio's son, Chiquinho (Mano Preto), who is of mixed race and has a romantic affair with a girl visiting from Portugal, is a key figure in this undertaking. By advocating that the younger generation of Portuguese and Cape Verdeans does not share the previous racial prejudices, the film evades touching on the historical conflicts apparent in the novel's title and its narrative.

Napumoceno's Will (1997) is another adaptation, but the first film to include Brazil as co-producer. In contrast to *Isle of Contempt*, the novel by Germano Almeida from 1989 is told from the point of view of a Creole upstart. In the hands of Portuguese television director Francisco Manso it turns into an amusing but re-mythifying farce on the idiosyncrasies and fetishes of this new class.

In both book and film the main character Napumoceno (Nelson Xavier) constructs a prosperous life through petty crimes in commerce. He admires American consumer culture and technology, loves Portuguese cooking and is a hypocrite with a double moral. Even though the adaptation demonstrates some of the character's contradictions, it is not interested in his emotional dilemmas explored in the novel that reveals the reasons for his ridiculous conduct, as well as his regrets at the end of his life. Not only did he imitate European and American behaviour patterns in order to become rich and socially recognized; he had to negate his own identity, humble origin and emotional life.

His illegitimate daughter is only recognized after his death and becomes the heir to his fortune. This human side is neglected in a film that prefers to suggest that his attitudes are common features of Creole identity. With a commercial success in the lusophone world in mind, Manso cast television stars from Brazil's famous soap operas who speak with their natural Brazilian accents. What is more, due to the Brazilian casting, the stereotyped Creole identity becomes valid for all former colonies. Historical references to tensions between colonizers and the Cape Verdean population present in the novel are also extinguished in this Luso-African 'pudding'[116].

The desire to negate one's self in favour of a European identity is even more evident in the bilingual *Dribbling Fate* (1998) by Portuguese director Fernando Vendrell. Based on a true story and produced in realist style, the film centres on Mané (Carlos Germano), a bar tender who is unsatisfied with his life. He despises his culture for its laziness, leisure and alcohol abuse. When a young man, he was invited by one of Portugal's most important soccer clubs, Benfica, but declined in order to marry and stay in his country.

The first scenes of the film demonstrate that his life and marriage are poisoned by feelings of regret and failure. To compensate for his error he has become an obsessive soccer fan. But not even this fulfils him anymore and he decides to give his life some meaning. Parting from the principle that Portugal is the promised land of soccer, he travels to Lisbon where he wants to suggest a young player whom he coaches to Benfica. During his journey he re-encounters Américo (Horácio Santos), the friend who took his place at Benfica. He now conducts a poor life since he did not take advantage of this opportunity. This gives Mané the possibility to reassess the past and free himself from the idea that he lost the chance of a lifetime. According to the film, it was Américo's Cape Verdean bohemian lifestyle and not difficulties in adapting to Portuguese society that made him fail to conquer fame and fortune.

There are in fact many scenes in which the receptivity of the Portuguese and the possibility of assimilating with ease into its society are underlined. Mané's son Alberto (Daniel Martinho), for example, is happily married to a white woman and perfectly at home in Lisbon; a condition not quite the rule, as many films by Pedro Costa[117] suggest. But the trip makes the main character realize that he misses and values his life in Cape Verde, mainly its sociability and happiness. He returns from the trip in peace with himself and certain of his strong bond with Portugal. Since his idea that Portugal is the

---

[116] The film resembles European co-productions that are considered Euro-puddings because of their fuzzy identity politics.

[117] See for example *Bones* (1997), *O Quarto da Vanda/Vanda's Room* (2000) and *Juventude em Marcha/Colossal Youth* (2006), which will be discussed in the chapter that compares national and coproductions.

better place for soccer is not shattered, he insists that his young athlete leave the country and play at Benfica. Soccer serves as an identity bridge and makes it possible to fully ignore the fact that at the time when Mané was invited to play in Portugal, Cape Verde was still a colony and the PAIGC was trying to liberate the country from colonial rule.

Figure 10: Carlos Germano in *Dribbling Fate* (Courtesy David & Golias)

In his adaptation *Slave's Island* (2008), based on the nineteenth century novel *O Escravo* (The Slave) by Portuguese author José Evaristo de Almeida from 1856 that is considered the first novel with Cape Verde as a topic, Francisco Manso employed again a cast of well-known television actors from Portugal, Brazil and PALOP and turned the historic account of an organized upheaval against slavery into a flashy melodrama.

The original text that exalts the qualities of a young creole, Maria, the daughter of a rich farmer, is only an inspiration. The most important feature of the novel, her falling in love with a slave, is eliminated so as to give space to the political conspiracy and a different romance. The film centres on a Portuguese villain, Albano Lopes (Diogo Infante), who is the grandson of a much-feared landowner. He comes to the Island of Santo Antão with the prospect of re-establishing the rule of the *Miguelistas*, the followers of the deposed King, *dom* Miguel. But Lopes is like his grandfather a man without ethics and betrays first the Portuguese soldiers and then the slaves who he involves in the revolt.

The film was first televised as a series. This is perceptible in its melodramatic structure, stereotyped characters and lack of cinematographic interest. Even though in terms of narrative a minor film, it puts forward an uncommon discourse with regard to the hybridity of Cape Verdean identity that goes beyond the affirmation of luso-tropicalism. The main character has blood relations with almost all the other important characters because of his grandfather's sexual relationships with slave women. This includes Maria (Vanessa Giácomo), whom he falls in love with, as well as her slave (Ângelo Torres), who falls in love with her. While the blood linage is acknowledged, it is shown to be repressed: it does not have any meaning for the characters, since the interest in the abolition of slavery remains political. The factual abolition would, in effect, come more than a decade later, in 1869. Instead of resolving social tensions, luso-tropicalism – the supposed harmonious mixture of different races and cultures – has no effect, and the film ends, on the contrary, with a deep divide between the Portuguese and the Cape Verdeans.

Conscious of their oppression, *Slave's Island* tries to give space to the colonial others: the closure applauds the cry for freedom uttered by Mestre Tesoura (Milton Gonçalves) and shows the successful flight from slavery of a group of Africans. But the African characters are, however, little more than caricatures and the scenes that depict religious rituals or the fight for liberation are indebted to the most stereotyped representations of voodoo practicing 'negroes' from Hollywood B movies. As a result, the subversion of the luso-tropicalist discourse is overshadowed by this anachronistic and involuntary racist portrayal.

Mozambique

Given the predominance of Portuguese directors in the Luso-Mozambican co-productions, European perspectives dominate there as well. Vendrell's second feature, *A Drop of Light* (2002), is based on a short story with the same title, written by Leite de Vasconcelos who also signed responsible for the screenplay. The film takes a more critical stance towards the relationship between former colonizer and ex-colony than in his earlier *Dribbling Fate*.

Figure 11: Filipe Carvalho in *A Drop of Light* (Courtesy Cinemate)

Set in Mozambique in the 1950s, the sophisticatedly photographed film tells the coming of age of an adolescent boy, Rui Pedro (Filipe Carvalho). His rite of passage to an adult self is marked by a twofold disillusionment: on the one hand, with regard to his father (João Lagarto), who exploits the country as administrator of a cotton plantation, and, alternatively, by his surrogate father Jacopo (Amaral Matos), a wise African who uses the tribal right to kill his own daughter Ana (Alexandra Antunes) after she brought shame over the village.

Ana, who works for the boy's mother (Teresa Madruga), is married to another great friend of his, Guinda (Alberto Magassela), an assimilated African, but falls in love with his initially racist Portuguese cousin (Marco D'Almeida). Consequently, the film compares the exploitation practiced by

Portuguese colonialism with an archaic African custom. This cultural relativism insinuates that both cultures are in fact cruel and liberates Portugal by means of one African homicide from five hundred years of oppression, genocide, slave trade and abuse. The film concludes with the suggestion that the boy should construct his own identity by parting from a synthesis of both cultures, given that each of them has become obsolete on its own.

Nelio's Story, a film made in 1998 by Solveig Nordlung, a Swede who has been living in Portugal for more than thirty years, parts from the same principle: the necessity of a new identity based on both African and European cultures. The adaptation of Henning Mankell's novel, a Swedish author of best-selling crime stories who lives part of the year in Mozambique, depicts the country's civil war by flirting with magical realism and by ignoring the colonial past and its legacy.

Nélio (Evaristo Abreu), a little boy from a village, flees to the city after a guerrilla fighter savagely killed his entire family. During his trip to the capital African spirits guide him, but, once he arrives there, finds refuge inside the statue of a Portuguese general, as if the leftovers from colonialism could protect him. When trying to survive with a gang of street kids, Nelio discovers his supernatural healing powers, which are highly appreciated by the poor and turn him into a much-required healer.

Even though true to the plot, Nordlund makes some major changes with regard to Nélio's characterization as a boy with exceptional powers and decontextualizes the references to animistic African culture. In the novel the poor consider him a healer, but Mankell is very clear about him being only a charismatic little boy. There is only one supernatural character, while the film turns another two into representatives of animistic culture. Nelio's now exceptional powers come to a sudden end when he is mortally wounded by the guerrilla fighter who killed his family, while in the book he is shot by the security personnel of the theatre.

After this incident, the references to Africa's animist culture are in fact substituted with the idea of Christian salvation, and Nélio assumes the model identity of Christ, when the baker who found him in agony burns his dead body to bake bread. This bread is shared among the street children in a Eucharist feast, so as to make them aware that they possess the same powers as Nélio. Once more, a co-production puts forward the naïf idea that cultural fusion could lead to a new identity capable of overcoming the difficulties of post-colonial African countries in crisis. Its refuge in magical realism, which distinguishes it from the much more sober and instructive original romance, to solve the burning social problems actually proves that the European filmmaker does not believe in real solutions.

While the first two co-productions were made by Portuguese filmmakers, two recent features were directed by filmmakers with a closer relationship to African reality. Portuguese director Teresa Prata, who spent her childhood in Mozambique and Brazil and now lives in Germany, as well as Mozambican director João Ribeiro both adapted novels on the civil war by Mia Couto (*Terra Sonambula/Sleepwalking Land*, published in 1992, and *O Último do Flamingo/The Last Flight of the Flamingo*, published in 2000), renowned Mozambican writer of Portuguese descent. *I Want To Be a Star* (2010) directed by Portuguese José Carlos de Oliveira is the third film he shot in Mozambique, but his first co-production. A melodramatic thriller it engages with the exploitation of young African women who are given the prospect to become models only to be forced into prostitution. The trafficking of adolescents is shown to be a business run together by Africans and Portuguese in this fast-paced commercial film.

Sleepwalking Land (Teresa Prata 2007) is subtler in its identity discourse, but, in accordance with its literary source, suggests in tune with the earlier films that Mozambique's future identity is (or should be) Euro-African. Muidinga (Nick Lauro Teresa), the hero of the film, is of mixed race, a mulatto who has lost any memory of his parents due to a disease. He was saved from near death in a refugee camp and adopted by Tuahir (Aladino Jasse), an elderly man who worked during colonial times for the Portuguese railway company.

The recovery of the boy's identity is told, in line with Couto's book, in two intertwined stories. When Tuahir and Muidinga take shelter in a plundered bus on the deserted road, they find the notebooks of one of the dead, Kindzu (Hélio Fumo), and read his story. After leaving his war torn village, Kindzu met Farida (Ilda Gonzalez) who had been raped by a Portuguese landowner, even though his wife had raised her like her own child. Since the two fall in love, Kindzu promises Farida to find the child, which she gave away out of despair and shame. The circular closure reveals what Muidinga had already guessed from the notebooks: that he is in fact Gaspar, the mixed-race son who Kindzu envisions just before dying.

African cosmology features strongly in the book, setting up a background for the understanding of the cultural and racial implications of the civil war. Concentrating on Muidinga's adventures while he lives in or tries to depart from the bus, the film cuts most of the complex cultural references – the belief in the importance and presence of the ancestors – as well as allusions to culturally and politically relevant characters and events. The civil war turns into a circumstantial reference that remains in the background, as does the discussion and search for a future post-colonial and post-war identity. Although Mia Couto's original idea that both Africa and Portugal are responsible for the civil war because they are both characterized by violence is open to discussion, the film distorts his arguments and presents Muidinga uncritically as the representative of a promising Euro-African identity whose relation with the civil war is obscured.

Guinea-Bissau

In contrast to the Mozambican co-productions, one national filmmaker, Florentino 'Flora' Gomes, directed the films produced with Guinea-Bissau[118], which are all spoken in Creole. His first trans-national film, *The Blue Eyes of Yonta* (1992), is a low budget multi-narrative about the difficulties of constructing a post-colonial identity in Guinea-Bissau. The war hero Vicente (António Simão Mendes), his comrade (Pedro Dias) and children, Yonta (Maysa Marta) and Amílcar (Mohamed Seidi), engage with the conflict between remaining faithful to the ideals of the anti-colonial struggle and the pressures of market economy.

The film is far from being nostalgic and recognizes the necessity to reevaluate and renegotiate the countries' identity by pinpointing the conflicts that stem from the influences of western consumer culture, the desire to migrate and the traditional African values and costumes. The existing paradoxes are discussed through the relationships between the characters and craftily resumed in the last dreamlike scene.

This scene turns evident that it is neither desirable nor possible to fully assume western life-style, because the young people who are keen on its commodities and status symbols already constructed a proper identity in which

---

[118] See Murphy and Williams (2007) for biographical details of the filmmaker and a discussion of his entire filmography.

traditional African values, respect for their own society and the memory of the anti-colonial past are integrated. In contrast to the synthesis suggested in other Luso-African films, Guinean society is the basis into which elements from other cultures can be incorporated without them being able to distort its cultural self-understanding.

Flora Gomes' following film, *Tree of Blood* (1996), abandons the anti-colonial context and focuses on the negative effects of western technology on African identity. This parabolic film develops a poetic imaginary, which results from its references to visual and oral African symbolism, traditions and believes.[119] The harmonious cultural life of a village – expressed at the beginning of the film in its paintings, carpentry and stories – is being threatened. First, because of the death of the twin brother of the main character N'te (Djuco Bodjan), who disrespected his antecedents and traditional costumes; and second, because he attracted men from the capital who want to exploit the village by setting up a lucrative wood trade.

The threat on the collective identity of the villagers makes them leave their home and embark on a symbolic voyage that takes them through a desert. They only return when the son of the main character is born – as had been foreseen by N'te's mother (Bia Gomes) – and after encountering another group of people from another village, also on the quest for a new life. The return to the village leads to an open end that avoids easy answers about the future of their traditional identity and how to resolve the conflict between tradition and modernity, modern western technology and ancestral knowledge.

Gomes' last fiction feature, *My Voice* from 2002, which has also been the countries' last fiction film, takes a completely different approach. The colourful and stylized musical returns to *Yonta*'s optimism, but adds a more marketable perspective on identity, comparable to other Luso-African productions on cultural synthesis. Shot without subsidies from Guinea-Bissau[120]

---

[119] As David Murphy and Patrick William (2007: 142) note, '*Po di Sangui* is simultaneously more modern (in terms, particularly, of higher cinematic production values) and more traditional (the film is set in a deliberately allegorically stylised African village, whose name means "tomorrow is far away")'.

[120] Due to the political and military conflict on 7 of June 1998, the film was entirely shot in Cape Verde and did not receive any funding from Guinea Bissau. But since

the film encounters in western culture and technology the chance to overcome obsolete African ideas and to construct a new identity.

Using one of commercial cinema's most popular genres, the musical, *My
Voice* is visibly directed towards a globalized audience. The beautiful main
character, Vita (Fatou N'Diaye), leaves Guinea-Bissau to study in France.
Before her departure she says farewell to her family and friends. Musical
numbers – composed by famous Cameroon musician Manu Dibango – present the wide range of contemporary social problems that Guinea Bissau is
facing: the difficulty in dealing with the memory of the heroic fight for independence, corruption, the coexistence of Animism and Catholicism, and the
unemployment among young people with university degrees.

Just like in *Yonta* the society seems incapable of keeping track with the ideals of the anti-colonial fight. These are remembered with a light-hearted
running gag in which two characters try to find a place for the statue of the
political leader of the PAIGC, Amílcar Cabral, that grows each time it is
moved around.[121] In this post-colonial constellation, Vita's route of migration seems to be the only escape.

Once in Paris she falls in love with a young music producer (Jean-
Christophe Dollé) and by singing one of his compositions leaves behind an
old family superstition that says that women of her family died when they
sang. With the purpose of dealing with the offence and after having become
a European music star, she returns with her boyfriend and band to her
hometown. By staging her own funeral, she simultaneously respects and
transgresses her mother's (Bia Gomes) belief and conception of identity. In
tune with the genre, the film presents a vibrant and utopian Africa that embraces western culture and technology without hesitations. The resulting
hybrid identity has the key failure that it is restricted to stardom.

---

the film is dedicated to the city of Guinea Bissau and was shot by Flora Gomes, *My
Voice* will here be considered a Luso-Guinean co-production.
[121] In 2007 Flora Gomes returned to the issue of the colonial war and directed
together with Diana Andringa the documentary *As Duas Faces da Guerra/The Two
Faces of War*, which was entirely financed by Portugal. It shows the two sides of the
story, that is, the Guieneese and the Portuguese perspective on the war.

Conclusion

The sixteen Luso-African co-productions under analysis vary strongly in their discourses on identity. The case of Guinean Flora Gomes demonstrates most evidently that one director can accomplish the whole spectrum, ranging from a discussion of anti-colonialism as an important but also harmful element for post-colonial identity, a concern with the threat to traditional African identity, to the celebration of a new Euro-African hybrid identity. His last film might please European and African audiences alike, and the fact that it was made after an interval of six years, even though Gomes had earned worldwide praise for his earlier films, is suggestive about the possible pressures and concessions he had to make in order to find funding.

Due to a set of reasons that include its history, dimension and geographic situation, but mainly because they were made by a national filmmaker with an authorial signature, the co-productions with Guinea-Bissau differ strongly from the trans-national films with Mozambique. The three directors of the Mozambican features, Fernando Vendrell, Solveig Nordlund and Teresa Prata, are all from Europe and their inter-identity proposals that fuse traditional African with European values are closer to wishful thinking than to reality. When compared with Flora Gomes' films it becomes obvious that they are unaware of the contradictions and cultural clashes that African countries have been facing since independence.

Discourses that make the former colonizer or Western culture look better than they deserve are also a common feature in the Cape Verdean co-productions made by Portuguese directors. Given the genuine hybridism of Creole culture and language, the concept serves the need for a less stigmatized Portuguese identity, but obscures the historical conflicts present in the original literary texts, whose compelling stories are simplified by the cinematographic adaptations. The most disappointing example is António Faria's film, probably the least inspired start ever for a (trans)national film history. Fernando Vendrell's film exemplifies a market-oriented concept of hybridity and provides one of the few case studies where financial interests (mainly in the Brazilian market) are harmful to the development of a credible discourse on Creole identity. Cape Verdean Leão Lopes is the only director to keep some of the discomfort and historical incompatibilities between Creole and Europeans from the original text, but seems equally convinced that they are easily overcome by the post-colonial generation.[122] While the great majority of co-productions with Cape Verde could please a Portuguese audience with their luso-tropicalist discourse on harmonious cultural encounter, films by Portuguese directors are rather disappointing. Francisco Manso's second film subverts luso-tropicalism but its representation of African slaves is such a cliché that the critique of the political manipulation by the Portuguese villain is outweighed.

Directed by filmmakers from diverse backgrounds, the Luso-Angolan productions offer a greater variety of approaches towards the question of identity. Only the film by Portuguese director José António forwards a simplistic discourse on equality and brotherhood in its attempt to free Portugal from any kind of post-colonial responsibility. The Luso-African directors develop more cunning views. Not by accident, Ruy Duarte de Carvalho takes refuge from the war torn Angola in Cape Verde's Creole society, where he can celebrate the existence of a post-colonial Euro-African identity – which had been on the Angolan agenda only until the nineteenth century. Conversely, his film does not fail to remember that Creole hybridity is as much the product of historical clashes, as a result of the creative symbioses of African and European cultures, races and languages. Fortunato de Oliveira presents the entire landscape of Angolan identities and inter-identities, indicating that they were bound to enter into conflict after colonialism's end. The two Angolan filmmakers involved in trans-national productions are equally concerned with understanding the civil war, but instead of returning to colonial times they either look to the recent past or the present. Their discourses differ greatly: while Zezé Gamboa develops a positive perspective of reconciliation by using the remembrance of anti-colonialism as a bridge to the future, Maria João Ganga points out how deeply the war affected the (in)capacity of (re)constructing identity. The Luso-Angolan films confirm the earlier findings that the directors who live in Africa tend to develop more multilateral views than the only Portuguese filmmaker, who tries to forget the unpleasant colonial past as quickly as possible.

---

[122] Even though Cape Verde was not a theatre of war during the colonial war between 1961 and 1974, many of PAIGC leaders were Cape Verdeans. Thus, it is surprising that Isle of Contempt does not engage more openly with the conflicts that were responsible for the war and are analysed in depth in the novel that gave origin to the film.

Although seven of the twenty co-productions produced between 1980 and 2010 had input from other countries, it is rather difficult to observe influences by these producers. The only film where the impact is perceivable is *My Voice*, in which Vita migrates to the financial partner France. As mentioned above, within the context of Gomes' work, concessions to the foreign producer can be sensed. The presence of non-European countries is, on the other hand, too insignificant to offer conclusions. It is, nevertheless, noticeable that while the two co-producers from North-African countries participated in films with complex identity discourses, the participation of Brazil occurred in two productions with strong commercial interests and simplifying discourses.

Sophisticated productions targeting box office success or based on commercial television series are, however, rather the exception than the rule. The majority of the films analysed are low budget films with slow and contemplative narratives. Instead of having stars in their cast, non-professional actors perform. Production quality varies greatly, as do genres and styles that range from realist docudrama to stylized musical. Indeed, few films meet the average technical standards of European cinema. *A Drop of Light, My Voice, Napumoceno' Will* and *Slave's Island* stand out in terms of their elaborate photography and art direction, when compared with the simplicity of *Moia, The Hero, Sleepwalking Land* and *Hallow City*. This should not be mistaken for a judgment of the films' quality. On the contrary, the low-budget films are often more inspired and convincing than the more stylish productions.

In terms of language as an important distribution factor in the respective countries or within the lusophone market, seven films represent the complex linguistic set of the PALOP and are not spoken entirely in Portuguese: one Angolan production (*Moia*) and two Cape Verdean films (*Isle of Contempt* and *Dribbling Fate*) are partially spoken in Creole from the islands, as is one Luso-Guinean production (*My Voice*), whereas the other two (*The Blue Eyes of Yonta* and *Tree of Blood*) are entirely spoken in Creole from Guinea-Bissau. *Sleepwalking Land* uses one of Mozambique's native languages and Portuguese, spoken by the bilingual main characters.

The Creole language was recognized as a written language in 1998. More disseminated than Portuguese, initiatives to make it the country's official language persist. It is noteworthy that the Portuguese language is in actual fact not the first language for many people in the PALOP. [123] In Angola it is spoken by 60 per cent of the population, next to 11 linguistic groups and 90 dialects, and an estimated 70 per cent speak a native language as first or second language. In Guinea-Bissau approximately 15 per cent of the population speak Portuguese, while 44 per cent use Creole; in Mozambique it is first language of 6.5 per cent of the population and second language of 39.6 per cent, next to a wide range of Bantu languages. These numbers are obviously not contemplated in the Luso-African productions do not contemplate the restricted demand of Portuguese, with the exception of the Luso-Guinean productions that are in Creole. In other words, the trans-national films from Angola, Cape Verde and Mozambique were mainly produced for an audience that understands Portuguese.

The most striking characteristic of the co-productions between Portugal and its former African colonies is, nonetheless, the impact of the national or trans-national background of their directors, being trans-national filmmakers more inclined to develop ambivalent views. In contrast to anglophone or francophone productions, the influence through the mode of production seems to be less direct and is rather noticeable in the films directed by Portuguese filmmakers in the 1980s and 1990s.

The importance of hybrid identities is unquestionable, as much for unilateral as for multilateral points of view. Strikingly, inter-identities are seen as either being characteristic of independent cultures such as the Cape Verdean, or offer a desirable new Euro-African identity that might transcend problematic aspects of both cultures. The only case that deserts this view (*Slave's Island*) is unconvincing due to its typecast portrayal of the African characters. The desire to see ones identity valued and freed of historical guilt can be encountered in many films by Portuguese directors, especially in the productions by António and Vendrell. The problem with these films is the absence of contextualization, not only of the colonial history, but especially of its legacy. African and Luso-African filmmakers are more thoughtful in terms of contextualization and often pose questions about how to balance aspects of traditional African identity, the values that led to the anti-colonial

---

[123] There is much controversy on the correct numbers. These and the following can be found on a website hosted by the Universidade Federal do Rio Grande do Norte (http://www.linguaportuguesa.ufrn.br/pt_index.php).

armed fight and the attributes and values of (or their absence in) European identity. Actually, only *My Voice*, *Nélio's Story* and *The Hero* are optimistic and affirmative regarding the possibility of resolving the conflicts that result from the colonial legacy and African post-colonial and post-war reality.

In conclusion, the dependence on financial, material and human resources so evident in the number of co-productions between the PALOP and the former colonizer Portugal does not automatically have an effect on their identity discourses. However, few of the Luso-African feature productions explore transnationality's ambivalence through multilateral perspectives. Unilateral identity discourses are, in fact, almost the rule among European directors. Only a rather small number of films accomplishes fully the potential of the production mode, in the sense that they offer a transnational stage for challenging obsolete discourses on identity, be they European or African. The films *Canhoca Train*, *The Blue Eyes of Yonta*, *Tree of Blood* and, with some restraints *Moía, Hollow City*, *The Hero*, *A Drop of Light* and *Nelio's Story* develop, in actual fact, compelling discourses on social, cultural and historical issues that engage with post-colonial tensions and offer a dialogue between the former colonizer and the ex-colonies.

Lusophone monologues or transnational dialogues: the Luso-Brazilian literary adaptations (1995 – 2008)[124]

Introduction

Since Brazil declared its independence from Portugal in 1822, there have been a number of political initiatives to straighten the bonds between the former colony and its ancient colonizer. From 1825 onwards, law projects, treaties and agreements were developed to promote or extend the idea of brotherhood between the two nations. Some projects even tried to re-establish the union from colonial times: in 1917 there was a plan for a Luso-Brazilian Confederation and in 1943 a project for double citizenship.

Regardless of these proposals and the wishful thinking of neo-colonial unification, Brazil's general lack of sympathy towards the former colonizer is, as Sandra Brancato (2003: 443–4) notes, as significant as the shared colonial history: 'A história comum, é preciso que se tenha presente, estava marcada não apenas pela identidade de língua e por algumas marcas culturais, como também por uma hostilidade muito latent'.[125]

Profound differences between Portuguese and Brazilian viewpoints are also diagnosed by Eduardo Lourenço (1999b: 135): Portugal's discourses on Brazil tend to be ecstatic, while Brazil's discourses are more often than not informed by resentment. The Portuguese euphoria can be linked to Vieira's idea of the Fifth Empire in which Brazil features as Portugal's future (Lourenço 1999a: 22). Brazilian resentment towards Portugal is, in contrast, the result of a nationalistic stance after independence in order to affirm a proper identity: 'being "Brazilian" or "Portuguese" was a discursive construction that justified each ones positioning within the new country's emerging socio-political system' (Rowland 2002: 378).

---

[124] This is a revised and updated version of a Portuguese text published with the title 'Monólogos lusófonos ou diálogos trans-nacionais - O caso das adaptações luso-brasileiras' as a conference minute in *Anais do XI Congresso Internacional da Abralic 2008: São Paulo, SP* – Tessituras, Interações, Convergências, Ed. Sandra Nitrini et al. e-book.

[125] ('One has to keep in mind that the common history has not only been marked by the identity of its language and some cultural landmarks, but also by a very latent hostility.')

The first Brazilian identity discourses used various strategies, ranging from the suggestion of a native identity, the recognition of the continuity of Portuguese laws and institutions, an either critical or affirmative perspective on the miscegenation between natives, Africans and Europeans, to the idea that Brazil had little in common with Portugal since it had developed its very own kind of colonial society. In general terms, the discourses have shaped an imaginary in which Brazilians consider themselves as their own creation, not only politically independent from Portugal but also historically and culturally. Lourenço (1999b 140) clarifies, however, that the Brazilian discourses based on the assumption of self-invention, self-sufficiency and cultural independence actually repress the country's historical involvement with its colonizer: 'ocultando, menosprezando ou, com mais verdade hoje, ignorando o seu nódulo irredutível e indissolúvel português'[126].

The opposite idea – present in Gilberto Freyre's already much discussed concept of luso-tropicalism – that argues that Brazilians and Portuguese are tightly interrelated, survived mainly in Portugal. In contemporary times it has gained an excessive, obsessive and sometimes fantastic dimension. Lourenço (1999b: 137) deems the insistence on strong fraternal bonds 'uma pura alucinação nossa'[127], and the celebration of a nonexistent Luso-Brazilian community nothing more than 'designações com alguma verdade afectiva, mas, no fundo, inadequadas'[128].

The chance to develop a factual and systematic cultural relationship appeared in 1994 when Brazil and Portugal signed the *Protocolo Luso-Brasileiro de Co-produção Cinematografica* (Luso-Brazilian Agreement on Cinematographic Co-productions), establishing an instrument for their 'vontade de concretizar as relações cinematográficas'[129], which was reformulated in 1996 and in 2007 (Ancine 1996, ICAM 2007). The protocol is based on an earlier agreement on co-productions, the *Acordo de Co-Produção Cinematográfica Luso-Brasileira*, signed in 1981, and aims for the production of feature films in different genres, including fiction, animation and documen-

---

[126] ('suppressing, scorning or, especially today, ignoring the irreducible and inextricable ties with Portugal')
[127] ('our very own hallucination')
[128] ('partly true in terms of affection but, actually, inadequate')
[129] ('the desire to make the cinematographic relationships become reality')

tary films. As I mentioned in the previous chapter on the Luso-African co-productions, it was, in fact, the first agreement to be signed with a former colony.

Nowadays the agreement foresees financial support for four films per year, two of which receive major and two minor funding from each country.[130] The most important criteria for the selection process consists again in the relevance of the project from the point of view of the cultural relationships between the two producing countries (see Ancine 1996). It is important to bear in mind that this agreement, which has produced twenty six trans-national films between 1995 and 2008, was brought back to life out of politi-cal reasons: the diplomatic crisis which followed Portugal's signing of the Schengen Treaty in 1993. I will discuss this crisis in more detail in the fol-lowing chapter that offers a detailed analysis of one of the first co-productions, *Foreign Land* by Walter Salles and Daniel Thomas.

Comparable to the Luso-African co-productions, the Luso-Brazilian feature films offer a further case study for transnationality's ambivalence. The imag-inary web of identity discourses outlined at the beginning of this and ex-plored in earlier chapters is similar: the idea of lusophony as a cultural histo-ry, which is readily used to pacify the complex and ambiguous colonial leg-acy in the political arena, on the one hand, and the Brazilian *and* Portuguese endeavour to characterize themselves as being less violent than the rest of the world by taking turns in developing luso-tropicalism, on the other.

There is, however, a set of reasons why the co-productions between Portugal and Brazil differ from those with the PALOP. An important factor is the long tradition of Brazilian identity discourses based on the notion of auton-omy, resulting not only from Brazil's early independence but also from its economic potential and recent consolidation. In addition, Brazil can look back on an extensive and, at times, intense film history.[131] That is to say that there is no comparable financial or technological dependency for filmmak-ing. Nonetheless, the endurance of the discourses discussed, besides the political reason for the re-establishment of cinematographic ties that oc-

---

[130] This number is rarely achieved. Some of the films took much longer to be produced than planned or did not pass the preproduction stage.
[131] For an exhaustive study of Brazilian cinema in English see Shaw and Dennison (2007) .

curred in a moment in which Brazil was facing a crisis of film production, are aspects that could turn the co-productions easily into yet another opportunity for Brazilian resentment or undue Portuguese affection.

Taking into consideration transnationality's ambivalence might, then again, be a way to accomplish the reassessment of the discourses wished for by Lourenço (1999b). As in my analysis of Luso-African co-productions, this will be the guiding principle in my assessment of an important part of the new chapter of trans-national film history that is being written jointly by Brazil and Portugal. There are two reasons why I will focus on literary adaptations. First, more than half of the twenty-six Luso-Brazilian co-productions[132] – fifteen films – are based on literature. The great majority – eleven films – draws on novels or writings whose authors are either Brazilian or Portuguese and will be subject to my analysis.[133] Second, the films make a wide range of statements on the historical and, in particular, cultural and linguistic Luso-Brazilian bonds.

As mentioned earlier in this book, literature has always been appealing to cinema. The most important aspects are its recognized cultural value, the existence of a story that has proved attractive and might guarantee success, the chance to rewrite or comment on an existing book of varying aesthetic significance, as discussed in the first chapter on Fernando Lopes' adaptations of canonical texts. Given the fact that the adapted books might put forward celebratory discourses on the Luso-Brazilian relationship or even

---

[132] Ten co-productions have been motivated by financial interests and do not present any kind of discussion of these bonds.

[133] Four films will be left out, since two films are based on African authors (*Nepumoceno's Will*, 1997 and *Slave's Island*, 2008) and have already been subject to analysis in the chapter on Luso-African co-productions. *O Veneno da Madrugada/In Evil Hour* (2004), adapted by Ruy Guerra from the novel *La Mala Hora* by Gabriel Garcia Marquez and *O Misterio da Estrada de Sintra/The Mystery of Sintra* (2008) by Jorge Paixão Costa, on the other hand, do not engage with Brazil and its relationship with Portugal. Guerra's film transcends, like *Estorvo/Turbulence*, national identity in favour of a discussion of Latin-America's political, religious and sexual ideologies, whereas Costa's film, based on a *folhetim*, first published by Eça de Queirós and Ramalho Ortigão in the journal *Diário de Notícias* in the form of anonymous letters, picks on Portugal's relationship with Great Britain and Spain.

lusophone utopias, or else, engage in either challenging or nationalistic readings, Luso-Brazilian literary adaptations present a particularly rich field for analysis.

I will now draw a map of the films co-financed by Brazil and Portugal that are either based on literary works or on both the biographies and writings of famous authors. My question is whether they are affirmative monologues on cultural myths that use the trans-national mode of production as an alibi to ignore conflicts and differences, or if they establish transnational dialogues that use their production mode to overcome obsolete and nationalistic discourses.

The films

Nine of the eleven literary adaptations based on lusophone literature were directed by Brazilian filmmakers, two of them being from trans-national backgrounds (Ruy Guerra is a Mozambique-born Portuguese and Alain Fresnot gave up his French nationality only recently).[134] Most are based on novels (seven), one draws on travel literature, and three films engage with both the works and biographies of canonical authors who not only travelled between Portugal and Brazil, but belong to both in terms of cultural identity.

The authors are Father António Vieira – orator, diplomat and missionary in Brazil during the seventeenth century – in the already discussed *Word and Utopia* (2000) by Manoel de Oliveira; António José da Silva – a Brazilian born Jew who became Portugal's most celebrated playwright of the eighteenth century – in *O Judeu/The Jew* (1995) by Brazilian filmmaker Jom Tob Azulay, and Manuel Maria Barbosa du Bocage – the most important Portuguese poet and *enfant terrible* of the same century – in *Bocage – O Triunfo do Amor/Bocage –Triumph of Love* (1997) by Brazilian filmmaker Djalma Limongi Batista. Having been persecuted by the Portuguese Inquisition, it is certainly no coincidence that they were chosen as main characters shortly after the end of the dictatorships in both countries.

---

[134] Since the nine productions are part of fourteen trans-national films directed by Brazilian filmmakers between 1995 and 2008, a strong interest in literature can be sensed, especially when compared with the Portuguese filmmakers who used literature only twice as their source in a total of twelve co-productions.

When it comes to the literary adaptations based exclusively on books, most Brazilian filmmakers choose to adapt contemporary national novels that discuss the relationship between Portugal and Brazil. Most of these novels are, however, historical. The only director to opt for a Portuguese author is Helvécio Ratton, who adapted in *Amor e Cia./Love and Co.* (1998) a lesser known and posthumously published novel, *Alves & Cia*, by one of Portugal's most celebrated authors, Eça de Queirós. The story is transferred from Lisbon to the Brazilian state Minas Gerais, but no changes with regard to the period in which the story is set were made. The Portuguese directors rely exclusively on national literature with trans-national topics. Manoel de Oliveira on Father António Vieira, and Leonel Vieira on a novel from the twentieth century by Ferreira de Castro for his homonymous film *A Selva/The Forest* (2002).

As a result, most of the Luso-Brazilian adaptations are costume films, mainly set in the colonial period. Together with the persecution by the Inquisition in the seventeenth and eighteenth century, the formation of Brazil in the sixteenth century is a recurring theme. It is present in *Hans Staden* (1999) by Luiz Alberto Pereira, who used the famous report by the homonymous German author on his two journeys to Brazil as reference, as well as in *Desmundo* (2002) by Alain Fresnot, based on the homonymous novel by Ana Miranda. National formation is also the subject matter in *Diário de um Novo Mundo/New World Diary* (2006) by Paulo Nascimento, adapted from the novel *Um Quarto de Légua em Quadro* by Luiz Antônio de Assis Brasil on the misadventures of the Azorean colonizers in the south of eighteenth century Brazil.

The nineteenth century – when Brazil gained its independence – is unrepresented and serves mainly as scenic backdrop for the comedy *Love and Co.* It is explored in greater detail for means of parody in another comedy, *O Xangô de Baker Street/The Xango of Baker Street* (2001), written by Jô Soares and directed by Miguel Faria Jr., where the emperor *dom* Pedro II and the famous English detective Sherlock Holmes have an imaginary encounter.

Two films are set in the twentieth century: *The Forest*, which denounces the exploitation of workers in a rubber tree plantation in the Amazon around 1914, and *Sonhos e Desejos/Carnal Utopia* (2006), an adaptation of the novel *Balé de Utopia* by Álvaro Caldas, directed by Marcelo Santiago, which depicts the resistance against Brazil's dictatorship in the 1970s. *Estorvo/Turbulence* (2000) by Ruy Guerra, based on the homonymous book by

Chico Buarque, is the only film set in contemporary times.

Despite the fact that the film's subject matters are often historical, none of the films fits the genres of history film or epic, whose plots focus traditionally on a past event with an unmistakably ideological function regarding national identity. Most films mix genres but use melodrama as narrative motors. The films based on the biographies of canonical lusophone authors are also neither traditional history nor biographical films in which extraordinary characters fight for a vital cause. On the contrary, while most of the films follow the model of classic narrative film, this group presents two authorial approaches: *Bocage* and *Word and Utopia*, being *Turbulence* the third film with a distinguished handwriting in the group of twelve literary adaptations.

Films designed to reach larger audiences become almost the rule after the year 2000, when big budget productions are given preference in the selection process. *The Forest*, Portugal's most expensive film ever, and *Xango*, which had a record budget for its set design and costumes, are obviously targeting box office results. The films from the middle of the 1990s had, on the contrary, difficulties to gain financial support in their native countries and both *The Jew* and *Bocage* were actually saved by the Luso-Brazilian protocol in a moment in which Brazil cut its film subsidies. The pioneering films – but also the last adaptation – are, indeed, as I will now demonstrate, the most conscious of transnationality's ambivalence.

The Jew

The Jew (1995)[135] by Tom Job Azulay tells the story of Antônio José da Silva (Filipe Pinheiro), who was born in Brazil, but became Portugal's most famous playwright of the eighteenth century. He left Brazil accompanying his mother, accused of Judaism by the Portuguese Inquisition. In the six texts that are performed with marionettes in different moments of the film, select-

---

[135] The film looks back on a long production history (see Ewald Filho 1999: 6–7). Originally a project by Antônio Cavalcanti (who travelled to Lisbon for research in 1978), Jom Tob Azulay got interested in making the film in the 1980s. Shooting started in 1987 but was interrupted until 1994. It was designed to be a Luso-Brazilian co-production from the start, based on the first treaty from 1981, but only gained funding from the IPACA during the second part of the production process (the first part in the 1980s received financial support from the Ministry of Culture through the responsible institution Embrafilme).

ed from the eight existing operas, fun is poked at the justice system, as well as at the slave trade. The scenes of the performances are used to advocate that the critical content of his writings were, in fact, the reason for da Silva's accusation by the Inquisition and not his supposed practice of Judaism.

The film traces the chronology of the playwright's life from his childhood in Brazil to his death on the bonfire in Lisbon and develops the political intrigue that leads to his condemnation in a subplot. It is featured by the priest *dom* Marcos (José Neto) who leads the accusation against the 'Jew' for the Inquisition. By means of this character, the rhetoric of the Church and its abuse and manipulation of the Catholic faith is exposed. Initially a devoted and ethical man, *dom* Marcos discovers the plot of the Inquisition, but makes a deal in order to climb up the hierarchical ladder of the Church. The playwright represents a challenge to this kind of power play: he ridicules the governors in his operas and expresses the cleverness of the lower classes.

The conflict of the film has a national connotation, although it takes place before Brazil's independence. It divides the representatives of the two future countries into repressive forces – represented by the Catholic Church and the Portuguese Inquisition – and innovative forces – represented by the two men born in colonial Brazil: the artist Antônio José da Silva and the secretary of *dom* João V (Mário Viegas), the diplomat Alexandre Gusmão (Edwin Luisi), who tries to save the artist from the bonfire, but fails due to the submissiveness of the King.

Although the idea that Brazil is a more advanced place from where liberal ideas come to pass is put forward in the film, it is rather used as an analogy for repressive and progressive ways of thinking than as national allegory. The production period, which started in 1987 – two years after the end of the Brazilian dictatorship – and was finally completed in 1995, serves as an explanation for the film's portrayal of the colony as the birth place of creative and progressive men who try to eradicate the ancient power structures associated with the political and cultural backwardness of the matrix Portugal. This becomes most evident in the role of the Inquisitor, *dom* Nuno da Cunha (José Lewgoy), who is played, not by accident, by a Brazilian actor who remains his accent. That Portugal's authoritarian power structure is part of Brazil's heritage and needs to be dealt with is the key point made by the film.

Bocage – The Triumph of Love

In both *The Jew* and *Bocage – The Triumph of Love* the main characters are linguistically linked to Brazil, since both were cast with Brazilian actors (Felipe Pinheiro e Víctor Wagner) who speak with their natural accents. *Bocage*[136] has, however, a less biased approach in terms of the characterization of the two countries. Loosely based on life and poetry of one of the most famous and controversial Portuguese poets of the eighteenth century, Manuel Maria Barbosa du Bocage, the film does not have a plot which proceeds according to cause and effect but, according to its subject, a conceptual structure divided into a prologue, three *cantos* and an epilogue. To build its story it uses themes and characters from Bocage's erotic, satirical and love poems, as well as allusions to real events (his journeys as second-lieutenant to Brazil, Mozambique and Goa from where he deserted and travelled to India, China and Macau, his bohemian life in Lisbon and his early death at the age of forty), in addition to biographical elements from people of his time (representatives of the Portuguese monarchy that condemned him for *lèse-majesté*, the lower clergy that gave him shelter or his different lovers).

While not following a coherent or chronological scheme, *Bocage the Triumph of Love* is a tale about the poet's coming of age: from a scandalous, emotionally reckless yet recognized poet, Bocage learns through the experiences in his public and private life that it is not by celebrating and practicing sexual liberation that one is set free and becomes an author of uncontested standing; rather, it is necessary to praise love as an analogy of political freedom.

Bocage is one of the first films of the so-called *Retomada*, the revival of Brazilian film production, which resulted from the new Audio-visual Law launched in 1995. Among the transnational literary adaptations it is out-

---

[136] Due to the Brazilian film production crisis in 1990, which will be described in detail in the following chapter on *Foreign Land*, the film faced like *The Jew* a difficult production process. Djalma Limogni Batista explains that the film was saved by the television channel HBO Brazil, as well as by the Portuguese producer António da Cunha Telles who helped to turn the film into a co-production with the subsidy of the ICAM (see Nadale 2005: 188–9).

standing, since it actually establishes a dialogue with the ancient colonizer by offering a new perspective on myths of transnational cultural identity. The film is transgressive in all its aspects: linguistically, visually and in relation to the (sexual) politics of its famous protagonist.

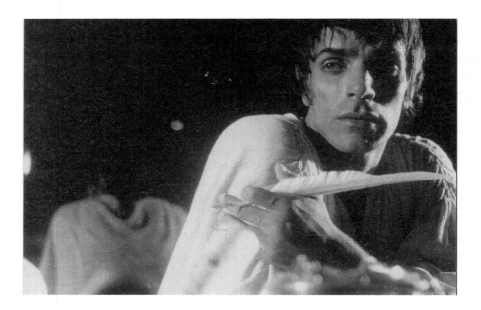

Figure 12: Víctor Wagner in *Bocage – The Triumph of Love* (Courtesy Djalma Limogni Baptista)

Linguistically, *Bocage* discloses the richness and variations of the Portuguese languages, instead of implying the neo-colonialist notion that a shared language corresponds to a shared culture. The dialogue consists mainly of Bocage's poems, but Asian, African, Arabian, Brazilian and Portuguese characters speak them with multiple accents and inflections. The existing bonds between these people from the different places explored and colonized by Portugal are expressed visually in all their complexity. Indeed, the editing establishes the most unimaginable spatial connections, cutting, for example, in the same sequence from a hut in the Amazon to a church in Portugal – the famous *Igreja Bom Jesus do Monte* outside Braga – and then to the statues of the 12 Prophets by Aleijadinho – the famous Brazilian Baroque sculptures that stand in front of the Sanctuary of *Bom Jesus de Matosinhos* in Minas Gerais. Shot in cinemascope, the film consequently not only suspends linear time but also the coherence of space, establishing an imaginary geography that is both testimony to (post-)colonial distance and proximity.

Accordingly, the lusophone world appears to be intertwined not by its language, but by the crossing of borders. This is initially related to the individuals' passions and sexual relationships (Bocage's adventures with Mantegui, a concubine from the Persian Gulf in the first *canto*; the *ménage à trois* between Bocage, Olinda and Alzira in the second *canto*; and the liaison between Bocage and Jocindo in the third *canto*), but becomes allegorical and political in the end. The third *canto* brings the political bonds to the foreground: on the one hand, regarding the colonial and imperial past and, on the other, concerning the long awaited end of the authoritarian regimes that characterized the twentieth century in both Portugal and Brazil. This is when the protagonist begins to comprehend a number of restraints: first of his erotic poetry and his desire to become an immortal poet, and then of his country's imperial splendour. Only when he comes to recognize art as being political, in the sense that love is a metaphor of both individual and collective freedom (in a sequence that alludes to the Carnation Revolution of 1974 and the recent end of Brazil's dictatorship), does he qualify for immortality and is crowned in the epilogue with an olive branch.

Aesthetically stunning and politically daring, Djalma Limongi Batista's film does not look directly at power structures, as *The Jew*, but is political in the sense that it proves lusophony wrong by declaring that Portuguese is in fact a plurality of languages that are related but autonomous from its matrix. The shared cultural patrimony by Portuguese speaking authors – in this case Bocage's – can be expressed and interpreted in different ways. One looks at a transnational universe in all its ambivalence, bound together by the prospect that the love celebrated in Bocage's poetry can lead to liberation.

Word and Utopia

By comparing *Word and Utopia* with *Bocage*, it becomes evident how conventional Manoel de Oliveira's celebration of Vieira and his contradictory utopia of the Fifth Empire remains[137]. Since the film has been analyzed in detail in the third chapter of the first part, I will only make some brief comments on its importance within the context of Luso-Brazilian literary adaptations.

The historical character António Vieira transcends like Bocage Portuguese culture – not only because of his biography (let me remember: he moved to Brazi as a six-year-old boy and worked there as a missionary) – but mainly due to the cultural importance given to his sermons and other writings in which he criticized the Portuguese colonialism and developed his prophecy. But in contrast to Batista's film, which is aware of problematic and contradictory aspects in Bocage's life and poems, Oliveira ignores any inconsistencies with regard to his famous subject and his writings.

I argue in the chapter on European expansion that Oliveira's film sees in Vieira's persona and discourse an outstanding example of courage and humanistic engagement with the colonial other, without considering the paradoxical elements of his writings and the cultural repression inherent in his Christian mission. Oliveira actually reveals himself as a prominent representative of the euphoric Portuguese brotherhood discourse whose excessive, obsessive and fantastic dimension Eduardo Lourenço so rightly criticizes.

It can be added that Oliveira's use of three different actors of both Portuguese (Ricardo Trepa, Luís Miguel Cintra) and Brazilian (Lima Duarte) nationality and inflection for the role of the famous priest favours this discourse even more and indicates yet another difference in relation to *Bocage*'s take on language as a signifier of cultural difference. By employing the different accents as though they were interchangeable, the diversity between the two countries is further eradicated in favour of a naive commemoration of the 'emperor of the Portuguese language' and one of the founding fathers of lusophony.

---

[137] Part of the commemorations of the 'Discovery' of Brazil, the film received financial support from the ICAM and the Cultural Ministry of Brazil, and from the *Instituto Camões* and the *Comissão Nacional para as Comemorações dos Descobrimentos*/National Commission for the Commemorations of the Discoveries. Additional financial support came from Ibermedia and Euroimage.

Hans Staden

The famous travelogue *True Story and Description of a Country of Wild, Naked, Grim, Man-eating People in the New World, America*, from 1557, was written by the German mercenary pike man Hans Staden. The book was highly popular in its time, but not, as in the case of the three earlier authors, because of its outstanding aesthetics or defying politics. While it is indebted to the comic tradition of the Spanish picaresque novel, it is also characterized by an excessive Protestant religiosity. Within this imaginary, the Tupinambá Indians, who held Staden their prisoner for nine months so that they could eat him as a ritual feast, are portrayed as cruel and wild natives and Staden himself as a favourite of God who, thanks to the direct contact that he establishes in his prayers, keeps on saving him miraculously.

The film[138] concentrates on Staden's (Carlos Evelyn) time with the Tupinambás and takes the Quixotesque adventure with great realism and ethnographic precision pretty seriously.[139] Nonetheless, some changes, related to the relationship between Staden and the Indians, as well as between Staden and the Europeans, shift the book's perspective. The portrayal of the cultures becomes relativist, and the Europeans are as appalling as the savage natives. The Portuguese are responsible for Staden's captivity because they killed his Indian servant violently and senselessly; and the French could not care less about their fellow European. One Frenchman even encourages the Indians to eat Staden and another tradesman (Sérgio Mamberti) only cares about his economic interests.

Staden himself is opportunistic and his religiosity is evidently a survival strategy[140], despite some moments in which he demonstrates compassion and

---

[138] Produced by Jorge Neves Produção Audiovisual and Lapfilme with funding from ICAM and SDAV.

[139] Some researchers discuss the contradictions of the ethnographic fidelity and foreground the problems of the film's European perspective (see Stam 2003, Nagib 2003) by comparing it to *How Tasty Was My Frenchman* by Nelson Pereira dos Santos (1971) that is partially inspired in Staden's book.

[140] Eduardo Morettin (2000: 53) also suggests that Hans Staden 'recorre a vários expedientes, dentre os quais Deus, para sobreviver em um determinado grupo' ('takes advantage of divers resources, among them God, to survive in a specific group').

feelings for the Indians or interest in their culture. The Indians, on the other hand, remain strange and sometimes ridiculous beings, even though a *pajé* (shaman: Stênio Garcia) is given space to express his discontent with the European invasion. In contrast to the book, no miracles save Staden. The film shows a disenchanted world where cultures and individuals simply try to survive and do so as egoistically as they can. Although high angle, aerial or crane shots are used with frequency so as to indicate a superior point of view, it observes unemotionally and without pity the cultures that either collide or try to make the best out of the fact that they are forced to live together. Although the film is contradictory in its illogical fidelity to the original, especially in terms of ethnographic details and the negative characterization of the Indians, the Brazilian filmmaker Luís Alberto Pereira's merit is to insist that the encounter between Brazilian Indians and Europeans was not only ambivalent, but that cultures are ambivalent in themselves.

Figure 13: Carlos Evelyn in *Hans Staden* (Courtesy Jorge Neves Produções)

Desmundo

Desmundo (2003) by Alain Fresnot, a Frenchman who was raised in Brazil and later acquired Brazilian citizenship, is based on the homonymous novel by Ana Miranda. The book is set in the middle of the sixteenth century. In order to recreate the period, the film is spoken in archaic vernacular with subtitles in modern Portuguese. While this establishes a greater fidelity to the linguistics of the time, it also distances the contemporary spectator from the characters and their identity issues. By stressing the common origin of Brazilians and Portuguese, the film suggests that this has to be seen as distant in time.

Oribela, the main character of the novel, is, like Staden, excessively religious. From her delirious Catholic imagination, Indians and Muslims emerge as monsters. She is part of a group of Portuguese orphans, sent to Brazil to be wed to the settlers and thus help avoid miscegenation with the native women. Historically speaking, the story is an exception to the rule. Brazilian historians describe miscegenation as widespread in the first centuries of colonization, whereas references to envoys of European women can only be found in footnotes (see Prado Jr. 2008: 102).

In contrast to Staden's ancient book, the contemporary novel deems it possible to adapt to the New World and overcome cultural boundaries. After the initial cultural shock Oribela engages in a multifaceted adaptation process, contrives friendship with an Indian woman and falls passionately in love with a Muslim. The novel expresses Oribela's viewpoint with a dense language that testifies her subjectivity, contradictions and introspection. The film approaches this subjectivity only vaguely by employing point of view shots by Oribela (Simone Spoladore) and close up shots of looks and gazes that the characters interchange.

Oribela's delirious religiosity and the cultural adaptation process are left out in the film.[141] It only takes advantage of the novel's main plot and the characters, but introduces substantial changes even there. The young woman

---

[141] It took Alain Fresnot four years to raise the money for *Desmundo* (Fresnot 2006: 339). The film gained additional financial support from multinational companies based on tax reductions (according to the *Lei de Incentivo à Cultura* and the *Lei do Audiovisual*/Cultural Incentive Bill and the Audiovisual Bill), and received subsidies from the Brazilian SDAV and the Portuguese ICAM.

remains rebellious and opposes herself to being married with the first groom, only to accept the hand of a farmer, Francisco (Osmar Prado), who falls in love with her because of her disobedient nature. He himself opposes any kind of authority, be it the Monarchy or the Church. But while Oribela flees her husband in the book because she desires to return to Portugal, encounters the Muslim and falls in love with him, the film makes her fall in love with another man before her matrimony, whose religious identity is changed into that of a *cristão novo* (Ximeno Dia: Caco Ciocler), a converted Jew who still practices his faith.

To accomplish the dramatic turning points in the film, Oribela flees twice. First, she tries to embark to Portugal after Francisco violated her when he discovers her desire for Ximeno. Her second escape takes place after she realizes that Francisco is a man without morals and that his sister is the result of an incestuous relationship with his mother. This time she hides at Ximeno's, who had been the object of her desire ever since she saw him for the first time as an interpreter between colonizers and natives. Although his capability of bridging cultures and relative autonomy from the Monarchy makes him attractive to her, he is the promise of a cultural alternative impossible to be kept.

Compared to the novel, colonization is presented from a much more negative point of view in the film and contrasts strongly with the utopian perspective on cultural and religious assimilation in the novel, which ends, nevertheless, tragically like the film. Indeed, the conclusion of the film highlights the oppression of any other culture by the newly created Brazilian identity represented by Oribela's husband. After killing Xiamen when he tries to take her to a ship that sails to Portugal, Francisco accepts the child Oribela is bearing. Looking for the freedom to construct his new identity – not only based on the disrespect for other cultures but for any kind of authority other than his own – he then takes his family and Indian slaves deeper into the country, where he will be a cornerstone of the patriarchal and oligarchic society in which Brazil is still rooted.

Edmunds's discourse on identity formation during the first years of Portuguese colonization tells the story of Brazil's self-invention and self-sufficiency. It is criticized as being one of repression and submission, since characters that represent moral and humanistic values have their subjectivity either negated or eliminated. Accordingly, the film presents, as Ismail Xavier (2006: 268) resumes, 'a arqueologia da família patriarcal brasileira e revolve seu subsolo de violência'.[142] In contrast to earlier cinematographic representations in Brazilian cinema, for example the famous film *Como era Gostoso o meu Francês/How Tasty Was My Frenchman* (1972) by Nelson Pereira dos Santos, the film insists that Brazil's society has European and Jewish roots, a fact rarely acknowledged in Brazilian culture, which has given greater importance to the miscegenation with natives and Africans.

New World Diary

New World Diary (2005)[143], directed by Brazilian filmmaker Paulo Nascimento, picks another rather exceptional chapter from the history of migration to Brazil: the intensification of the colonization of the country's south. In contrast to the colonization process in the rest of Brazil, families that came mostly from the Portuguese Azores practiced agriculture and cattle holding and neither used slave labor nor mixed with other ethnic groups. As a result, the south is, until today, less hybrid and more European.

The film has been described as 'um filme de uma confrangedora mediocridade'[144] (António 2008). In truth, the novel on which it is based is already rather weak. It tells the colonization process from the point of view of an Azorean doctor, Gaspar de Froes, presenting mostly stereotyped characters, a reductionist view of the Indians and a pathetic love story between the doctor and Maria, the wife of a Portuguese lieutenant. However, its complex accounts of the broken promises to the Azorean people by the Portuguese crown, of the many obstacles, dramas and transfers they faced in order to obtain their promised land, of the conflicts between Portugal and Spain because of the demarcation of the southern boarders, as well as of the first signs of Brazil's aggressive oligarchy are of interest.

---

[142] ('the archaeology of the Brazilian patriarchal family and brings its underlying violence to the foreground')

[143] The film is a co-production between Brazil, Portugal and Argentina. It did not only receive subsidies from the official organs of film financing (ANCINE, ICAM and INCAA), but also from the regional governments of the states Rio Grande do Sul and Santa Catarina. Its status as super-production was possible due to the additional financing by Ibermedia and money coming from national and international private and public companies, such as banks, energy plants, etc. by means of the Cultural Incentive Bill and the Audiovisual Bill.

[144] ('a distressingly mediocre film')

The film simplifies these accounts to the extreme. It changes Gaspar de Froes' (Edson Celulari) Portuguese background into a trans-national story: he came as a child to Brazil, studied medicine in Coimbra, married and worked on the Azores. Given that he is Brazilian, the problem of assimilation is almost eliminated. The only biographical detail maintained is that in 1752, when his young wife dies, he decides to depart with one of the ships that take Azorean families to Santa Catarina in the south of Brazil.

With the intention to focus on the love story between the doctor and Maria (Daniela Escobar) and to heighten the dramatic potential, the film stresses the conflict with Spain and lessens the problems of the colonizers. These are reduced to a few defying dialogues between the protagonist and the representatives of colonial power, designed to typify him as a hero. The art direction is also of little help, since it turns the uncomfortable and dirty forts and villages into picturesque museum pieces.

Similar to *Desmundo*, but lacking its critical perspective, the film tells the story of Brazil's self-invention and self-sufficiency. The construction of the protagonist's subjectivity is crucial in this operation. He is presented as a dynamic and self-contained man and either defies the governors with regard to the situation of his countrymen, challenges the Spaniards during the War, or ignores general moral standards by having a passionate affair with a married woman. His disrespectful behaviour is seen as bravery and justified by the stereotyped antagonists, whose wicked conduct free him from any moral predicaments: the treacherous Spaniards, the unfaithful and now syphilitic husband of Maria (Rogério Samora) and the untrustworthy Portuguese crown.

The allegorical identity discourse of the film implies that the southern state of Santa Catarina did not result from the migration of poor and desperate Azorean families, but from the encounter of vigorous and daring men and women like Gaspar and Maria. The effort to impose a contemporary cinematographic style, which consists mainly in the excessive use of wide angles, slow motion and a soundtrack that features an electric guitar, enhances the impression of inconsistent artificiality. Deprived of its epic elements, the story is reduced to a predictable romance, as though it was necessary to have amnesia to be able to talk from a Brazilian point of view about a shameful chapter of Portugal's colonization.

The Forest

The Forest (2000), directed by the Portuguese filmmaker Leonel Vieira, was the most expensive Portuguese film production ever.[145] With a commercial outlook that resembles *New World Diary*, the adaptation also ignores the historical elements present in the homonymous novel by Ferreira de Castro. The remarkable book continues to a certain degree the discussion of the formation of Brazil, even though from a Portuguese perspective and by portraying a post-colonial episode: the exploration of rubber tappers in the Amazon during the decadence of the rubber extraction business at the beginning of the twentieth century. Alberto, a young monarchist and law student who had to leave Portugal because of his political ideas, is send by his uncle to work as a rubber tapper on one of the smaller rivers in the Amazon forest. After getting to know the hard work of the tappers, he is promoted and becomes the bookkeeper's clerk. In this more acceptable social position, he remains allied to his former colleagues and begins to express socialist ideas.

The book is a *Bildungsroman* in which Alberto slowly develops morally and psychologically until he changes his monarchist standpoint and reproaches the injustice of the internal colonialism. The absence of women on the plantation – a strategy by its owner to incite alcohol consumption and thus regain the small wages from the workers – is of some significance in the novel, since it makes the young man fantasize about the wife of the bookkeeper, Dona Yayá. This desire is condemned in the book, but becomes one of the major events in the film, explored in scenes of sex and nudity.

Many secondary references – the unanswered desire for Dona Yayá (Maitê Proença), an attack by the Indians, the escape of a group of rubber tappers lead by Firmino (Chico Diaz) – become main plot points so that the protagonist can assume heroic dimensions. Alberto (Diogo Morgado) actually turns everything into practice what the book character avoids: he seduces Dona Yayá, assumes that he helped the tappers to escape, is rebellious against his boss, Juca Tristão (Cláudio Marzo), and kills the gunman Velasco (Karra

---

[145] *The Forest* was co-produced with subsidies from Brazil, Portugal and Spain, provided not only from the ICAM and the Brazilian Ministry of Culture, but also from the Secretary of Culture and Tourism of the Amazon, Ibermedia, Portuguese and Spanish television channels (RTP, Canal+ and TVE) and Portugal's prestigious Instituto Camões.

Elejalde). While both novel and film end with the old slave Agostinho (Zé Dumont) killing his patron by setting his house on fire after he tortured the dissident tappers, the film stresses Alberto's protagonism by having him interfere and liberate his former colleagues.

Alberto's audacity and virile attitude is shown to be the very essence of his unruly character. It is closely linked to his Portuguese nationality and the social class he comes from. The literary adaptation simply forgets about the main character's process of growth in favour of a superficial heroism inspired in Hollywood blockbusters, from which the films also takes its aesthetic cues.

As a result, the film's identity discourse that suggests that the Portuguese clerk is a masculine role model in the most conventional sense of classic narrative cinema contrasts with the typically negative and folkloric stereotype usually associated with the clerks and traders who migrated in huge numbers from Portugal to Brazil at the end of the eighteenth century. Rowland (373) subsumes the discourse on this kind of migrants, developed in popular culture (especially music) and novels, as that of the rich and parasitic Portuguese. It actually expressed growing post-colonial tensions when Portuguese merchants began to monopolies the distribution of food, as well as the housing business in Rio de Janeiro in the late nineteenth century. The identity discourse from Vieira's 2003 film apparently tries to free the country from any such negative view or association with neo-colonialism. But apart from criticizing the Brazilian neo-colonialist exploitation, it puts forward a unilateral monologue on Portugal's moral superiority.

Carnal Utopia

Resembling *New World Diary* and *The Forest*, *Carnal Utopia*[146], directed by Brazilian director Marcelo Santiago, employs the commercial formula of a love triangle and some sex scenes, by simultaneously ignoring historical details concerning the opposition against the Brazilian dictatorship in the 1970s. But this time the literary adaptation goes in tune with the intentions of the book.

---

[146] The ICAM presents the film as a co-production in its catalogue from 2006. The generics of the film, however, only mention ANCINE, Ibermedia, Brazilian Paramount and MGM as financial sources. The Portuguese production company *Fado Filmes* appears, on the other hand, as co-producer.

Balé de Utopia by Álvaro Caldas already takes advantage of the political resistance to set up an erotic climate. A young revolutionary, Vaslav is shot and hidden in the apartment of a militant couple, consisting of the revolutionary leader Saulo and his very young wife Cristiana. Wanted by the police, Vaslav cannot reveal his identity to the young woman and hides his face under a cap. This cap becomes an erotic fetish, which, together with his dance routines as a ballet dancer arouse Cristiana, while her husband is battling off screen with the growing repression. Her attraction is, naturally, responded. The novel describes the erotic tension in an affected poetic language that sounds unnatural and corny. It also serves to compare persistently artistic creativity with political opposition against the authoritarian regime.

Based on the book, the film narrative engages very little with the fight for political freedom. It offers two different levels: the auto-diegetic perspective of Cristiana (Mel Lisboa) that shares her emotional bewilderment and the progression of her sexual attraction towards Vaslav (Sérgio Marone) in voice-over, and the scenes between the characters. Since the film focuses stronger on her emotions than the book, the political resistance by Saulo (Felipe Camargo) and the struggle for a democratic country are drowned even more in her feelings and desires than in the original text.

While the book mentions no relationship with Portugal, it is established by turning a mentally disturbed revolutionary into the Portuguese activist Roco (Ricardo Pereira), who has a brief appearance. Apart from the acknowledgment that both nations suffered dictatorships by means of the inexpressive character, the film's monologue is literally all-inclusive: individual satisfaction overpowers political resistance and makes a reflection on the Brazilian dictatorship, let alone its connection with Portugal's regime, impossible.

Love and Co.

The change of its title from *Alves and Co.* to *Love and Co*[147], already indicates that Helvécio Ratton's adaptation of a minor novel by Eça de Queirós also deals light-heartedly with social power relations. In fact, it sweetens the text of the master of irony, who famously remarked that the Brazilian language was like speaking Portuguese with sugar. While the short novel carries the main preoccupation of its protagonist in its title – the importance of a

---

[147] The production received subsidies from ICAM and SDAV.

good name and the prosperity associated with the business that bears this name – the film reduces the biting satire of the original to a rather unexciting romantic comedy.

Love and Co. follows the main plot points of the novel to tell the story of two business partners[148], Alves (Marco Nanini) and Machado (Alexandre Borges), whose professional and personal relationships suffer a short-lived blow due to the affair of Alves' wife Ludovina (Patrícia Pilar) with Machado. The period remains the nineteenth century, but the love triangle is transferred from the Portuguese metropolis Lisbon to a quiet little town in Minas Gerais. Significant changes in relation to the characters, the infidelity and the closure give the cinematographic narrative its sugary taste.

The generous and sentimental Alves becomes ridiculous and clownish, whereas the young elegant lover turns into an inoffensive womanizer. It is the bored, frivolous and materialistic wife trying to escape from her tedious marriage who suffers the profoundest changes by becoming a good-looking, goodhearted and charming lady. Where the novel does not leave the slightest doubt about her infidelity, the film suggests that the affair never happened. Ludovina is neither responsible for her husband's suspicions, nor does she want to recover her comfortable life style; her only ambition is to return to the man she loves and whose child she delivered without his knowledge during their separation. Whereas the novel is keen on showing that the pragmatic reconciliation occurs only to preserve the good name, maintain appearances and the prosperous company by sacrificing honour and cowardly avoiding a duel, the sticky sweet reconciliation of *Love and Co.* reunites the romantic lovers with the business partner in one big happy family.

The adaptation substitutes the acid Portuguese study of the high price of bourgeois life, its surrender to financial wellbeing and social stability, with the cliché of Brazilian kindliness and good-hearted nature in a film that lacks grace. Although apparently inoffensive, the adaptation is quite a statement on the differences between Portuguese and Brazilian cultures, perpetuating the myth of self-invention by replacing a critical analysis of class with a self-indulgent perspective on identity.

---

[148] The fact that the commercial partners export to colonial Africa, and thus live from colonialism, is acknowledged in the book, but disappeared completely from the literary adaptation.

The Xango from Baker Street

In comparison with *Love and Co.*, *The Xango from Baker Street*[149] seems to have made only the necessary changes in order to adjust the 350 pages of the original text to a film that lasts almost two hours. The story on the theft of a Stradivarius violin from the baroness Maria Luiza (Cláudia Abreu), the lover of the emperor Pedro II (Cláudio Marzo), which brings the famous English detective Sherlock Holmes (Joaquim de Almeida) to investigate what turns out to be the first serial killer, suffers a few cuts, but keeps most of the main plot and all of the characters.

The characters are all, according to the genre, ridiculous. The Europeans are slightly more preposterous than the Brazilians who are presented as a lively society trying to tackle important social issues such as the abolition of slavery. The great actress Sarah Bernhardt (Maria de Medeiros), who is touring Brazil and asks her friend Holmes for intervention, is gossipy; Sherlock Holmes, who speaks Portuguese with an accent from Portugal, is incompetent; Doctor Watson (Anthony O'Donnell) is pedantic. Many of the gags and pleasantries, almost always based on national stereotypes or sexist remarks, derive predominantly from Holmes' and Watson's droll encounters with what seems exotic to them: Brazilian clothing, food, drugs (hashish), sensual women, and the Afro-Brazilian religion *candomblé*.

The film's key pun is that the famous European detective is unable to re-solve the case on Brazilian soil, even though the significance of the circum-stantial evidence is almost rubbed into his face. This is coupled with the idea that Jack the Ripper was in actual fact Brazilian, because a crime of such sexual perversity can only have been invented in Brazil. Europe and Brazil are presented as opposed cultures whose differences are impossible to be bridged. What is more, Europeans are incapable of deciphering the South-American country. Brazil is literally inscrutable for Holmes – as much in term of the unsolved case, as in relation to his unfulfilled sexual desire for Ana (Thalma de Freitas), a sensual *mulata*. Holmes' casting with a Portu-

---

[149] The film was financed with help from the Cultural Initiative Bill and the Audiovisual Bill. A large number of multinational companies are cited as sponsors during the generics. The co-production between MGN and RTP received further subsidies from ICAM and the prefecture of Rio de Janeiro, where the film was partially shot.

guese actor brings a double edge to the character, associating him not only with Europe, but also with the ancient colonizer. But the portrayal of Brazil is even less flattering: in contrast to the impotent Europe, it becomes the birthplace of sexually inspired serial killing. Notwithstanding this demeaning presentation of cultural difference, the film opts for an aesthetic that mimics the famous Brazilian soap operas and thus manages to wipe out the aggressive discourse on cultural identities, hiding it rather well beneath a shallow surface.

Figure 14: *The Xangô form Baker Street* (Courtesy Skylight Filmes)

Turbulence

Ruy Guerra's *Turbulence* (2000) could not be more different in its perspective on identity. It follows the homonymous novel by Chico Buarque de Holanda with great precision, but encounters an ingenious cinematographic approach to translate the perturbation of the book's protagonist. The main character, who is referred to as I (Jorge Perugorría) in the casting list, is a young man who comes from a traditional upper-class family. After a failed marriage and without occupation, he lives isolated in an apartment of a city that bears the traces of three metropolises from the co-producing countries: Rio de Janeiro, Lisbon and Havana. When a strange character (Xando Graça) disturbs him in his sleep, he is alarmed by a familiar gesture that he sees through the peek hole and embarks on a paranoid perambulation. It takes him to a couple of familiar places that fail to offer him shelter: the posh house of his sister (Bianca Byington), the workplace and apartment of his ex-wife (Leonora Rocha), the apartment block of an old friend, and the abandoned country house of his family that is now being occupied by drug dealers.

The shattered family relationships in both book and film stand for Brazil's contemporary society, where alternatives to the patriarchal structure that cause the protagonist's crisis are lacking. The main character's drama derives from rejecting this patriarchal social structure after his father's death, but also from the fact that he has no supplementary project. Since he is paranoid, emotionally and financially dependent on his family, especially on his sister, he is unsuited for the defiance that he intends to make. What is more, his revolt is restricted to a pact with criminals who live on the family property and to whom he tries to sell jewels stolen from his wealthy sibling.

The upper class, which sustains the patriarchal society, is portrayed as neurotic and perverted. They lead a ghettoized lifestyle to protect themselves from the results of the social injustice they nourish and react brutally to assaults on their belongings. Symptomatically, the protagonist's brother-in-law denounces not him but the criminals when he burgles their home. The character who triggers off the protagonist's roaming in fact turns out to be a policeman who ends the problem of theft and occupation by means of a massacre. With the reappearance of the strange character the narrative takes the shape of a cycle and it remains unclear if the story starts at its end.

The cyclic structure stresses that the young man's revolt leads ironically to the reestablishment of the social order. It is uncertain if he actually dies when he flees from the scene of the execution to a bus stop and runs into the knife of a startled traveller, or whether this happened before he was disturbed at home, or if everything was only a dream. In any case, the film states that patriarchy is under threat by dissidents like the protagonist, even though he proves ineffective in his anarchic action which implicates him in a crime and is, ultimately, self-destructive. The impact of both film and book lies in demonstrating this dilemma.

Figure 15: Jorge Perugorría in *Turbulence* (Courtesy Skylight Filmes)

There are some alterations with regard to the original novel that expand the main character's crisis of belonging to a profoundly patriarchal and authoritarian society and turn his problem into a transnational issue. *Turbulence* was filmed in three different cities. Since these cities are not recognizable in the shots, this creates the impression that the film could take place in any bigger Ibero-American metropolis and that the story is valid for a larger cultural context. Another strategy to enhance the story's geographical impact occurs on the linguistic level and consists in the use of an eccentric mixture of Portuguese and Spanish by some characters, particularly by the protagonist.

Two additional cinematographic strategies participate in the amplification and transnationalization of the protagonist's conflict. The first consists in the duplication of the character into the performing protagonist and an auto-diegetic narrator. The result is twofold. On one hand, it serves to express the schizophrenic state of the protagonist. On the other, the use of Ruy Guerra's own voice-over and Mozambican accent to articulate the thoughts of the protagonist bears the traces of his transnational belonging, raising multiple questions on authorship. By involving the filmmaker, the film becomes self-referential, not only in terms of indicating the participation and presence of the author of the film, but also in the sense that the filmmaker incorporates the identity drama proposed by the book's author. The merging of the two voices, the authorial – the double voice of consciousness – and the protagonist's, which occurs when the latter is unintentionally stabbed at the end of the film, proposes that he reaches a higher level of understanding at the end. The second strategy derives from shots and images that express the perturbation of the main character by using unfocused lenses, fast camera movements, a vast amount of close-up shots, high paced editing, to name but the most relevant.

Given this set of strategies, it might be argued that the film's aesthetic principle points towards a disturbance that is not only related to the protagonist's Ibero-American crisis, but, more generally, a result of the contemporary world. In the tradition of Franz Kafka's literature that battled with the archaic authoritarian mechanisms in the modern world, the film transcends the national towards the transnational by exploring the contemporary paranoid mind.

Conclusion

In the group of eleven Luso-Brazilian literary adaptations no clear trend can be detected with regard to the chosen writers. Canonical authors who transcend national identity in their biography and writings, like António Vieira, Bocage and the 'Jew', or writers who represent it in an absolute manner, like Eça de Queirós, can be found next to bestseller authors, be they historic like Hans Staden, whose book was translated into several languages and had ten reprints within five years in the sixteenth century (Bueno 2008: 9), or contemporary authors like the television comedian Jô Soares, who has two of his novels on the list of the top one hundred Brazilian books of the 1990s (Reimão n.d.). Nonetheless, authors of critical acclaim outweigh more popular writers. Ana Miranda and Chico Buarque have been praised as important authors of their generation, and the same is true for the Portuguese Ferreira de Castro. Consequently, seven writers are of reputation, four of them canonical; two are bestseller authors and two are novelists of minor importance

(Álvaro Caldas and Luiz Antônio de Assis Brazil).

The strongest reason for the choice of the texts for co-production is, however, to be found in the cultural encounters explored in the book's narratives or their author's lives. The majority of the literary adaptations tell stories of the contact between native Brazilians and Europeans, or between Brazilian born colonizers and Europeans. Their encounters occur for the most part during the colonial period and almost exclusively in Brazil, but also stretch over the eighteenth and nineteenth centuries into the present.

When looking at the films in the chronological order of their historical setting, specific periods feature rarely more than once, while certain topics are quite persistent. Forming, in fact, a mosaic of significant moments within Brazil's history, the films revisit mainly the problem of cultural encounters or conflicts, and the social predicaments of authoritarianism and patriarchy, being the almost a-historical *Love and Co.* the only exception. These issues suffer variations that can be presented in the following order of past events: the clash of cultures (*Hans Staden* in 1549), the formation of Brazil's patriarchal society (*Desmundo* in 1552), the role of the cultural encounter for the (future) identity of Portugal (*Word and Utopia*, between 1623 and 1697), the authoritarian and repressive mechanisms of its governors (*The Jew*, between 1713 and 1739), the conflicts related to the colonization of the south (*New World Diary*, between 1752 and 1753), the Portuguese language and its diversity (*Bocage*, between 1785 and 1805), the clash of cultures after independence (*The Xango from Baker Street* in 1886), the inoffensiveness of the Brazilian bourgeoisie (*Love and Co.* at the end of the nineteenth century), the persistence of authoritarian mechanisms in the twentieth century (*The Forest*, between 1912 and 1918 and *Carnal Utopia* in the 1970s) and the difficulty to overcome Brazil's patriarchal society (*Turbulence*, around 2000).

Albeit a concentration on these themes, the identity discourses in the films are extremely varied and often ambiguous. *Hans Staden*, for instance, does not engage with Brazil's national identity directly, since the film comments on cultural relativity in general. It implies that the Europeans imposed themselves on the natives, questioning as such the luso-tropical idea of cultural harmony. Luso-tropicalism is present and remythified in *Word and Utopia* and turns Manoel de Oliveira's monumentalization of António Vieira into one of the most biased adaptations of the group. Focusing strongly on Brazil's national identity in the same historical moment, *Desmundo* develops a critical perspective, comparable to that of *Hans Staden*. The film demonstrates the disrespect and oppression of the Other in the very moment in which the country's patriarchal society was founded.

Shortly before Brazil's independence, *The Jew* is the only film set in Portugal. It criticizes the colonial matrix and develops the promise of a new Brazilian identity based on progressive and liberal ideas. The film is, however, not biased, since it remembers that challenges to authoritarianism, put forward by an artist and a diplomat, are rather the exception than the rule. *New World Diary* recycles, in contrast, the good old monologue on Brazil's self-invention and self-sufficiency, even though it spotlights only the south of the country.

Bocage can be added to the list of unbiased films, next to *Hans Staden*, *Desmundo*, *Turbulence* and *The Jew*, since the myth of lusophony is detoured with the help of an author who is more often than not a canonical reference within the lusophone world. Myths and mythmaking are, however, fundamental in *Word and Utopia*, *New World Diary*, *Love and Co.* and *The Forest*. It is quite impressive how their filmmakers reiterate the respective national discourses on identities. The veteran Manoel de Oliveira and the newcomer Leonel Vieira both insist on the moral superiority of a representative from their country, although the first does so with an authorial approach and the second in a Hollywood simulation. While the two Brazilian filmmakers Helvécio Ratton and Paulo Nascimento have rather opposing views, they both develop affirmative perspectives on Brazilian identity within their commercial productions. Setting his film during colonization, Nascimento underlines the bravery of his new Brazilians; whereas Ratton can already count on the cordiality of his countrymen who have prospered and settled in socially a century later.

The differences between Ruy Guerra's and Marcelo Santiago's films are more profound. In fact, they represent two extreme points on the scale of unbiased and biased discourses within the group of the eleven filmmakers under study. Directed by a veteran from Brazil's *cinema novo*, *Turbulence* offers a challenge to national identity, not only because it shows that its social structure, patriarchy, is questioned, but mainly because the film transcends the country's identity problem by pointing out that Iberian culture, if not the entire modern world, should be included in the discussion of the persistence of patriarchal social structures. *Carnal Utopia*, on the other hand, is, in tune with its English title, a hymn on the victory of individualism and a death song to political utopias. Even though these are absent in *Turbulence*'s story, which does not seem to believe in leftist ideology and mentions it only in passing, they materialize, in the tradition of avant-garde films, in the film's aesthetic.

Bearing in mind Lourenço's (1999b) remark on the biased discourses regarding the Luso-Brazilian relationships, it might come as a surprise that almost half of the films (*Hans Staden*, *Desmundo*, *The Jew*, *Bocage* and *Turbulence*) engage in varying degrees with perspectives that search for a multilateral, that is, transnational dialogue. They are aware of the ambivalences of cultural encounters and offer, especially in the cases of *Turbulence* and *Bocage*, startling reinterpretations of Brazilian hegemonic identity and lusophony.

The co-productions that are driven by resentment or delirium are, nonetheless, more frequent. When the discourses are absent in the original texts they are either added in the adaptation process (*New World Diary*, *Love and Co.* and *The Forest*), or lose their ambiguity (*Word and Utopia*). Historical amnesia with regard to historical elements from the original stories is another trait of the films that present common places for easy digestion (*New World Diary*, *The Xango of Baker Street* and *Carnal Utopia*). The popularity of biased views reveals how deeply rooted they still are in the imaginary of a significant number of filmmakers from both sides of the Atlantic.

One of the strongest reasons for the monologues on national identities is the desire of commercial success, detectable in the big budget productions with their sophisticated technical paraphernalia that proliferate from 2000 onwards – the symbolic year of the celebrations of the 'Discovery' of Brazil. The fact that the Luso-Brazilian co-productions are the result of a political initiative now aiming for prestigious results, is another important point to be made, given that the first and more interesting films (*The Jew*, *Bocage*) were co-produced in a moment when the agreement had not really kicked in on an institutional basis.

Although the trend indicates otherwise, one can only hope that in the future there will be less lost opportunities for transnational dialogues that outwit the soliloquies on national pre-eminence still dominating the imaginary of the Portuguese-speaking world. By taking better advantage of its ambivalent potential, the Luso-Brazilian co-productions could participate in the promotion of a critical and constructive meaning of transnationality in film studies.

The limits of Luso-Brazilian brotherhood: Fortress Europe in *Foreign Land* (1995) by Walter Salles and Daniela Thomas[150]

Introduction

Globalization is an exterior *and* interior process The Brazilian sociologist Renato Ortiz (1996: 83) notes that not only the power of organization escapes the territoriality of a unique urban zone or country when articulated dynamically into the global capitalist system. The loss of former spatial limits through de-territorialization of the nation state also implodes its moral, mental and cultural unity. In consequence, national identity loses its privileged position as source of meaning. Contradictions reach new dimensions and, along with a sensation of rootlessness, multiple references emerge that offer themselves for a necessary re-territorialization.

Walter Salles and Daniela Thomas' Luso-Brazilian co-production *Terra Estrangeira/Foreign Land* from 1995 offers itself as a case study of the consequences of Brazil's globalization. It spotlights how the exterior and interior crises of its main characters turn the ancient colonizer Portugal again into a possible reference for identity construction. This is obviously complicated by the fact that the economic attractiveness of the recent EU member coexists with out-dated discourses and socio-cultural practices – as much in relation to the ex-colonies as to the European co-members. As we just saw in the previous chapter, the colonial bonds had never really been cut off after Brazil's declaration of independence in 1822, even if they remained largely on an ambiguous discursive level. I have also mentioned in earlier chapters Portugal's identity fluctuation between an underdeveloped prosperized Caliban, who turned his back on Europe for centuries, and a calibanized Prospero, whose inter-identity politics made it difficult for its colonized to develop anti-colonialist discourses. What is more, the EC's increasingly restrictive migration politics, which have been referred to in social sciences as the creation of a 'Fortress Europe', put even the most exalting discourses on the historical, cultural and parental bonds under strain.

Foreign Land is a complex account of the negotiation of identity discourses.

---

[150] This chapter is a revised version of an article published under the same title in 2006 in *Third Text*, 2.6: 731–41. Reprinted by permission of Taylor & Francis.

Consequently, the film received much critical attention by national and international scholars, comparable to that of its Portuguese counterpart *No or the Vain Glory of Command* by Manoel de Oliveira, discussed in the first part of the book. Both films strike a note, since they call for a revision of national identity construction and an assessment of the colonial relationships as a consequence of the profound socio-economic changes set off by the re-democratization processes – in 1985 and 1974 respectively.

While the Portuguese production *No* is mainly a result of the adhesion to the European Community, the co-production *Foreign Land* focuses on the effects of the savage economic measures put into practice in 1990 by the recently elected Brazilian government. It is worth noting that the difficult financial circumstances turned the Brazilian film project into a trans-national production that goes beyond the questioning of national identity put forward by *No*. As I will argue on the following pages, *Foreign Land* not only positions itself within the contradictory cultural discourses and lines of power that result as much from the contemporary globalization processes as from the legacy of colonial and neo-colonial practices; it actually demonstrates the potential of the co-production mode, by engaging with the problem of supra-national and trans-national identity construction within the context of 'Fortress Europe'.

Foreign Land

Brazil's de-territorialization

The film begins on 13 March 1990, two days before the first Brazilian civil government elected by direct vote since the military coup in 1964 took office. Its president Fernando Collor de Mello immediately implemented a plan to modernize the Brazilian economy according to the neo-liberal recipe of global capitalism. The plan resulted in mass unemployment, the temporary freezing of salaries and savings, and the extinction of foundations and public companies such as the national film enterprise *Embrafilm* and the national Film Council *Concine*. Needless to say that this had a strong effect on national film production, which was reduced from over 100 films per year to the release of only two films in 1992 (Moisés 2003: 7). What is more, the policies of Collor de Mello (Collor Plan) produced an enormous number of Brazilian emigrants, estimated between 400,000 and one million.

The main character in *Foreign Land*, Paco (Fernando Alves Pinto), a young physics student who actually aspires to become an actor, will become one of them. He is introduced in the first sequence of shots as an insignificant speck in the centre of São Paulo where the Minhocão, a highway viaduct, cuts right through the apartment blocks. Capitalism's presence is much more evident, when 'Hope' appears as the brand name of an underwear firm promoting consumerism with a huge hoarding on one of the buildings. Paco is rehearsing the lines of Goethe's unsatisfied Faust and his desire to go beyond the boundaries of human nature: 'levem-me daqui para uma vida nova e variada! Que um manto mágico seja meu e me carregue para terras estrangeiras'[151] (Thomas, Bernstein and Salles 1996: 8).

The significance of this speech changes its meaning when Paco's mother (Laura Cardoso), a Basque immigrant from San Sebastián, watches the announcement of the Collor Plan on television. It jeopardizes her plan to return to her roots and literally kills her. In his grief, Paco still tries to audition for Faust but cannot pronounce a single word from this majestic figure of the Western canon. Transposed from his insignificance into the spotlights, an extreme close-up of his sweating face reveals that he cannot cope with being centre-stage, his world having just imploded.

But the part of Faust is assigned to Paco by reality. Without other prospects in a country in which (at least for an English speaking spectator) hope is the name of a consumer good, Paco takes on his mother's desire to return to San Sebastián. Igor (Luís Melo), an antiques dealer who has Portuguese and Brazilian citizenship, offers him a trip to Lisbon in exchange for the delivery of a violin. The first step towards Paco's re-territorialization is marked by the fact that in order to return to his alleged European origin he has to make a pact with the devil that tempts him in the disguise of a trans-national diamond smuggler.

Portugal between colonial past and European future

Although the Collor plan radicalized the globalization of Brazil's economy, the 1980s had already been a period of emigration to Portugal. Other characters are already abroad and are introduced in a parallel narrative set in Lisbon: Miguel (Alexandre Borges), an unsuccessful avant-garde musician with

---

[151] ('Take me to a new and different life. I wish I owned a magic coat to take me to Foreign Lands.')

a drug habit, who has taken on smuggling diamonds for Igor; and Alex (Fernanda Torres), his girlfriend, also from a middle-class background, who is exploited as a waitress in a traditional restaurant. Jean-Claude Bernardet (1996: 86) has argued that *Foreign Land* is the most romantic portrayal of the country ever made by a foreign filmmaker, but the circumstances of the characters are far from charming. By no means have they encountered the better place that they expected Portugal to be.

Portugal likes to see itself as the initiator of the modern globalization processes with its maritime enterprises. However, incapable of competing with the European markets, it soon turned its back on Europe (Lourenço 1999a: 17). Only during Cavaco Silva's conservative government in the late 1980s and early 1990s, which looked more to Europe, Portugal began to renegotiate its position. The Brazilian anthropologist Bela Feldman-Bianco argues that Portugal's process of re-territorialization within its ancient geographic frontiers on the Iberian Peninsula was almost concurrent with its de-territorialization into the space defined by the EU.

As a result, the country had to subordinate itself to European migration politics. *Jus sanguinis* replaced *jus solis* as early as 1981 and was developed into a new law for foreigners in 1992.[152] Fortress Europe was put into action in 1993 when, after signing the Schengen agreement, Portugal started to block unwanted immigrants from the Portuguese-speaking African countries (PALOP) and from Brazil at the airports. This was, in fact, an illegal act, as it ignored the Bilateral Agreement of Equality signed with Brazil in 1972. The earlier agreement had been indispensable for the Portuguese imperialist regime since it offered thousands of settlers in the African 'ultramarine provinces' – a euphemism used for the colonies – a new home in Brazil during and after the colonial war. The already ambivalent relationship between the ancient empire and its former colony subsequently turned into what Feldman-Bianco (2002: 388) calls a 'family drama'.

But Portugal is no homely place for the Brazilian characters in *Foreign Land*. Orphaned by their own country, they are marginalized in Europe and survive only by trying to make their living outside the law. Portugal's membership in the EU is, in fact, equivalent to being a stage for criminal activity on which nationals from wealthier European nations, namely France and

---

[152] Currently immigration law is being changed again in favour of *jus solis*.

Spain, act. While their supra-national identity bestows on them the possibility to transgress the legal system, Portugal's traditional role as subaltern colonizer is foregrounded and Brazil finds itself in the lowest position as henchman.

The Portuguese characters are mere accomplices to the crimes of the other Europeans. Igor, who passes the borders between Brazil and Portugal with ease, is dis respected by his European bosses. Miguel and Paco find themselves in the position of messengers. Their Calibanesque powerlessness is repeatedly demonstrated in situations that manifest their incapacity to play leading roles and their irrelevancy is captured visually as they meander through the sites from which Europe's colonial history began.

Instead of encountering inter-identities promised by defenders of lusophony and luso-tropicalism, the Brazilians actually lose their sense of self. José Carlos Avellar (2003) uses a striking example by describing a scene set at the sanctuary of Cape Espichel. Within the colonial architecture and set against the impressive natural spectacle of cliffs and sea Alex only repeats [to Paco] what the image shouted before: 'I am nobody. And you even less! And the other nobody [Miguel] died three days ago' (Avellar 2003: 59).

Myths of Luso-Brazilian brotherhood

According to the already cited Gilberto Freyre (n.d..: 13), the reassuring idea of transcending national identity was Brazil's trans-national fantasy after the end of Portuguese colonialism: 'Brazilians and Portuguese have a common destiny: It goes beyond the mythic limits of nationalism.' Colonizer and colonized appear as equals, but it is the generous colonizer who inspires the latter – an idea on which the dictator Salazar picks up in his luso-tropicalist speech cited in the chapter on *No or the Vain Glory of Command*.

As mentioned in the previous chapter, since the years of independence there has been no lack of Brazilian discourses hostile towards this point of view. In their discussion of *Foreign Land*, Brazilian film scholars notably refer to more recent and more ambivalent discourses, whose authors acknowledge rather a feeling of discomfort and orphanage in relation to the European bonds: the conservative nineteenth-century abolitionist Joaquim Nabuco and the father figures of Brazilian film criticism, Paulo Emílio Salles Gomes.

In her film analysis, Andrea França Martins (1997: 94) invokes Nabuco's idea that Brazilians were condemned to instability caused by their lack of history: while their feelings were Brazilian, their imagination was European.

She agrees that *Foreign Land*'s characters encounter themselves in a similar state of gloomy instability, but stresses that the fatherland (*patria*) loses its significance as territorial reference in the film and is redefined by the characters' journey in which other emotional communities are delineated. The loss of a centre was not fitting for Nabuco's time in which the replacement of external with internal colonialism needed to be theorized.[153]

At the beginning of the 1970s, Salles Gomes (1980: 88) stressed that the difficulty in constructing a proper national identity was based less on a sense of indebtedness to Europe than on a feeling of alienation: 'we are neither Europeans, nor North Americans, but lacking an original culture, nothing is strange to us, given that everything is. The thorny construction of us is developed within the dialectic of being and not being.' This observation expressed worries about the future of the Brazilian cinema that had promoted the debate on identity and affirmed itself a modern cinema – *cinema novo* and *cinema marginal*. It also proves that after centuries of brotherhood discourses, which were reinforced during post-coloniality, it is impossible to think Brazilian identity without acknowledging Europe.

With regard to *Foreign Land*, scholars develop different views on Salles Gomes' questioning of prevailing discourses on inter-identities and his outlook on Brazilian national cinema. Denise Lopes (2000: 66) affirms that the film is perhaps *the* national film, which takes Salles Gomes' affirmation most literally. França Martins (1997: 93) describes, alternatively, the problem as being transnational and related to how Brazil should now position itself to the outside world in general terms, that is to say, to any other, which cannot be seen as different anymore.[154] André Parente (1997: 195-203) brings an anti-colonialist perspective into the discussion by declaring that *cinema novo* and other cultural strategies like Anthropophagy and Tropical-

---

[153] Due to the weak colonialist performance of the chaotic and absent Prospero, substitute Prosperos emerged in Brazil in what can be regarded as one of the most conservative and oligarchic independences on the Latin-American continent (Sousa Santos 2001: 44–5). Nabuco's discourse expresses more strongly than Freyre's the contradiction between the still existing desire of the Brazilian elite to maintain a European imaginary in order to be a substitute Prospero and the emergence of a national identity.

[154] According to França Martins, Paco's movement towards a reaffirmation of identity is the other side of the experience of globalisation.

ism had already been successful in resolving this Hamletian dilemma in the 1960s and 70s.

Anthropophagy and Tropicalism were fundamental in opposing colonialism and neo-colonialism. Oswald de Andrade's patriotic and parodist *Manifesto antropófago* of 1928 formulated the idea that the colonized can defend and strengthen his own cultural identity by incorporating the colonizer's power and culture in a cannibalistic manner (see Boaventura). Tropicalism, which took shape in the 1960s as a reaction against the military dictatorship and a statement on the modernist explosion of urban centres and consumerism, subsequently adapted and integrated aesthetic ideas from opposing contexts in a neo-cannibalistic manner that questioned national myths (see Xavier 2001: 29–33). Owing to the impact of these avant-garde movements on literature, visual arts and film, as well as the cultural changes they implied, Parente argues that the cinema of the 1980s and 1990s is a step back. Contemporary films are incapable of affirming Brazilian identity, whereas *cinema novo* liberated itself from the labyrinth of inter-identities.

Are there new insights with respect to Salles Gomes' question of 'being and not being' in theses analyses of *Foreign Land*? For Lopes the problem remained more or less in the same shape as it did thirty years ago. The same is true of Parente's who measures contemporary films according to former historical circumstances. What is more, he affirms *cinema novo*'s identity politics from the 1950s and 60s as still valid. His criticism, which includes a comparison with anti-colonialist and anti-imperialist cultural movements, nonetheless, makes an important observation possible. Any discussion of the relationship between *cinema novo* and the 'new Brazilian Cinema, has to keep in mind that the earlier film movement (as well as in more general terms Anthropophagy and Tropicalism) took place under neo-colonialism and dictatorship. The *Retomada,* the so called revival of Brazilian film production in the mid-1990s, which resulted from the new Audiovisual Law launched precisely in 1995 and of which *Foreign Land* is an inaugural part, takes place under democracy and globalization – certainly a new form of imperialism but without an identifiable centre. Even though related, these are two very different sets of circumstances that imply the rethinking of identity. The new coordinates of the problem, which consist in throwing the (national) self back on itself due to the loss of a centre, are only pointed out by França Martins.

Indeed, the characters negotiate and articulate complex and contradictory perspectives on inter-identities related to brotherhood and national identity throughout the film. The avant-garde artist Miguel, for example, denigrates luso-tropicalism by calling Lisbon conceitedly a 'cabaret of colonies'. He is a cynic whose music, in an obvious contrast to Tropicalism's popularity, is not fashionable at all. He sees Portugal as a calibanized Prospero and dislikes it mainly for being economically and culturally underdeveloped. For the ambitious Miguel, Portugal is just a hole in the Fortress through which he wants to make it into the genuine Europe. Conversely, his girlfriend Alex is completely disillusioned about Europe as the Promised Land and her desire to return home intensifies during the narrative. By stating that her Brazilian pronunciation creates frontiers rather than feelings of brotherhood, she demonstrates that lusophony is a fraud. Alex most strongly expresses her frustration about Brazil as a country that went wrong. But, in contrast to Miguel, she does not blame the ancient colonizer but acknowledges respect for the courage of the colonial enterprise.

Figure 16: Alex (Fernanda Torres) in *Foreign Land* (Courtesy Videofilmes)

The characters have in general no feelings of belonging to the former colonizer or its post-colonial imaginary, the lusophone community. This is made evident in Paco's relationship with Loli (Zeka Laplaine), a friendly African character. Loli not only helps Paco, but tries to make him aware of his self-pity by telling him about his people's suffering in the civil war that followed Angola's independence from Portugal. Paco feels rather bothered by him at first. The European descendant changes his approach when he feels in need of a friend. But not for long. When the violin is taken away from him, Paco violently accuses the African of being the thief, unaware that his real antagonist is the Portuguese character Pedro.

Pedro (João Lagarto), a friend of Alex and Miguel, is the only character who reminds us of the sentimental relationships between Portugal and Brazil. He is in love with Alex and helps her out, thus betraying his friend Igor. When confronted with violence, he ends up betraying Alex as well. Evidently, there are no enduring bonds. The trans-national antiques dealer Igor, who travels easily between the two continents and switches from a Brazilian to a Portuguese accent, is an unmistakable example of a perfect substitute Prospero who admires the colonialist project. It is no coincidence that Igor keeps up the habit of smuggling diamonds in statues of saints or other cultural objects as was common during the colonial period. Furthermore, Igor complains about the end of history, because his privileged position that allows him to exploit his own people is called into question.

Frustrated re-territorialization

Besides discussing Luso-Brazilian brotherhood, *Foreign Land* shows that taking Europe as a reference for re-territorialization is actually fatal to its characters. Miguel dies because in his anti-colonialist overconfidence and European ambition he underestimates the criminals of real Europe who kill him for trying to keep the money made from smuggling. This complicates Paco's situation, since he cannot hand over the violin. When he encounters Alex by chance, she tries to help him to sell the violin. Although they end up spending the night together, Alex is preoccupied with her survival and she rejects Paco the next day. National bonds are also jeopardized in a situation in which both characters fear for their lives. It is nonetheless their relationship that becomes paramount later in the film. Before this happens, Paco is confronted by his Mephistopheles and the Europeans who manipulate his strings regarding the whereabouts of the precious stones. At this point, he is able to give sense to Faust's lines and speaking them helps him escape. Paco then tries to return the violin, but is panic-stricken when he discovers that

Alex gave it away in a naive act of sabotage. Their lives are now really in danger and Paco decides that they need to flee to Spain.

During their journey they recover the capacity to establish a relationship based on inter-subjectivity. The emblematic shot of their embrace in front of a stranded ship is not only a visual expression of their shipwrecked return to Europe but also of a possible new beginning. The Portuguese literary critic Margarida Calafate Ribeiro (2004: 40) has pointed out that the discoveries turned the opportunity for self-discovery offered by the encounter with the Other rapidly into the desire for expansion and power. Subsequently, the 'balsamic construction of Portugal as an Empire was used to elude the country's peripheral European existence. The very contrary is the case here. The shipwreck, which has been interpreted by Jorge Ruffinelli (qtd. in Elena 2003: 214) as a metaphor for economic stagnation and personal distress, can also be seen as a metaphor for the invalidity of Eurocentric myths about supra or trans-national identities in times of globalization. This opens up the possibility of a re-territorialization, which could consist in the reconstruction of identity by recognizing the *national* Other as subject *without* taking the colonizer into account.

But the new identity project, which delineates an emerging community that experiences economic crises as well as emigration, proves to be fragile. Given the lines of power of globalization and the residues of the European dream still present in the attempt to go to San Sebastián, it is ultimately impossible for the characters to complete this kind of resistance identity. Set before the Schengen agreement, the European borders are still effective and Alex cannot cross them because she has sold her passport. When the criminals get hold of the couple, Alex attacks Igor with a fork and a bottle, while Paco shoots the other accomplice and gets wounded. Portugal not only turns these Brazilians finally into assassins but also is inevitably lethal for the men who try to affirm themselves on the European stage. Paco's use of Faust's speech, which might be described as an anthropophagic act, reveals itself only momentarily successful.

The resolution of the film maintains an ambivalent tone. Alex drives across the border with the wounded Paco on her lap and thus violates the nationally imposed frontiers. But her desire to take Paco home is not very realistic. Alex' and Paco's last sequence ends with an aerial shot of their car driving off into an uncertain future. Alberto Elena (2003: 218) observes that this shot, a possible homage to Glauber Rocha's 1964 *Deus e o Diabo na Terra do sol* (*Black God, White Devil*), only makes the difference between the *Cinema novo* film and *Foreign Land* more visible.

Whilst Rocha's film had a prophetic and optimistic ending, the latter and more recent film is incapable of indicating a prospective outcome or a promising future. Elena also points out that the song *Vapor Barato*, which accompanies the shot, was written by Waly Salomão, a poet close to the Tropicalist movement and became the anthem for a generation whose fight against the military dictatorship brought many of them into exile. Alex and Paco's migration is a completely different case, which results from political and economic disillusion. And Paco's tragic fate attests to the fact that the hopes of the former generation have not come true. The generation that is now living under democracy is again on the road, with less orientation than before. With this ambivalent ending *Foreign Land* makes evident not only the fatality of the Luso-Brazilian brotherhood discourses but also the need to rethink the strategies of former counter-culture movements.

Aesthetic of mourning

Many interesting remarks have been made on the aesthetic elements of the film. Walter Salles (qtd. in Nagib 2002: 419) has commented on the use of black and white to express a contradictory mood as well as the film's feel of documentary in the sense of an urgent portrayal of a whole generation. Avellar (qtd. in Elena 2003: 216) has highlighted the film's indebtedness to *Cinema novo* in terms of 'hand-held-camera, natural light, shooting on location, setting the operator in the middle of the scene as any other character in the film, action that seems to be improvised or created in that moment, etc.' The expressionist tone of the metaphorical shots and the complexity of cinephile allusions to genres and styles of the road movie, neo-realism or authors such as Michelangelo Antonioni, Wim Wenders, Nicholas Ray, Glauber Rocha or Nelson Pereira dos Santos have been analyzed in detail by Elena (2003: 215–19).

I would like to add to these analyses a reading that explores my point on the failure of trans-national or supra-national identity construction. Wendy Everett (1996: 108) has argued that the self-conscious recognition of the process of remembrance reflected in the linking of memory and journey is widespread in contemporary European films and serves to acknowledge European memory and myth. Likewise, *Foreign Land*'s road movie structure acknowledges myth but by interrogating Brazil's bonds with Europe. Furthermore, the journey is shot in black and white and its documentary aesthetic foreground the film's quality as memory. The de-territorialization suffered by the characters and the impossibility of using Europe as a reference for re-territorialization is presented as a past and painful event. And, like memory, *Foreign Land* is open-ended. For that reason, I believe hat what has been considered a romantic portrayal is indeed mourning, an active grief about the indispensable, but at the same time excruciatingly factual and imaginary loss of Europe as a reference point after the national identity crises that followed the Collor Plan. Five years after the actual events *Foreign Land* is a flashback to the traumatic events, and like any return to trauma, its memory is intended to trigger off a healing process.

The Luso-Brazilian co-production shares the idea that the colonial history needs to be mourned with *A Portuguese Farewell* by João Botelho. But the comparison with both Botelho's and Oliveira's films on the colonial war manifests that *Foreign Land* goes a step further. Alex is capable of recognizing the 'Discovery of Brazil ' as an extraordinary accomplishment. However, it is very clear to her that neo-colonial practices – especially the diamond smuggling – are still taking a high toll on the ex-colonized. This is why she gives the violin away and we see people stepping on them unconsciously in the last sequence of the film. The film proves that mourning needs not be related to a remystification of the colonial bonds by exalting again an inexistent ideal cultural history.

Conclusion

While most of the subsequent films by Walter Salles, some in partnership with Daniela Thomas, offer solutions that run the danger of remystification and simplification[155], *Foreign Land* restages the discussion of Brazil's trou-

---

[155] *O Primeiro Dia/Midnight* (Walter Salles and Daniela Thomas 1998) deems it utopian to bridge Brazil's different social classes by engaging with the national other. *Central do Brasil/Central Station* (Walter Salles and Daniela Thomas 1998), however, offers the possibility of re-territorialisation by recycling national myths. *Abril Despedaçado/Behind the Sun* (Walter Salles 2001) develops on this optimism and underlines the need for individual freedom. *Diários de Motocicleta/Motorcycle Diaries* (Walter Salles 2004) returns to the past by means of a nostalgic recovery of a resistance identity that could not affirm itself politically.

bled identity and dilemma of being and not being with an original twist. First, because the film chooses the very moment that makes the change from neo-colonialism to globalization visible. The implementation of Collor de Mello's neo-liberal economic strategies entails the end of the dream of a self-sufficient, democratic and progressive country and triggers off a national identity crisis. Second, because the resulting desire for reorientation takes the migrating characters to Portugal – or, more generally, to Europe – in order to lay bare the invalidity of the ambiguous and contradictory discourses on trans-national Luso-Brazilian brotherhood, such as lusophony and luso-tropicalism. Third, because in this new set of circumstances *Foreign Land* distances itself from former critical discourses *and* anti-colonialist practices such as Antropophagy and Tropicalism by adopting a different aesthetic approach. This approach mourns the previous references for identity construction and replaces them by suggesting the recognition of the *national* other as subject.

There is another interesting point to be made. As one of the first films of the *Retomada*, *Foreign Land* drew some criticism for having been filmed abroad (see Parente 1997: 199). But such criticism is based on a stable and fixed concept of national identity and national cinema that *Foreign Land* shows to be in jeopardy. Orphaned by the extinction of *Embrafilm*, the film is a Luso-Brazilian co-production by *Videofilmes* (Brazil) and *Antimatógrafo* (Portugual) that demonstrates the potential of dealing with the contradictory legacy of colonialism, just like *Comboio da Canhoca*, *The Blue Eyes of Yonta*, *Tree of Blood* in the preceding chapter on Luso-African co-productions, or other Luso-Brazilian films such as *Hans Staden*, *Desmundo*, *The Jew*, *Bocage* and *Turbulence*. Due to its rejection of out-dated discourses on inter-identity, its aesthetic of mourning and search for inter-subjectivity, *Foreign Land* re-establishes or rather re-defines its contradictory European bonds and thus, in parts, breaks the borders set by Fortress Europe.

Identities adrift: lusophony and migration in national and transnational films[156]

Introduction

Due to its journeys of discoveries and its many colonies spanning Brazil to Macau, but even more because of its weak socio-political and economic situation from the eighteenth century onwards, Portugal has always been a country of massive emigration. Still distant from the social and economic standards of first world nations after the end of its empire, Portuguese emigration to Brazil, richer European countries or the United States of America have not ceased. Accordingly, the portrayal of migrants has a tradition in Portuguese national cinema.[157] Fiction films on the relatively recent impact of immigration – as for example the co-production *Foreign Land* discussed in the previous chapter – are only a recent phenomenon.

While the decolonization process is usually interpreted as the main reason for the explosion of immigration, it rather led to an inverted migration process, since Portuguese citizens who had moved to the African colonies now returned in large numbers. The amount of non-Portuguese citizens remained small after the PALOP and East Timor gained independence so that, in 1981, only 54,414 foreigners, of which thirty percent came from Europe, were registered with the *Serviço de Estrangeiros e Fronteiras* (Service of Foreigners and Frontiers).[158] By 2006 the number had multiplied by eight (434,887) and immigrants represented 4.1 per cent of the entire population and 5.1 per cent of its work force (Peixoto 2008: 27).

The growth of immigration is a consequence of the economic boom that followed Portugal's entry into the European market and its subsequent de-

---

[156] This article is a revised version of 'Identities Adrift: Lusophony and Migration in National and Trans-national Lusophone Film'. *Polyglot Cinema: Migration and Transcultural Narration in France, Italy, Portugal and Spain*. Eds. Verena Berger and Miya Komori. Berlin/München/Wien/Zürich/London, LIT Verlag, 2010: 173–92.

[157] At least twenty films have narrated emigrants' stories in the thirty-two years since re-democratisation when the average yearly cinematographic production has totalled twelve feature films.

[158] Portuguese National Institute of Statistic (www.ine.pt).

mand for mainly unskilled workers, for the most part in the construction industry, as well as a result of the growing political conflicts in the former colonies. The civil wars in Angola (1975–2002) and Mozambique (1975–1991), and the constant political instability in Guinea Bissau were responsible for the influx from the PALOP, as was the severe economic crisis in the early 1990s for an increase in Brazilian migration[159].

In addition to the PALOP (45.1 per cent of all immigrants in 1981, 40.2 per cent in 1991, 44.7 per cent in 2001) that represented 26.6 per cent of all working immigrants in 2006, and Brazil (10.8 per cent in 2001) that represented 19.8 per cent in 2006, from the end of the 1990s onwards Eastern Europe began to supply workers to fulfil the demand for foreign labour; and the number of Ukrainian immigrants equalled that of working Brazilian immigrants (19.8 per cent) in 2006 (Malheiros 2002, Peixoto 2008: 27). The former leaders of the list, the Cape Verdeans, who have since the 1960s traditionally found work in the construction and manufacturing industry due to their special status as assimilated Africans within the Portuguese colonial system, dropped to the third place (9.7 per cent).

While there is a trend towards diversification, the immigration from the PALOP has not changed in numbers but in terms of origin (Malheiros 2002). The Cape Verdean community has shrunk by half, mainly because of the tightening of immigration control on the islands and in Europe, but also because many Cape Verdeans moved on to richer European countries like the Netherlands and France (see Carling). Due to the constant economic and political crises, the number of Angolan immigrants has more than doubled and the community from Guinea-Bissau was in 2002 four times the size it was in 1981.[160] Given the shortage of domestic labor, the increase of illegal immigration, the fragile economy and, most importantly, the European Union's immigration policies since the Treaty of Schengen in 1993, Portugal's openness towards foreign workers during the 1980s and 1990s has changed dramatically and immigration is today a polemic issue in Portuguese society.

---

[159] Feldman-Bianco (2002: 159) cites Baganha e Góis who observe that while the immigrant population from Brazil integrate into the higher levels of Portuguese society, those from the PALOP can be found at its base.

[160] According to Malheiros (2002), Angola represented in 2001 9.9 per cent, Cape Verde 22.3 per cent and Guinea-Bissau 7.6 per cent of legal immigrants.

The numbers above confirm that in contrast to many other European countries, except France and Great Britain, contact between migrants and the Portuguese population still results strongly from colonialism. Almost half of the legally working immigrants (46.4 per cent) come from Portuguese-speaking countries. The chapter on *Foreign Land* already pointed out the complicated set of discourses on the historical, linguistic and cultural bonds that these migrants from Brazil and the PALOP have to face. It is now time to have a closer look at the question of lusophony – the idea of a unifying Portuguese idiom – which has already been glanced at in several occasions in this book.

Within the context of literary studies, Eduardo Lourenço was the first[161] to identify the misuse of Fernando Pessoa's already referred phrase 'A minha pátria é a minha língua'[162] from which the concept takes its symbolic and political power. It is invoked when Portugal needs to tighten the bonds with its ancient colonies (as the examples of the creation of the CPLP and the agreements on co-productions described in earlier chapters illustrate). But any political instrumentalization of Pessoa's phrase in a neo-colonialist and nationalistic fashion has to be considered absurd, since the poet's expression was personal and unpatriotic. For Lourenço (1999b: 126), Pessoa's writing was a linguistic adventure and the Portuguese language offered the possibility to invent ones identity beyond national restraints:

> Isto não abre para nacionalismos tribais, para patriotismos de exclusão da universalidade alheia. A nossa relação com a língua é de outra natureza e é outra a pátria que nela temos ou donde somos. Por isso a tão famosa frase quer dizer apenas: a *língua portuguesa*, esta língua que me fala antes que a saiba falar, mas, acima de tudo, esta língua que através de mim se torna uma realidade não só viva mas *única*, a língua através da qual me invento Fernando Pessoa, é ela a *minha pátria*.[163]

---

[161] It is quite revealing that a critical attitude towards lusophony had already been under way in coproductions, for example in *Foreign Land* from 1995 and in *Bocage – The Triumph of Love* from 1998.

[162] ('My country is the Portuguese language.')

[163] ('This does not offer a basis for tribal nationalisms or patriotisms that exclude universalism. Our relationship with language is of a different kind, as is our fatherland that we inhabit and from which we come. The famous phrase only wants

Lourenço (1999b: 131–3) is conscious of the fact that language always played an extraordinary role in Portugal's cultural formation and served as a source of feverish exaltation and secret suffering. But while imperial in vocation, it remained provincial and never achieved the influence of other languages such as English and French. After decolonization, it is now necessary to rephrase Pessoa: one should not speak of one Portuguese language but of a plurality of countries, peoples and languages. The diversity of the Portuguese languages – and cultures – that resulted from profound linguistic and cultural transformations in Africa and Brazil needs to be recognized. Only then is it possible to avoid the unconscious neo-colonial idea that sharing a language implies sharing a culture. Given that language is a privileged place for identity formation, Portuguese has to be seen as a pluralized language (Lourenço 1999b: 121).

Developing on earlier chapters, my aim here is to offer a comparative study of the national and trans-national films that, by choosing immigrant main characters, engage with the relation between language and culture, and thus with the construction of post-colonial lusophone identities. I will part from the factual diversity of the Portuguese languages – their diverse accents and grammars – and consider the more profound changes it suffered – in the different Creole languages with Portuguese as its matrix – in order to survey if the films with migrating protagonists do likewise.

So far, few Portuguese filmmakers have dedicated national feature films to immigrant main characters: Pedro Costa, author of *Casa de Lava/Down to Earth*, 1994 (set mostly on the Cape Verdean *Ilha de Fogo*) and of the *Fontainhas* trilogy – *Bones*, 1997, *No Quarto da Vanda/In Vanda's Room*, 2000, *Juventude em Marcha/Colossal Youth*, 2006 – about the lives of Cape Verdean immigrants and their descendants in the Lisbon slum *Fontainhas*; Teresa Villaverde, whose interest in the future of adolescents made her choose an African descendant as one of the three main characters in *The Mutants* (1998) – analysed earlier in the book – (and, exceptionally, a young Russian woman in *Transe* 2006); and Leonel Vieira who offers a mainstream portrait

---

to say that the Portuguese language, the language that speaks me before I learn to speak, and, more importantly, that becomes not only a living reality through me but the *only* reality – in other words: the language that I use to invent myself, Fernando Pessoa, this language is my country.')

of the second generation of Angolan immigrants in *Zona J/J Zone* (1998). Additionally, there is a small number of Luso-African and Luso-Brazilian co-productions on the subject of migration. Directed by filmmakers of diverse backgrounds, they tell stories about Brazilians and Africans who migrate to Europe. The trans-national films include the already discussed *Foreign Land* (Walter Salles and Daniela Thomas 1995), *Dribbling Fate* (Fernando Vendrell 1998) and *My Voice* (Flora Gomes 2002), as well as *Tudo isto é Fado/Fado Blues* (Luís Galvão Teles 2003) and *Um Tiro no Escuro/A Shot in the Dark* (Leonel Vieira 2005).

In the following I will ask if these films replicate the neo-colonial discourse on cultural and linguistic homogeneity and harmony or if they engage with the existence and potential conflicts that derive from diversity. This concluding chapter offers for the first time a comparison between the different production modes, and my question will therefore extend on their influence on the films' take on lusophony.

Portuguese cinema

Pedro Costa is one of the most internationally recognized Portuguese filmmakers of his generation. The discourses on lusophony in his films are at once varied, paradoxical and intriguing. His first film on the subject, *Down to Earth*, engages with Leão (Isaach de Bankolé), a Cape Verdean construction worker, who is accompanied by a Portuguese nurse, Mariana (Inês Medeiros), back to his island after he falls into a coma after a failed suicide attempt. Although money was sent to pay for his return, nobody takes an interest in him when he arrives, and Mariana invests some time and effort to discover his relatives and his relationship with a Portuguese woman, Edith (Edith Scob).

This other Portuguese woman's story indicates a bigger picture of transcultural relationships since she also came to the island as the wife of a political prisoner who was sent to the legendary concentration camp Tarrafal during the dictatorship. Jacques Lemière (101) stresses that Pedro Costa is, thus, 'o primeiro a pôr em cena uma figura e um local até então ausentes do cinema português de ficção'[164]: the migrant worker and the prisoner camp from colonial times.

The Cape Verdean Creole is an important element in the cultural encounters in this highly visual and elliptic narrative. Like other Creole languages, Creole with Portuguese as its base is a result of linguistic encounters during colonization. From a grammatical point of view it is a differentiated and autonomous language, which, once it was formed, became the symbol of Guinea Bissau's and Cape Verde's identity.[165] After the separation of the two countries in 1980, it was recognized as a written language in Cape Verde in 1998 and, as mentioned earlier, there are initiatives to declare it the country's only official language.

In *Down to Earth* Creole is a means to manifest Mariana's struggle in dealing with what is seen to be a different, even strange, culture, as well as her changing relationship with it. She seems to understand everything said in Creole when she arrives, but her difficulties in getting a deeper comprehension of Cape Verdean culture is perceptible in her oscillating command of its language. There is no doubt that Cape Verdean culture and language remember only on the surface its Portuguese roots and lexica.

Notwithstanding her initial comprehension, when circumstances become more complex, especially Leon's relationship with other characters, Mariana suddenly needs an interpreter. Interpretation is easily provided since almost everybody is bilingual and thus always a step ahead of Mariana. She also demands that the Portuguese characters speak to her in her mother tongue, especially Edith, whose adaptation to Creole culture and language and her role as Leão's lover Mariana does not understand in the beginning. When she has a passionate encounter with Edith's nameless son (Pedro Hestnes), who was born on the island and speaks only Creole, Mariana asks him to speak to her in the native tongue, enjoying the erotic connotation of its strangeness. By and large, Mariana takes up a rather aggressive stance towards Cape Verdean culture and expresses her resentment also by attacking its language: during a fight with Leão she denigrates him by saying that she

---

[164] ('the first to stage a character and a place, which had been absent from Portuguese fiction film')
[165] See for further information on the formation of Creole with Portuguese as its base: Web: http://cvc.instituto-camoes.pt/hlp/geografia/crioulosdebaseport.html.

understands his cowardly language.

The film depicts cultural conflicts between Mariana and the Cape Verdeans, or between her and the Portuguese characters that live on the island, as conflicts of language. It demonstrates the main character's initial unwillingness to integrate and suggests that she becomes more and more enchanted with the people's crude emotions that are, in fact, not unlike her own. The open ending hints at the possibility that she will remain on the island and become a part of its culture, like Edith and her nameless son, who, by only speaking Creole, ignore (or have, at least, forgotten) their Portuguese origin.

Portuguese and Creole cultures are both apprehended in their ambivalence. Mariana is overconfident (especially in her profession as a nurse), 'paternalistic and intrusive, but also engaging and caring. The African characters are depicted with more stereotypical features that indicate a gender divide – on the one hand complicity among the hard working women, and on the other the lack of responsibility by the men who are absent, seductive and violent. However, they all share the desire to migrate.

But the Fire Island and its extreme and arid nature is also a metaphor for a more complex, even though mysterious and – especially from Mariana's European perspective – incomprehensive culture, whose most striking characteristics challenge binary oppositions: there is a close relationship between death and desire, but also a passive, gloomy, yet relaxed and festive attitude towards life.

Although conscientious of the cultural diversity that wipes out the lusophone imaginary of a unified culture and language, *Down to Earth* recognizes the desire of the Portuguese characters to submerge in another 'strange and initially hostile culture, in what might seem to be their luso-tropical predisposition. But this occurs with a twist better described with another concept: *cafrealização*. It has been used to stigmatize the adaptation of the Portuguese to African values, institutions and means of production. Sousa Santos 2001: 54) explains: 'é uma designação oitocentista utilizada para caracterizar de uma maneira estigmatizante os Portugueses que, sobretudo na África Oriental, se desvinculavam da sua cultura e do seu estatuto civilizado para adoptarem os modos de viver e pensar dos cafres, os negros agora transformados em primitivos e selvagens'[166]. Costa obviously gives the concept a positive meaning.

Mariana and Edith – even though much earlier – are aware that they are getting lost in the new surroundings. In Edith's case it is a conscious choice of abandoning culture through choice of place and language and her psychological motivation is to forget the repressive past that made her loose her husband. Mariana's motives are left unspoken and her resistance to Creole culture turns only slowly into a sense of liberation from European conventions and pressures.[167]

One of the last shots shows Leão and Edith together in the house of lava (of the original title in Portuguese), suggesting that there is a shared place by based on reciprocal feelings, that is to say, a possibility for a communion in the daunting African environment. This communion is again based on language, but, this time, on Creole, which has both an African and a Portuguese matrix. Costa's Portuguese characters, nonetheless, escape both luso-tropicalism and lusophony, either by fighting against or by embracing the possibility to engage with the Other and adapt to their culture.

As analyzed in greater detail in the chapter on the adolescents as allegory, *Bones* follows up on *Down to Earth*'s gender divide within African culture, but offers an almost opposite perspective on intercultural communication due to the change of location: Pedro Costa now looks at the second generation of Cape Verdean immigrants in Lisbon who live in the shanty town *Fontainhas*, constructed in the 1970s by the first migrants.

Even though all the characters now speak Portuguese, the cultural and, particularly, economic barriers between the former colonizer and the descendants of the migrants from the colonies or elsewhere are here impossible to be overcome. There is no such thing as the house of lava, that is, a metaphoric but also linguistic space in which the two cultures meet and unite. In fact,

---

[166] ('It is a designation from the eighteenth century used to stigmatise the Portuguese who abandoned, mainly in West Africa, their own culture and civilised status in order to adapt to the ways of living and thinking of the Kaffirs and black Africans, transforming themselves into primitives and savages.')

[167] Jonathan Rosenbaum (2009: 127 and 130) compares Marina's motivation to stay on the island with Pedro Costas' who has commented repeatedly on the importance of his Cape Verdean experience for his personal and professional life.

only the nurse is capable of moving freely between the two separate worlds that cannot be bridged by the Portuguese language.

Language plays again a complex role. There is a generalized lack of communication and the characters hardly ever speak. The Creole community is bilingual, but Tina, Clotilde and the Father speak exclusively Portuguese, even among themselves. There are actually only two characters that express themselves in Creole: Clotilde's husband, who is portrayed as a stereotypical macho, her son and a friend of her husband. Even though Creole neither draws a line nor unifies the Portuguese and Cape Verdean characters as it does in *Down to Earth*, it expresses the alienation between the men and women of the migrant community. Portuguese is nothing more than a means of communication, with no inter-subjective potential, while Creole separates because of its association with chauvinist attitudes. Language is incapable of establishing culture in a world that João Miguel Fernandes Jorge has described as 'restos de civilização'[168].

The closure of the film demarcates the shift from a discussion of the social relationship between former colonizers and colonized, paramount in *Down to Earth*, to a demonstration of the gendered relationship within the community. Instead of an intercultural liaison that results from the adaptation to a language that draws as much on Africa as on Portugal, *Bones* presents an inter-communal sisterhood that shuts doors and windows to both Cape Verdean men and Portuguese society, in spite of the fact that they speak the same languages.

In Vanda's Room, the second part of the *Fontainha's* Trilogy, enters radically into Vanda Duarte's, the actress of Clotilde, life with the intention to show a less melancholic but cruder picture of the second generation depicted in *Bones*. The film accompanies Vanda's drug habit, her job (selling groceries from door to door), her conversations with friends, as well as other drug users and the destruction of their neighbourhood *Fontainhas*, which is being demolished so as to give space to social housing apartment blocks. Jacques Rancière (2009: 54) remarks that Costa renounced from this film onwards 'a explorer a miséria como objecto de ficção. Instalou-se nesses lugares para aí

---

[168] ('civilization's remains')

ver viver os seus habitants, ouvir-lhes a palavra, apreender-lhes segredo'.[169]

The movie was filmed with a digital camera in long static, beautiful and dense shots whose scarce lighting is used to create interiors reminiscent of seventeenth- and eighteenth-century paintings. They allow the spectator a long reflection on the complex and unexpectedly beautiful details of this marginal world. Inscribed in the romantic tradition, it gives voice to the underdogs of Portuguese society whose unhappy lives are given 170 minutes of time and space, bestowing dignity and meaning to their troubles, drug addiction and social exclusion that they are usually denied.

In contrast to both *Down to Earth* and *Bones*, *In Vanda's Room* does not have a gendered discourse. Both men and women suffer from marginalization, use or sell drugs, look for places to stay or tell their sad stories. The fact that Vanda is the daughter of immigrants is not even directly acknowledged; on the contrary, she identifies with Portugal's language and culture and questions certain features of its society as being typical of her country. Language features only in the background, but when it comes to the fore, at one specific point, it puts forward a powerful argument on the reasons for the second generation's marginal lives.

There is exactly one scene in which the African heritage is strongly remembered. While Vanda's mother, Lena Duarte, and sister, Zita Duarte, are skinning a rabbit in the yard, we hear a man's voice in off lecturing Vanda in Creole. He questions her lack of respect and tells her that in Cape Verde she would have received a lesson for her behaviour, because only in Portugal there was no justice and everyone did as they liked. A cut to Vanda's room shows her sitting on her bed, preparing to smoke crack. The voice goes on questioning her lifestyle – she spends all day in bed and does not work. Another cut shows in a medium close up part of the man's body – an arm, his violin and part of his dress – and his voice tells Vanda about the hardships on his Cape Verdean island where men and women get up at three o'clock in the morning and work all day. The man leaves by saying that it was useless to talk to her and the film cuts back to Vanda who goes on smoking, mumbling that he must have been mistaken in the door.

---

[169] ('to explore misery as a fictional subject matter. He settled in these places to see how its inhabitants live, hear what they have to say, capture their secrets.')

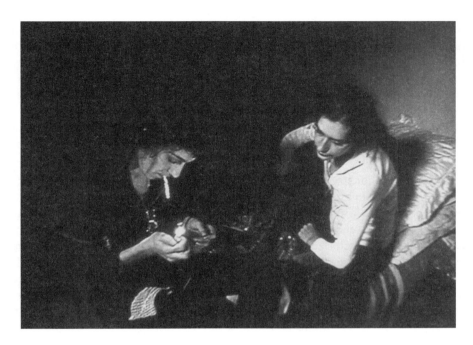

Figure 17: Zita and Vanda Duarte in *Vanda's Room* (Courtesy Pedro Costa)

It is not clear if the man is her father or a father figure, but he introduces a moral judgment that is absent in the rest of the film where the drug habit is a natural gesture – like eating, drinking, working and talking – and its users complex, ill and unhappy creatures. Dissimilar to the usage of Creole in *Bones*, *In Vanda's Room* suggests, not unlike *Down to Earth*, that Creole culture is, literally, more down to earth and a residue of popular wisdom that contrasts with the superficial and, in actual fact, destructive modern Portuguese culture. In the earlier film the lesson is learned by the Portuguese character Mariana that becomes permeable to this culture, while the second-generation character Vanda seems to ignore it. The argument here is that the adaptation process to European culture and language impoverishes and marginalizes the African descendants, while Creole culture remains, albeit its strange surface, not only more open but also more enriching. The fact that the second generation does understand but not answer in Creole is another means of expressing their alienation.

Colossal Youth follows up on this idea through its main character, Ventura, a first generation immigrant. The Creole language features strongly in the film and expands on the perspective that Cape Verde's language and culture are a reservoir of traditional values and virtues. It develops the thought already present in *Bones* and *In Vanda's Room* that the values represented by this simple man are endangered by the destruction of the neighborhood *Fontainhas*. Breaking the boundaries between documentary and fiction even further than *In Vanda's Room*, *Bones* or *Down to Earth*, the film's hybrid structure reconstructs without temporal or spatial linearity the past and present life of an immigrant from the times of the first influx in the 1960s.

Ventura was a construction worker and helped to build one of the most important cultural institutions in Portugal, the Calouste Gulbenkian Foundation, which hosts a museum, a library and a centre for the arts, as well as other institutions related to the country's scientific and artistic development. He is mainly characterized by his relationships to young characters that he considers his children. It is again not evident if these young people – including Vanda – who he visits or talks to are (all) his biological offspring or if he is a father figure to them, but they construct Ventura as a patriarchal reference that represents the Cape Verdean value system of hard work, solidarity and dignity. However, there is a hint at gender conflict at the beginning of the film, when a woman – presumably his wife – throws his furniture out of the window and sets off his rootless wandering.

The film does not have a story but aims to paint a dignifying portrait of this immigrant who dedicated his life to the development of Portugal. Instead of presenting a plot on Ventura's social contacts, past experiences and misfortunes, *Colossal Youth* is a massive visual experience that turns the Creole worker into a living monument. Notwithstanding the fact that the title refers to a slogan of the Cape Verdean liberation movement against colonialism, and the playing of a political song in Creole, 'Labanta Braço', in one of the scenes, the film's politics are linguistic and visual.

Critics have celebrated the film's aesthetic as outstanding, arguing that its choice of angles, long shots and lightning challenge conventional perception (see Gardnier; Rancière). Indeed, Costa creates an atmosphere in which the shots of Ventura and the other characters resemble masterpieces from the history of European Art – a valorization of spaces and characters that becomes even more obvious when the main character visits his former work place, the Gulbenkian Museum of Art.

The paintings in exhibition suggest a close comparison between Ventura and the honoraries or renowned characters depicted by Rubens and Rembrandt, as well as between the artist's canvases and the filmmaker's iconography. Jacques Rancière (2009: 58) offers an explanation for Costa's aesthetic choices that stress the beauty of the places that his marginal characters inhabit by noting that the sequence is not only a comment on the ingratitude of the museum with regard to the construction worker, but that the film generally tries to recover the richness of his sensual experiences.

Just like *In Vanda's Room*, a marginalized and unspectacular character is given centre stage; only this time we are not confronted with the negative results of migration – a generation without perspective lost in drug consumption – but with the earlier diligent age group and his little rewarded hard work. Nonetheless, Ventura resembles Vanda, since he is caught within a similar process of deteriorating identity that stems from his condition as immigrant. And, in contrast to the visual celebration of his personality, this occurs on the linguistic level.

Ventura's longing to return to Cape Verde is introduced through a letter written to a loved one on the islands – which had already appeared in *Down to Earth* – and expresses the collective hope to return full of money and with gifts. The letter merges, actually, two sources: a letter written from a Nazi concentration camp by the French poet Robert Desnot to his wife and the letter of an immigrant. It thus establishes not only a relationship between Leão and Ventura, but also a political context that juxtaposes resistance against political repression and the migrant's situation.

The letter is repeated various times like a *leitmotif* and is the most evident sign of how language reveals that his identity is adrift. When the letter is composed for a friend while they are playing cards, it is first recited by Ventura in Creole and then repeated in Portuguese. It is then cited another five times – three of them in Portuguese – as though the speaker would try to overcome the distance created by the new life and language through repetition, at the same time as it manifests the impossibility to do so. While in my understanding the letter is used to (unsuccessfully) resist the ambivalences of migration, other authors interpret it as Ventura's artistic accomplishment, his poem (see Rancière 2009: 59, Guerreiro 2009: 204).

Throughout the film, the choice of language indicates whether the character belongs or not to Portuguese society. Vanda, who is now a mother and drug free (with the help of Methadone), tells the story of the birth of her child in both Portuguese and Creole, depending on whether she addresses Ventura or is relating her dialogue with the Portuguese nurses. She is more rooted – due to her new home, working husband and child – and seems more capable of dealing with her double identity as both Portuguese citizen and Cape Verde-an descendant. Ventura, on the other hand, speaks mainly Creole and only the longing letter reminds us of his plurilingualism. He is rather in limbo, an in-between, and his choice of Creole expresses that he does not see himself belonging to the two cultures as Vanda does.

Figure 18: Ventura and André Semedo in *Colossal Youth* (Courtesy Pedro Costa)

Portuguese culture is again exclusive and mainly associated with the destruc-tive modernization of the neighbourhood and the construction of clean and anonymous apartment blocks that extinguish the Cape Verdean culture and community life cultivated by Ventura. The strongest metaphor for this loss is the new empty apartment in which Ventura lives without any relatives, given that his supposed children have apartments of their own, and, like Vanda, are coping better with this change.

The film's aesthetic strategies try to counterbalance Ventura's limbo by attributing to him and his generation the place that they deserve, that is, within the portray gallery of distinguished personalities. Because of this feature – the integration of the worker into a bourgeois aesthetic sense of high art –, the filmmaker has been accused of elitism (Krivochein 2008). Jacques Rancière (2009: 55) believes that this argument has no point, since Costa's aesthetic aims for a questioning of high and low and other binary oppositions, developing instead a poetic based on exchanges, correspondences and dislocations.

Colossal Youth is, indeed, of a striking beauty that attributes to Ventura an unquestionable dignity. It goes beyond the believe in cultural harmony that can be encountered at the end of *Down to Earth*, but is – as *Bones* and *In Vanda's Room* equally suggest – only possible on African soil. In contrast to *Bones*, where the women reject as much the Portuguese nurse as the men from their own community, the film accepts ambivalence and does not try to resolve Ventura's paradoxical situation. Besides using visual references that either assimilate the Cape Verdean migrant partly into the European iconographic system or depict the shanty town partially according to its aesthetic principles, it also points linguistically at the main character's difficulties to integrate and visually at the contribution of the first generation of immigrants to Portuguese society, as well as at the (rather ugly) destruction of his home.

The films by Teresa Villaverde (*The Mutants*) and Leonel Vieira (*J Zone*) are equally concerned with the integration of African descendants. Since their immigrants face no linguistic barriers or memories, the filmmakers' concern is to encounter ways to express aesthetically their rejection in Portugal's society. However, the approaches of Villaverde, an acclaimed auteur like Costa, and Vieira, a producer of blockbusters[170], could not be more dif-

---

[170] *Zona J*, a co-production with the private television channel SIC achieved the highest box office takings in the year of its release, 1998. According to the Portuguese Film Institute ICAM (2002: 172) 246,073 spectators saw the film,

ferent.

The Mutants, discussed in depth in the chapter on adolescents as post-colonial allegory, demonstrates that the boy of African descent, Ricardo, is the most vulnerable of the three main characters. Similar to *Bones*, there is no affirmation what so ever of lusophony's mythic idea of a shared place, apart from the fact that all share the same language. The film clearly indicates that within Portugal's post-coloniality racism endangers Luso-Africans even more than the already predisposed adolescents.

J Zone offers a similar discourse in terms of the impossibility of integration of an adolescent of African descent who not only speaks Portuguese as his mother tongue but also holds Portuguese citizenship, but believes naively in another myth: that racial mixture as a solution to racism. The film's protagonist is the eighteen-year-old António (Félix Fontoura), son of hard-working immigrants from Angola who live in an apartment block at Lisbon's outskirts, the J Zone, part of the suburb Chelas. His relationship with Portuguese society is explored through his romance with Carla (Nuria Madruga), a white middle-class girl, and through his involvement with his group of friends, who live from petty theft and are planning a major crime.

Even though António comes from a stable home, his story ends just like Ricardo's in *The Mutants*: with his death. Due to some rather unbelievable plot points – Carla gets pregnant, his father loses his job and gets involved in diamond smuggling to Angola – the boy decides to participate in a jewellery robbery where he is wounded. The film actually presents criminality as the only possible survival strategy for both the first and the second generation of African immigrants. Portuguese society is literally black and white; and this is presented as permanent and unchangeable. It is also suggested that António never really wants to be part of Portuguese society and culture: his room is decorated with posters of Africa and he exalts the continent during a visit to a bookshop with his friends. When he is wounded during the assault, it is clear to him that he does not want to remain in Portugal and he tries to travel with Carla to Angola without taking into consideration that she needs a visa to enter the country of his parents.

---

placing it fourth in the ranking of the ten Portuguese films with the biggest audiences.

The box office success of *J Zone* is easily explained by the film's conventionality, its 'visually attractive' and 'engaging narrative', referred to by the critic Eurico de Barros. Indeed, the film manages to present a demanding topic in an entertaining format, so that the spectator can easily escape the challenge to engage critically with the exclusion of the Luso-Africans. Albeit its denunciation of xenophobia, the closure effortlessly dismisses the second generation as a lost cause and passes on to the unborn third generation that Carla is expecting. The last sequence shows António dying in Carla's arms while she looks symbolically to the horizon, holding her hand over the unborn in her womb. Instead of offering a solution, this rhetoric of positive racial mixture puts forward the luso-tropicalist discourse in a different disguise. Race is seen to be a stronger element of division than language could ever be a form of unification. Portuguese is merely a means of communication that offers no deeper engagement with Portuguese culture and society, hostile against its immigrants because of their skin colour.

Lusophone Co-productions

Analyzed in detail in the chapter on *Foreign Land*, Walter Salles' and Daniela Thomas' film was the first co-production after the agreement was established between Portugal and its former Brazilian colony. More than any other film, it discusses critically the linguistic and cultural ties between Portugal and Brazil, and each character serves the purpose of challenging either lusophony or luso-tropicalism.

Miguel's hatred of the ancient colonizer's backwardness is associated with Brazil's underdevelopment and calls attention as much to the flaws of the shared matrix as to its arrogant offspring. His girlfriend Alex sees less identity than difference, especially in linguistic terms, but pays tribute to the courage of the discoverer Portugal. Loli, an Angolan, is used to develop the idea of diversity in the Portuguese-speaking world. He not only demonstrates the discrepancies between Portugal and Africa, but also between Africa and Brazil. Pedro, a friend of Alex and Miguel, reminds, then again, of the sentimental bonds between Portugal and Brazil, but proofs also that they are not enduring. The antiques dealer Igor, who celebrates cultural intimacy and considers himself as both Portuguese and Brazilian, does so to take advantage of the idea of cultural and linguistic identity and exploit his fellow Brazilian countrymen.

The sympathetic but conventional *Dribbling Fate* by Fernando Vendrell discussed in the chapter on Luso-African co-productions, offers a different discourse on linguistic belonging by revisiting Pedro Costa's idea in *Down to Earth* that the Cape Verde islands are a place where African and European cultures embrace after some resistance. Mané's plurilingualism – he speaks Creole and Portuguese with the same ease and chooses it according to the country he is in – helps him recover the lusophone bonds based on which he comes to peace with his own culture. Since the idea that Portugal is the better place to live (at least for soccer players) is not shattered, he keeps on living the dream of cultural harmony and linguistic unity.

My Voice, the colourful and optimistic musical by Flora Gomes – whose films have been subject to a more detailed analysis in the chapter on Luso-African films – also develops an affirmative discourse on intercultural and linguistic exchange. But it remains concerned with Guinea Bissau's post-colonial social problems and colonial history. It even remembers one of the central figures of anti-colonial resistance in what is now the PALOP, the Cape Verdean Amilcar Cabral. In his earlier films like *The Blue Eyes of Yonta* (1992) or *Tree of Blood* (1996) cultural conflicts were central to the narratives and Creole the only language spoken. Gomes' last fiction, in contrast, depicts the encounter between African graciousness and Western music and technology that offers the possibility to overcome out-dated cultural practices, namely, African superstition and European racism. Although the two languages spoken in the film are Creole and French (instead of the official language Portuguese), the main character, the beautiful Vita, speaks the foreign language like her mother tongue and switches between them with ease, demonstrating the same plurilingualism present in *Dribbling fate*.

Portugal's colonial presence in Africa is only shortly recalled by means of an eavesdropping Portuguese cleaner in Paris – a pun on the end of the hegemony of ancient colonizers in general. Vita is presented as a modern African woman who conquers her place in the French and European music market. Neither language nor culture are obstacles or represent boundaries. Everybody understands literally everybody, especially after the cultural problem of superstition is playfully overcome: Vita's boyfriend does not speak but understands Creole and her mother understands but does not speak French. The choice of language and the inoffensive discourse on Afro-European harmony and easy linguistic encounter are designed to gain access to the French market that has a long tradition of absorbing African art house cinema.

Fado Blues, a comedy by Luís Galvão Teles, is, on the other hand, a commercial project that not only lacks *My Voice*'s grace but also shows no sign of being preoccupied with the legacy of colonialism and the contemporary challenges of contemporary post-colonial societies. The film engages, like *Foreign Land*, with three different Portuguese accents. But instead of interrogating difference, it celebrates linguistic identity and attributes to Portugal the leading role in the happy encounter of ex-colonizer and ex-colonies.

All the characters in the film have an allegorical dimension: the Brazilian Leonardo (Danton Mello) who works in a video store in Rio de Janeiro but wants to follow in the footsteps of his idol Reis (João Lagarto), a Portuguese writer of detective stories; the African Amadeu (Ângelo Torres) who lives with Leonardo in Brazil because he wants to make big money by cheating on tourists; Reis's sensual daughter Lia (Ana Cristina de Oliveira) with whom both young men fall in love, but who gives in to the equally white and more romantic Leonardo; and, finally, Reis, the father figure who does not want to assume his role but ends up taking everybody under his wing in the good-hearted theft of a painting that had been stolen from Amadeu's former boss and friend, Salvador (Carlos Santos), and is now worth a fortune. According to another myth popular in the Portuguese-speaking world, all the characters, including Lia, are *malandros*, inoffensive little crooks with a big heart.

The story is as simple as its identity politics: Leonardo and Amadeu leave Brazil because it is a country with no economic perspective. Since they have Reis's address they invade his property and meet Lia who suggests to her father the plan of the perfect robbery. They steal the painting on the night of the finals of the World Cup in which Portugal and Brazil dispute the title. Given the celebratory discourse of the film it is no surprise that they manage to steal the painting – with the important intervention of Reis – Portugal wins the World Cup and all the characters celebrate the Luso-Afro-Brazilian harmony under Portuguese patronage on the streets.

It is important to add that the film is no satire. It is pretty serious in its perspective on Brazil as an economic fiasco and Portugal as the winning team in all instances. While Portugal embraces the other cultures – there is one light comment each to dismiss the factual discrimination of Brazilians and Africans (Leonardo's accent and Amadeu's skin colour) –, it is in fact superior, economically, culturally and even in terms of soccer, which is the most absurd statement of them all.

The wishful thinking of the film, in which all Africans are Portuguese – just like in colonial times – and the Luso-Brazilian love-story is inevitable due to the unconditional Brazilian passion for its matrix, is a perfect example of the delirious Portuguese discourse that Lourenço reproaches (when he speaks about the factual absence of links between Brazil and Portugal and the Portuguese perception of proximity with Africa). This discourse not only ignores reality but, particularly, the linguistic and cultural differences between the three continents involved. While minor cultural and especially economic differences are acknowledged, the Portuguese language is the glue that holds the characters together. Leonardo's admiration of Reis' literary skills, whose name is carefully chosen to remind of Fernando Pessoa's famous heteronym, is just another example of the film's celebration of lusophony.

A Shot in the Dark, Leonel Vieira's second film on migration, also mystifies Portugal's relationship with Brazil, but offers, at the same time, a severe critique of the country itself. The film begins again in Brazil: a young woman, Veronica (Vanessa Mesquita), leaves her four-month-old daughter for a moment with a stewardess (Margarida Marinho) on an airport toilet. The woman kidnaps the baby and we reencounter Veronica a year later in Lisbon in a stripper bar where she earns her living. After the shows she goes to the airport, hoping to spot the stewardess and thus to find her child. The film is unclear why she chose the profession: we never know if she was a stripper before or if she chose to work exposing her body – as with many female Brazilian migrants – so that she has a chance to return to Brazil with her daughter.

The melodrama turns into a crime movie when Veronica is fired and Carlos (Filipe Duarte), the bar's bodyguard takes her side and has to leave as well. His brother (Ivo Canelas) is a criminal who has just been released from prison and they end up forming a gang that robs banks. As the police are hunting them down, the detective (Joaquim de Almeida) who is working on the case turns out to be the husband of the stewardess who kidnapped the baby, finally spotted by Veronica at the airport. The suspense reaches its climax when the gang members shoot each other during the last robbery, which Veronica uses to mislead the detective in order to get her daughter back. In the final twist, the detective reaches the airport just before boarding, recovers the child, recognizes his wrongdoings and returns the girl. Veronica can finally leave with her daughter for Brazil.

A Shot in the Dark develops similar to *Fado Blues* a stereotyped and strongly gendered idea of both Brazil and Portugal. But the roles are now inverted: the Brazilian character is sensual (there are many scenes of Veronica stripping, taking a bath or having sex with Carlos), while the Portuguese are sterile, immoral and self-destructive (the stewardess and the detective lost their child and steal another one, the detective tries to use his position in order to conceal his wife's crime, and the gangsters are not only ignorant machos, but also incompetent and end up killing one another).

Whereas the comedy unites light-heartedly little crooks from three continents, *A Shot in the Dark* underlines (similar to *Foreign Land*) the dark side of migration to Portugal. The cultural proximity suggested by the common language is questioned: literally, when Veronica's accent is imitated by Carlos' brother and the other gangster (Miguel Borges), and indirectly when she is exploited by the stewardess and later by the bar owner who demands 5,000 Euros in return for her passport. Although the film is submerged in platitudes, it has a point when it suggests that Brazilians are regarded with envy (by women) or aggressive desire (by men). In contrast to *Fado Blues, A Shot in the Dark* also hints at the fact that the idea of economic and moral superiority expressed by the detective ('Maria is much better off with us than with a stripper') is an unconscious cover-up for deep feelings of resentment.

Conclusion

The discourse on lusophony is of Portuguese origin and aims to guarantee Portugal a place within the world outside its small post-colonial territory. One of the conclusions that can be drawn from the films analyzed in this chapter is that this one-sided discourse resists incorporation when the topic is migration. None of the national films under analysis considers language a unifying factor, and the majority of Luso-Brazilian films shares this perspective. Only the two Luso-African films (*Dribbling Fate* and *My Voice*), and one Luso-Brazilian production (*Fado Blues*) believe in cultural bonds and conflict free plurilingual communication, being that the films produced with the PALOP are also aware of cultural difference. Thus, only three out of the eleven films on migration suggest that African and Brazilian immigrants have a chance to become a part of Portugal's society.

Indifferent to their nationality, ideas or aesthetics (authorial films or blockbusters), the majority of the filmmakers of this study consent that their migrating characters (both first and second generation) are not welcomed and that they are either marginalized or feel alienated. In some cases migration to Portugal (or being a descendant from migrants) is actually fatal (*The Mutants*, *J Zone* and *Foreign Land*). While all Portuguese productions seem to agree that language is neither an obstacle nor of help, the reasons for exclusion and alienation vary. They are found in the loss of traditional values and ways of living (*In Vanda's Room*, *Colossal Youth*), in racism (*The Mutants*, *J Zone*) or in the machismo in the Cape Verdean community (*Bones*).

Pedro Costa presents varying perspectives on the impact of language on the intercultural relationships. In *Down to Earth* he shows that the Portuguese characters, in sharp contrast to his Cape Verdean characters, are capable of adapting, albeit initial resistance, to a different language and culture. Plurilingualism, on the other hand, is no guarantee for being part of a culture. It is used to express female discrimination and marginalization within the same culture (*Bones*), or estrangement from once roots (*In Vanda's Room*). Only in the last film is it explored in its ambivalence and serves as much as a sign for adaptation as for alienation from one's primary culture (Vanda and Ventura in *Colossal Youth*).

The Luso-African productions, shot by a Portuguese filmmaker and by an internationally acclaimed African director from Guinea Bissau, display, on the contrary, how the European languages and the contact with its cultures empower their characters. Due to intercultural exchange and their plurilingualist skills they become able to enjoy their respective cultures more fully. The Luso-Brazilian productions are less optimistic: only the comedy, directed by a Portuguese filmmaker, believes in harmonious trans-national encounters, while the other two films – directed by a Portuguese and a Brazilian director respectively – have a much more pessimistic and perhaps more realistic take on migration.

Interestingly, the Luso-Brazilian co-productions all deal with crimes, echoing either playfully or with a dark tone the shared colonial history and its abuses. Only once are the different cultures and languages portrayed as being compatible and the migrant characters successful in striving for a better life in Portugal (*Fado Blues*). Linguistic and cultural differences are either mentioned (*A Shot in the Dark*) or explored (*Foreign Land*), but always shatter lusophony's dream of a shared cultural history by indicating a deep divide between Africa, Brazil and Portugal.

The trans-national production mode is, however, no guarantee for a critical approach towards the complex bonds and historical relationships between Portugal and its ex-colonies that lead to migration from Africa and Brazil. Despite the wide range of perspectives on lusophony and the overriding critical stance, many films still look for an all-embracing identity and – one might guess – box-office success. Some are aware of diversity, but take rescue with stereotypes. The Portuguese productions are, then again, almost too convinced about difference and exclusion. In conclusion, one trans-national production and two national productions – *Foreign Land*, *The Mutants* and *Colossal Youth* – are the finest examples of the desire to distinguish between language and culture and thus come to terms with the burden of lusophony.

Works cited

Anderson, Benedict. *Imagined Communities: Reflections on the Origins and Spread of Nationalism*. London: Verso, 1983.

Andrade-Watkins, Claire. 'Portuguese African Cinema: Historical and Contemporary Perspectives – 1969 to 1993'. *Research in African Literature* 26.3 (1995): 134–50.

Andrade-Watkins, Claire. 'Le Cinema et la Culture au Cap Verte et en Guinée-Bissau'. *CinemAction* 106 (2003): 148–55.

Avellar, José Carlos. 'Brasil: para un espectador desatento/Brésil: à l'attention d'un spectateur inattentive'. *Cinémas d'Amerique latine* 5 (1997): 5–16.

Avellar, José Carlos. 'Pai, país, mãe, patria'. *Cinemais* 33 (2003): 55–86.

Azevedo, Cândido de. *A Censura de Salazar e Marcelo Caetano*. Lisboa: Caminho, 1999.

Baecque, Antoine de, and Jacques Parsi. *Conversas com Manoel de Oliveira*. Lisbon: Campo das Letras, 1999.

Balczuweit, Ronald. 'Le Soulier de Satin de Manoel de Oliveira'. *O Cinema Português através dos Seus Filmes*. Ed. Carolin Overhoff Ferreira. Porto: Campo das Letras, 2007.

Barthes, Roland. *S/Z*. Paris: Seuil, 1970.

Bauman, Zygmunt. 'From Pilgrim to Tourist – or a Short History of Identity'. *Questions of Cultural Identity*. Eds. Stuart Hall and Paul du Gay. London: Sage Publications, 1996. 18–36.

Benjamin, Jessica. 'Recognition and Destruction. An Outline of Intersubjectivity'. *Like Subjects, Love Objects: Essays on Recognition and Sexual Difference*. New Haven: Yale University Press, 1995. and Web 15 Sept. 2003. www.psychematters.com/papers/benjamin.htm.

Bernardet, Jean-Claude. '*Carlota Joaquina* e o Cinema Brasileiro'. *Imagens* 5 (1996): 85–91.

Bloom, Harold. *The Western Canon: The Books and Schools of the Ages*. New York: Harcourt Brace, 1994.

Boaventura, Maria Eugenia. *A Vanguarda Antropofágica*, São Paulo: Ática, 1985.

Botelho, João. 'João Botelho'. *A Guerra Colonial - Realidade e Ficção*. Ed. Rui De Azevedo Teixeira. Lisbon: Editorial Notícia, 2001. 493–5.

Botelho, João. 'Si la mémoire existe'. *Cahiers du Cinema* 393 (1987): 20–3.

Boxer, Charles. *Race Relations in the Portuguese Colonial Empire*. Oxford: Clarendon Press, 1963.

Brandlmeier, Thomas. *Manoel de Oliveira und das Groteske Melodram*. Berlin: Verbrecher Verlag, 2010.

Brasil, Luiz Antônio de Assis. *Um Quarto de Légua em Quadro*. Porto Alegre: Movimento, 1997.

Brancato, Sandra M. L. 'Aproximação Brasil/Portugal em 1953: reflexos na Espanha'. *Portugal-Brasil no século XX. Sociedade, Cultura e Ideologia*. Eds. Christiane Marques Szesz, Maria Manuela Tavares Ribeiro, Sandra Maria Lubisco Brancato, Renato Lopes Leite, Artur Cesar Isaia. Bauru: Editora da Universidade do Sagrado Coração, 2003. 443–53.

Briesemeister, Dietrich. 'José Cardoso Pires – Schriftsteller der Gemarkung Portugals'. *Portugiesische Literatur*. Ed. Henry Thorau. Frankfurt am Main: Suhrkamp, 1997. 377–406.

Bueno, Eduardo. 'Como era gostoso Hans Staden: um livro para devorar'. In Hans Staden. *Duas viagens ao Brasil*. Porto Alegre: L&PM Pocket, 2008. 7–13.

Butler, Judith. *Bodies that Matter*. London/New York: Routledge, 1993.

Cabral, Amílcar. *Unity and Struggle – Speeches and Writings*. New York/London: Monthly Review Press, 1979.

Cabral, Eunice. *José Cardoso Pires – Representações do Mundo Social na Ficção*. Lisbon: Edições Cosmos, 1999.

Caldas, Álvaro. *Balé da Utopia*. Rio de Janeiro, Garamond, 2006.

Camões, Luís de. *Os Lusíadas*. Lisbon, CentraLivros, 1997.

Castells, Manuel. *The Power of Identity*. Oxford: Blackwell, 1997.

Castro, Eduardo Viveiros de. 'Os pronomes cosmológicos e o perspectivismo ameríndio'. *MANA: Estudos de Antropologia Social* 2.2 (1996): 115–44.

Chevrie, Marc. 'Entre-Temps'. *Cahiers du Cinema* 393 (1987) 16–19.

Cinemateca Nacional da República Popular de Angola. *10 anos cinema angolano: filmografia 1975-1985*. Luanda: Cinemateca Nacional, 1985.

Cinemateca Nacional da República Popular de Angola. *Cinema angolano: um passado a merecer melhor presente*. Luanda: Cinemateca Nacional, 1986.

Cinemateca Portuguesa, ed. *Cinema Angolano*. Lisbon: Cinemateca Portuguesa, 1987.

Cinemateca Portuguesa, ed. *Cinemas de África*. Lisbon: Cinemateca Portuguesa, 1995.

Coelho, Eduardo Prado. 'O Círculo dos Círculos'. *O Delfim*. José Cardoso Pires. Lisbon: Publicações Dom Quixote, 2002. 9–29.

Costa, João Bénard da. *Histórias do Cinema*. Lisbon: Imprensa Nacional – Casa da Moeda, 1991.

Costa, José Manuel. 'Uma Abelha na Chuva'. *Textos Cinemateca Portuguesa* 60 (1999): 209–11.

Couto, Déjanirah; Enders, Armelle; Léonard, Yves. 'Lusotropicalisme: Du Mythe à l'Objet de Recherche'. *Lusotopie*, (1997): 195–7.

Cruchinho, Fausto. 'Os passados e os futuros do Cinema Novo – O cinema na polémica do tempo'. *Estudos do Século XX*, 1 (2001): 215–40.

Cruchinho, Fausto. *Fernando Lopes - Uma Mística do Olhar*. Porto: Mimesis, 2002.

Cruchinho, Fausto. *O Desejo Amoroso em Os Canibais de Manoel de Oliveira*. Porto: Mimesis, 2003.

Cruz, Liberto. *José Cardoso Pires - Análise Crítica e Selecção de Textos*. Lisbon: Arcádia, 1972.

Diawara, Manthia. *African Cinema: politics and culture*. Bloomington: Indiana University Press, 1992.

Diop, Samba. *African Francophone Cinema*, Los Angeles: University Press of the South, 2004.

Duarte, Fernando. 'Uma Abelha na Chuva de Fernando Lopes'. *Celulóide*, 173 (1972): 1–5.

Duarte, Fernando. 'Breve história do cinema moçambicano'. *Celuloide* 283–4 (1979): 307–10.

Eça de Queirós, José Maria. *Alves & Cia*. São Paulo: Editora Ática, 1998.

Elena, Alberto. 'Terra Estrangeira'. *The Cinema of Latin America*. Eds. Alberto Elena and Marina Díaz López. London: Wallflower, 2003. 211–20.

Everett, Wendy. 'Timetravel and European film'. *European Identity in Cinema*. Ed. Wendy Everett. Exeter: Intellect, 1996.

Ewald Filho, Rubens. *ISTOÉ, O Judeu – Fita e Revista*, edição n° 1578, 1999.

Fanon, Franz. *The Wretched of the Earth*. London: Penguin, 2001.

Faria, António. 'Ficção e Guerra Colonial: um filme'. *A Guerra Colonial - Realidade e Ficção*. Ed. Rui de Azevedo Teixeira. Lisbon: Editorial Notícia, 2001. 481–6.

Feldman-Bianco, Bela. 'Portugueses no Brasil, brasileiros em Portugal. Antigas rotas, novos trânsitos e as construções de semlhanças e diferenças culturais'. *Entre Ser e Estar – Raizes, Percursos e Discursos da Identidade*. Eds. Maria Irene Ramalho and António Sousa Ribeirio. Porto: Edições Afrontamento, 2001. 143–84.

Feldman-Bianco, Bela. 'Entre a 'fortaleza' da Europa e os laços afetivos da 'irmandade' luso-brasileira: um drama familiar em um só ato'. *Trânsitos coloniais: diálogos críticos luso-brasileiros*. In Cristina Bastos, Miguel Vale de Almeida, Bela Feldman-Bianco. Lisbon: Imprensa de Ciências Sociais, 2002. 385–415.

Ferreira, Carolin Overhoff. 'The adolescent as post-colonial allegory: Strategies of inter-subjectivity in Portuguese films of the 1990s'. *Camera Obscura* 59.20.2 (2005): 34–71.

Ferreira, Carolin Overhoff. 'Decolonizing the Mind? The Representation of the African Colonial War in Portuguese Cinema'. *Studies in European Cinema,* 2.3 (2005): 227–40.

Ferreira, Carolin Overhoff. 'Heterodox/Paradox : The Representation of the 'Fifth Empire' in Manoel de Oliveira's Cinema'. *Dekalog – On Manoel de Oliveira*. Ed. Carolin Overhoff Ferreira London: Wallflower Press, 2008. 60–88.

Ferreira, Carolin Overhoff. 'Pouco canónicas – As adaptações de Fernando Lopes: *Uma Abelha na Chuva* (1972) e *O Delfim* (2001)'. *Narrativas em Metamorfose: Abordagens Interdisciplinares*. Eds. Irene Blayer, Francisco Cota Fagundes. Cathedral Publicações: Cuiabá, 2009. 319–38.

Ferreira, Carolin Overhoff. 'Os Descobrimentos do Paradoxo: A Expansão Europeia nos Filmes de Manoel de Oliveira'. *Manoel de Oliveira: Uma Presença*. Ed. Renata Junqueira. São Paulo, Editora Perspectivas, 2010. 117-145.

Ferreira, Carolin Overhoff. 'Portugal, Europa e o mundo: condição humana e geopolítica na filmografia de Manoel de Oliveira'. *Revista dos Estudos Portugueses* 30.43 (2010): 109–40.

Ferreira, Carolin Overhoff . 'Non-inscription and Dictatorship in Non-canonical Adaptations – *A Bee in the Rain* (1972) and *The Daupin* (2001) by Fernando Lopes'. *Adaptation* 3.2 (2010): 112–31.

Ferreira, Carolin Overhoff. 'Identities Adrift: Lusophony and Migration in National and Trans-national Lusophone Film'. *Polyglot Cinema*. Ed. Verena Berger and Miya Komori. Berlin/München/Wien/Zürich/London: LIT Verlag, 2010. 173–92.

Ferreira de Castro, José Maria. *A Selva*. Lisbon: Guimarães Editores.

Fresnot, Alain. *Alain Fresnot – Um Cineasta Sem Alma*. São Paulo: Imprensa Oficial do Estado de São Paulo, 2006.

Freyre, Gilberto. Aventura e Rotina: Sugestões de uma Viagem à Procura das Constantes Portuguesas de Caráter e Ação. Lisbon: Livros do Brasil, n.d.

Gardies, André. Cinema d'Afrique Noire Francophone: l'Espace-miroir. Paris: L'Harmattan, 1989.

Gil, José. *Portugal, Hoje – O Medo de Existir*. Lisbon: Relógio D'Agua, 2004.

Gomes, Paulo Emílio Salles. *Cinema: Trajetória no Subdesenvolvimento*. Rio de Janeiro: Rio de Janeiro, 1980.

Guerreiro, António. 'A Suspensão e a Resistência'. In Ricardo Matos Cabo (ed.). *cem mil cigarros – os filmes de Pedro Costa*. Lisbon: Orfeu Negro, 2009. 203–205.

Gugler, Josef. *African Film: re-imagining a contintent*, Bloomington: Indiana University Press, 2003.

Hall, Stuart. 'Introduction: Who Needs 'Identity'?' In Stuart Hall, Paul du Gay (eds.). *Questions of Cultural Identity*. London: Sage, 1996. 1–17.

Hayward, Susan. *Key Concepts in Cinema Studies*. London/New York: Routledge, 1996.

Heath, Stephen. *Questions of Cinema*. Basingstoke: Macmillan, 1981.

Higbee, Will; Lim, Song Hwee. 'Concepts of transnational cinema: towards a critical transnationalism in film studies'. *Transnational Cinemas* 1.1 (2010): 7–21.

Hjoert, Mette and Scott MacKenzie, eds. *Cinema and Nation*. London/New York: Routledge, 2000.

Hollanda, Sérgio Buarque de. *Raízes do Brasil*. São Paulo: Companhia das Letras, 2007/1947.

ICAM. *Cinema2002*. Lisbon: ICAM, 2002.

Instituto Angolano de Cinema, ed. *1ª Mostra de Cinema Angolano*. Angola: Instituto Angolano de Cinema, 1982.

Kaplan, E. Ann. *Women & Film. Both Sides of the Camera*. London/New York: Routledge, 1988.

Johnson, Randal. *Manoel de Oliveira*. Urbana and Chicago: University of Illinois Press, 2007.

Johnson, Randal (2008). 'Manoel de Oliveira and the Aesthetics of Representation'. *Dekalog2 – On Manoel de Oliveira*. Ed. Carolin Overhoff Ferreira. London: Wallflower Press, 2008. 89–109.

Johnson, Randal. 'Oliveira Político'. *Aspectos do Cinema Português*. Eds. Jorge Cruz, Leandro Mendonça, Paulo Filipe Monteiro, André Queiroz Rio de Janeiro: Universidade Estadual do Rio de Janeiro – SR-3 – Edições LCV, 2009. 23–48.

Júdice, Nuno. 'O lado visível da palavra'. *Arte 7* (1991): 50–1.

Jorge, João Miguel Fernandes Jorge. 'Ossos'. *cem mil cigarros – os filmes de Pedro Costa*. Ed. Ricardo Matos Cabo. Lisbon: Orfeu Negro, 2009. 157–9.

Knopf, Jan. 'Verfremdung'. *Brechts Theorie des Theaters*. Ed. Werner Hecht. Frankfurt am Main: Suhrkamp, 1986. 93–141.

Lemière, Jacques. ''Terra a Terra' O Portugal e o Cabo Verde de Pedro Costa'. *cem mil cigarros – os filmes de Pedro Costa*. Ed. Ricardo Matos Cabo.Lisbon: Orfeu Negro, 2009. 99–111.

Lopes, Denise (2000). 'Terra Estrangeira, 'as cores do desterro' da era Collor'. *Contratempo* 4 (2000): 59-73.

Landes, David. *A Riqueza e a Pobreza das Nações*, Rio de Janeiro: Gradiva, 2002.

Lopes, Óscar; Saraiva, António José. *História da Literatura Portuguesa*. Porto: Porto Editora, 1965.

Lourenço, Eduardo. *O Canto do Signo – Existência e Literatura (1957-1993)*. Lisbon: Editorial Presença, 1993.

Lourenço, Eduardo. *Portugal como Destino seguido de Mitologia da Saudade*, Lisbon: Gradiva, 1999a.

Lourenço, Eduardo. A Nau de Ícaro seguido de Imagem e Miragem da Lusofonia. Lisbon: Gradiva, 1999b.

Magalhães, Isabel Allegro de. 'Carlos de Oliveira'. *História da Literatura Portuguesa. As correntes contemporâneas*, Vol. 7. Eds. Óscar Lopes and Maria de Fátima Marinho. Lisbon: Publicações Alfa, 2002. 331–3.

Marques, José Vieira. Cinema da Figueira da Foz. Lisbon: Associação do Festival Internacional de Cinema da Figueira da Foz, 1996.

Martins, Andrea França. 'Radicações políticas na imagem'. *Cinemais* 5 (1997): 83–97.

Martins, Andrea França. 'Entre o talent e a fome, entre a terra e a errância'. *Cinemais* 32 (2001) 87–98.

Matos-Crus, José de. *O Cais do Olhar: o cinema português de longa metragem e a ficção muda*. Lisbon: Cinemateca Portuguesa, 1999.

Matos-Cruz, José de. 'Cinema Português e a Guerra Colonial'. *A Guerra Colonial - Realidade e Ficção*. Ed. Rui De Azevedo Teixeira. Lisbon: Editorial Notícia, 2001. 487–91.

Matos-Cruz, José de and José Mena Abrantes. *Cinema em Angola*. Luanda: Caxinde Editora, 2002.

Melo, João. de. 'Kolonialkrieg und Befreiungskampf in den portugiesischsprachigen Literaturen'. *Portugiesische Literatur*. Ed. Henry Thorau Frankfurt a.M.: Suhrkamp, 1997. 478–500.

Miranda, Ana. *Desmundo*. São Paulo, Companhia das Letras, 1996.

Moisés, José Álvaro. 'A new policy for Brazilian Cinema'. *The New Brazilian Cinema*. Ed. Lúcia Nagib. London/New York: I B Tauris, 2003.

Monteiro, J.E. 'António de Sousa, Director de "Films Angola"'. *Imagem* 10 (1951): 9.

Morettin, Eduardo. 'Hans Staden: o indivíduo e a História'. *Sinopse* 2.5 (2000): 52–3.

Morley, David and Kevin Robins, Kevin. Spaces of Identity – Global Media, Electronic Landscapes and Cultural Boundaries. London/New York: Routledge, 1995.

Muhana, Adma Fadul, ed. *António Vieira. Apologia das Coisas Profetizadas*. Lisbon: Edições Cotovia, 1994.

Murphy, David and Patrick Williams. *Postcolonial African cinema. Ten directors*. Manchester: Manchester of University Press, 2007.

Nadale, Marcel. *Djalma Limongi Batista – Livre Pensador*. São Paulo: Imprensa Oficial do Estado de São Paulo, 2005.

Nagib, Lúcia. *O Cinema da Retomada*. Editora 34, São Paulo, 2002.

Nagib, Lúcia. 'O eu e o outro antropófago'. *A Utopia no Cinema Brasileiro*. São Paulo: Cosac&Naify, 2006. 93–117.

Naremore, James, eds. *Film Adaptation*. New Brunswick: Rutgers University Press, 2000.

Niang, Sada, ed. *Litterature et Cinema en Afrique Francophone: Ousmane Sembene et Assia Djebar*, Paris: L'Harmattan, 1996.

Oliveira, Carlos de. *Uma Abelha na Chuva*. Lisbon: Livraria Sá da Costa Editora, 2001.

Oricchio, Luiz Zanin. 'Bocage – O Triunfo do Amor'. *Cinema* 2.10, (1997/1998): 25.

Ortiz, Renato. Um Outro Território – Ensaios sobre a Mundialização. São Paulo: Olho D'Agua, 1996.

Parente, André. 'Terra estrangeira'. *Cinemais*, 4 (1997): 195–203.

Parsi, Jacques. *Manoel de Oliveira - Cinéaste portugais XXe siècle*. Paris: Centre Culturel Calouste Gulbenkian, 2000.

Partido Comunista Português, ed. *Cinema Africano: Angola, Mozambique, Guiné, Cabo Verde*. Lisbon: Célula de Cinema do Partido Comunista Português, 1981.

Peixoto, João. 'Imigração e Mercado de trabalho em Portugal: investigação e tendências recentes'. *Revista Migrações* 2 (2008): 19–46.

Pereira, Luís Miguel. '"Uma Abelha na Chuva' A banda sonora'. *Arte 7* (1991): 55–6.

Pessoa, Fernando. 'A minha pátria é a lingua portuguesa'. *Descobrimento – Revista de Cultura* 3 (1931): 409–10.

Pessoa Fernando. *Mensagem*. Lisbon: Parceria António Maria Pereira, 2004.

Piçarra, Maria do Carmo. 'Fernando Lopes – Exorcismo da ditadura'. *Premiere*, 7 (2001): 36.

Pina, Luís de. *História do Cinema Português*. Mem Martins: Publicações Europa-América, 1986.

Pinto, António da Costa. *O Fim do Império Português*, Lisbon: Livros Horizonte, 2001.

Pinto, Margarida Rebelo. 'O Triunfo do Amor'. *Diário Nacional* 13 Jun. 1998: 36.

Pires, José Cardoso. *O Delfim*. Lisbon: Publicações Dom Quixote, 1999.

Prado, Caio Jr. *Formação do Brasil Contemporâneo*. São Paulo: Brasiliense, 2008 [1942].

Quandt, James. 'Still Lives'. *cem mil cigarros – os filmes de Pedro Costa*. Ed. Ricardo Matos Cabo. Lisbon: Orfeu Negro, 2009. 29–39.

Ramos, Jorge Leitão. 'Cinema e História'. Eds. Nuno Figueiredo and Dinis Guarda. *Portugal um Retrato Cinematográfico*. Lisbon: Número – Arte e Cultura, 2004. 71–83.

Rancière, Jacques. 'Política de Pedro Costa'. *cem mil cigarros – os filmes de Pedro Costa*. Ed. Ricardo Matos Cabo Lisbon: Orfeu Negro , 2009. 53–63.

Reis, Carlos. 'Narrativa contemporânea del Neorealismo a la Revolución de los Clavos'. *História de la Literatura Portuguesa*. Eds. António Apolinário and José Luís Gavilanes. Madrid: Cátedra, 2000.

Ribeiro, José. 'Cinema e guerra colonial: representação da sociedade portuguesa e a construção do Africano'. *A Guerra Colonial - Realidade e Ficção*.

Ed. Rui de Azevedo Teixeira. Lisbon: Editorial Notícia, 2001. 285–96.

Ribeiro, Margarida Calafate. Uma História de Regressos. Império, Guerra Colonial e Pós-colonialismo. Porto: Edições Afrontamento, 2004.

Rosenbaum, Jonathan. 'Algumas erupções na *Casa de Lava*'. *cem mil cigarros – os filmes de Pedro Costa*. Ed. Ricardo Matos Cabo. Lisbon: Orfeu Negro, 2009. 125–32.

Rowland, Robert. 'A cultura brasileira e os portugueses'. *Trânsitos coloniais: diálogos críticos luso-brasileiros*. Eds. Cristiana Bastos, Miguel Vale de Almeida and Bela Feldman-Bianco. Lisbon: Imprensa de Ciências Sociais, 2002. 373–84.

Ruffinelli, Jorge. 'Brasil 2001 and Walter Salles: Cinema for the Global Village?' *Portuguese Literary and Cultural Studies* 4.5 (2000): 681–96.

Russel, Sharon A. *Guide to African Cinema*. Westport: Greenwood Press, 1998.

Sabine, Mark. 'Killing (and) Nostalgia: Testimony and the Image of Empire in Margarida Cardoso's *A Costa dos Murmurios*'. Eds. Cristina Demaria and Daly Macdonald. *The Genres of Post-Conflict Testimony*. Nottingham: Critical, Cultural and Communications Press, 2010. 249–76.

Said, Edward. *Culture and Imperialism*. London: Vintage, 1994.

Santos, A. Seixas. 'Seixas Santos'. *A Guerra Colonial - Realidade e Ficção*. Ed. Rui de Azevedo Teixeira. Lisbon: Editorial Notícia, 2001. 497–9.

Santos, Boaventura Sousa. *O Estado e a Sociedade em Portugal*. Porto: Edições Afrontamento, 1998.

Santos, Boaventura Sousa. 'Entre Prospero e Caliban'. *Entre Ser e Estar – Raízes, percursos e discursos de identidade*. Eds. Maria Irene Ramalho, Antóinio Sousa Riberio. Porto: Edições Afrontamento, 2001. 23–85.

Saraiva, António José. *História e Utopia: Estudos sobre Vieira*. Lisbon: Instituto de Cultura e Língua Portuguesa/ICALP, 1992.

Schlesinger, Philip. 'The Sociological Scope of 'National Cinema''. Eds. Mette Hjoert and Scott MacKenzie. *Cinema and Nation*. London/New York: Routledge, 2000. 19–31.

Shaw, Lisa and Stephanie Dennison, eds. *Brazilian National Cinema*. London/New York: Routledge, 2007.

Sherzer, Dina, ed. *Cinema, Colonialism, Postcolonialism: Perspectives from the French and Francophone World*. Austin: University of Texas Press, 1996.

Silva, P. da. 'Mourir oui, mais lentement'. *L'art du cinéma - Manoel de Oliveira*. 21.22.23 (1998): 109–17.

Shoat, Ella and Robert Stam. *Unthinking Eurocentrism - Multiculturalism and the Media*. London/New York: Routledge, 1994.

Silverman, Kaja. *Male Subjectivity at the Margins*. London/New York: Routledge, 1992.

Soares, Jô. *O Xangô de Baker Street*. São Paulo: Companhia das Letras, 1995.

Staden, Hans. *Duas viagens ao Brasil*. Porto Alegre: L&PM Editores, 2008.

Stam, Robert. *Film Theory: An Introduction*. Boston/Oxford: Blackwell Publishers, 2000.

Stam, Robert. 'Cabral and the Indians: filmic representation of Brazil's 500 years'. *The New Brazilian Cinema*. Ed. Lúcia Nagib. London/New York: I.B. Tauris, 2003. 206–28.

Tavares, Vítor. 'O Segredo da 'Abelha''. *Celulóide*, 131 (1968): 11–16.

Thackway, Melissa. *Africa Shoots Back – Alternative Perspectives in Sub-Saharan Francophone African Film*. Bloomington: Indiana University Press, 2003.

Thomas, Daniela, Marcos Bernstein, Marcos and Walter Salles. *Terra Estrangeira*. Rio de Janeiro: Rocco, 1996.

Torgal, L. Reis, ed. *O Cinema sob o olhar de Salazar*. Lisbon: Temas & Debates, 2001.

Turim, Maureen. *Flashbacks in Film: Memory and History*. London/New York: Routledge, 1989.

Ukadike, N. Frank. *Black African Cinema*. Berkley: The University of California Press, 1994.

Wa Thiong'o, Ngugi. *Decolonising the Mind: The Politics of Language in African Literature*. London: Currey, 1986.

Wall, Jeff. 'A propósito de Ossos'. Ed. Ricardo Matos Cabo. *cem mil cigarros – os filmes de Pedro Costa*. Lisbon: Orfeu Negro, 2009. 151–5.

Xavier, Ismail. *O Cinema Brasileiro Moderno*. São Paulo: Paz e Terra, 2001.

Xavier, Ismail. 'Do texto ao filme: a trama, a cena e a construção do olhar no cinema'. *Literatura, Cinema e Televisão*. Eds. Flávio Aguiar, Hélio Guimarães, Randal Johnson, Tânia Pellegrini and Ismail Xavier. São Paulo: Senac, 2003. 61–90.

Xavier, Ismail. 'Prefácio'. In: *Alain Fresnot, Um Cineasta sem Alma*. São Paulo: Imprensa Oficial, 2006. 15–35.

Xavier, Ismail. 'Humanizadores do inevitável'. *ALCEU – Revista de Comunicação, Cultura e Política* 8.15, 2007. 256–70.

Internet references:

Agência Nacional do Cinema. 'Protocolo luso-brasileiro de co-produção cinematográfica, 2007'. Agência Nacional do Cinema, 2007. Web 14 Jan. 2008. www.ancine.gov.br/media/protocolo_luso_brasileiro_julho_2007.pdf.

Agência Nacional do Cinema. 'Protocolo luso-brasileiro de co-produção cinematográfica, 1996'. Agência Nacional do Cinema. Web 30 Mar. 2006. www.ica-ip.pt/Admin/Files/Documents/contentdoc727.pdf.

Albuquerque, Rosana. 'Political Participation of Luso-African Youth in Portugal: some Hypothesis for the Study of Gender'. 2000. Web 10 Jan. 2004. www.bib.uab.es/pub/papers/o2102862n60p167.pdf .

Alves, Manuel dos Santos. 'Uma Abelha na Chuva da mudança ou a intersecção dos paradigmas'. Web 22 Sept. 2005. www.ipn.pt/literatura/zips/salves1.rtf.

António, Lauro. 'Diário de um Novo Mundo'. Web 29 Jan. 2008. www.lauroantonioapresenta.blogspot.com/2006/09/cinema-diario-de-um-novo-mundo.html.

Barros, Eurico. 'Sangue novo no celulóide'. 1998. Web 3 Feb. 2004. www.instituto-camoes.pt/arquivos/cinema/sangcine.htm.

Carling, John. 'Cape Verde: Towards the End of Emigration'. 2000. Web 10 Jan. 2004. www.migrationinformation.org/Profiles/print.cfm?ID=68.

Domingues, João Marco (1998). 'Identité, Cooperation et Influence: l'enterprise politique de la CPLP '. Diplôme d'Études Approfondies, Université de Paris 1. 1998. Web 22 Jun. 2000. www.terravista.pt/ PortoSanto/1646.

Jornal de Notícias. 'O meu cinema é o Americano - Entrevista com Leonel Vieira'. Web 3 Feb. 2004. www.bragancanet.pt/picote/portugues/imprensa/2000-04/jn_meu_cinema.htm.

Krivochein, Barnardo. 'Juventude em Marcha de Pedro Costa'. 2007. Web 14 Dec. 2008. www.zetafilmes.com.br/criticas.asp?id=328.

Madragoa Filmes. 'Críticas sobre Ossos'. Web 3 Feb. 2004. www.madragoa filmes.pt/ossos.

Malheiros, João. 'Portugal Seeks Balance of Emigration, Immigration'. 2002. Web 20 Jan. 2004. www.migrationinformation.org/Profiles/ print.cfm?ID=77.

Ministério das Relações Exteriores. 'Acordo de Co-Produção Cinematográfica entre os Governos da República Federativa do Brasil e da República Portuguesa'. Web 15. Jan. 2008. www2.mre.gov.br/dai/ portcine.htm.

O'Neill, Alexandre. 'Um Adeus Português'. Web 28 Feb. 2004. http://alegna.no.sapo.pt/Recanto_ da*Alegna*Ficheiros/Poesia_AON.htm.

Reis, José Eduardo. Vieira's Utopian millenarianism and the transliteration of the idea of the fifth empire in the seventeenth-century English treatises of the Fifth Monarchy Men. Web 2 May 2007. www.ln.edu.hk/eng/staff/eoyang/icla/Jose%20 Eduardo%20Reis.doc.

Torres, A. Roma. 'Ossos' – Filme de Pedro Costa '. Web 3 Feb. 2004. http://www.terravista.pt/Enseada/1014/cinema29.htm.

Reimão, Sandra. 'Os bestsellers de ficção no Brasil – 1990/2000'. Web 20 Feb. 2010. www.eventos.uevora.pt/comparada/VolumeI/OS%20 BEST_ SELLERS%20DE%20FICCAO%20NO%20BRASIL.pdf.

Index

Beiträge zur europäischen Theater-, Film- und Medienwissenschaft
hrsg. von Verena Berger, Andrea B. Braidt und Daniel Winkler

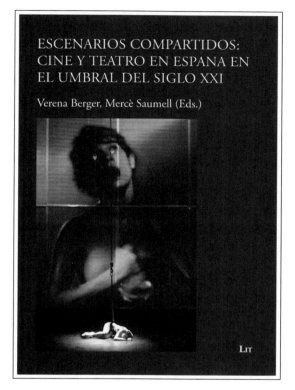

ESCENARIOS COMPARTIDOS:
CINE Y TEATRO EN ESPANA EN
EL UMBRAL DEL SIGLO XXI

Verena Berger, Mercè Saumell (Eds.)

LIT

Verena Berger; Mercè Saumell (Eds.)
Escenarios compartidos: Cine y teatro en España en el umbral del siglo XXI
Cine y teatro: ¿cómplices o rivales? Dieciocho ensayos de investigadores procedentes de España, Fran-
cia, Holanda, Gran Bretaña, Alemania y Austria ofrecen una visión de conjunto de las nuevas relaciones
entre ambos lenguajes artísticos y su evolución en España desde 1975. Pedro Almodóvar, Carlos Saura,
Ventura Pons, Pilar Miró, Achero Mañas, La Cubana, Els Joglars o La Fura dels Baus son, entre otros,
los temas que aquí se abordan desde la perspectiva que ofrecen conceptos teóricos tales como teatralidad,
performatividad, inter-, trans- o multimedialidad.
Bd. 1, 2009, 280 S., 24,90 €, br., ISBN 978-3-8258-0471-8

LIT Verlag Berlin – Münster – Wien – Zürich – London
Auslieferung Deutschland / Österreich / Schweiz: siehe Impressumsseite

POLYGLOT CINEMA
Migration and Transcultural Narration in
France, Italy, Portugal and Spain

Verena Berger, Miya Komori (Eds.)

LIT

Verena Berger; Miya Komori (Eds.)
Polyglot Cinema
Migration and Transcultural Narration in France, Italy, Portugal and Spain

Polyglot Cinema brings together a diverse group of scholars from Europe, Canada and the USA, resulting in a dynamic account of plurilingual migrant narratives in contemporary films from France, Italy, Portugal and Spain. In addition to the close analysis of key films, the essays cover theories of translation and language use as well as central paradigms of cultural studies, especially those of locality, globality and post-colonialism. The volume marks a transdisciplinary contribution to the question of cultural representation within film studies.

Verena Berger teaches Spanish and Latin American Studies at the University of Vienna. Her main research field is Film Studies and she recently co-published with Mercè Saumell Escenarios compartidos: *Cine y teatro en España en el umbral del siglo XXI* (2009).

Miya Komori is a lecturer at the WU Vienna University of Economics and Business. Her main research interests include semiotics, language and culture contact in Hispanic studies.

Bd. 2, 2010, 248 S., 24,90 €, br., ISBN 978-3-643-50226-1

LIT Verlag Berlin – Münster – Wien – Zürich – London
Auslieferung Deutschland / Österreich / Schweiz: siehe Impressumsseite